VOLUME 572

NOVEMBER 2000

THE ANNALS

of The American Academy *of* Political
and Social Science

ALAN W. HESTON, *Editor*
NEIL A. WEINER, *Assistant Editor*

PRESIDENTIAL CAMPAIGNS: SINS OF OMISSION

Special Editors of this Volume

KATHLEEN HALL JAMIESON
MATTHEW MILLER
Annenberg Public Policy Center
University of Pennsylvania
Philadelphia

 Sage Publications, Inc. *THOUSAND OAKS   LONDON   NEW DELHI*

Origin and Purpose. The Academy was organized December 14, 1889, to promote the progress of political and social science, especially through publications and meetings. The Academy does not take sides in controverted questions, but seeks to gather and present reliable information to assist the public in forming an intelligent and accurate judgment.

Meetings. The Academy occasionally holds a meeting in the spring extending over two days.

Publications. THE ANNALS of the American Academy of Political and Social Science is the bimonthly publication of The Academy. Each issue contains articles on some prominent social or political problem, written at the invitation of the editors. Also, monographs are published from time to time, numbers of which are distributed to pertinent professional organizations. These volumes constitute important reference works on the topics with which they deal, and they are extensively cited by authorities throughout the United States and abroad. The papers presented at the meetings of The Academy are included in THE ANNALS.

Membership. Each member of The Academy receives THE ANNALS and may attend the meetings of The Academy. Membership is open only to individuals. Annual dues: $61.00 for the regular paperbound edition (clothbound, $90.00). For members outside the U.S.A., add $12.00 (surface mail) or $24.00 (air mail) for shipping of your subscription. Members may also purchase single issues of THE ANNALS for $20.00 each (clothbound, $30.00).

Subscriptions. THE ANNALS of the American Academy of Political and Social Science (ISSN 0002-7162) is published six times annually—in January, March, May, July, September, and November. Institutions may subscribe to THE ANNALS at the annual rate: $375.00 (clothbound, $425.00). Add $12.00 per year for subscriptions outside the U.S.A. Institutional rates for single issues: $70.00 each (clothbound, $75.00).

Periodicals postage paid at Thousand Oaks, California, and at additional mailing offices.

Single issues of THE ANNALS may be obtained by individuals who are not members of The Academy for $30.00 each (clothbound, $40.00). Single issues of THE ANNALS have proven to be excellent supplementary texts for classroom use. Direct inquiries regarding adoptions to THE ANNALS c/o Sage Publications (address below).

All correspondence concerning membership in The Academy, dues renewals, inquiries about membership status, and/or purchase of single issues of THE ANNALS should be sent to THE ANNALS c/o Sage Publications, Inc., 2455 Teller Road, Thousand Oaks, CA 91320. Telephone: (805) 499-9774; FAX/Order line: (805) 375-1700. *Please note that orders under $30 must be prepaid.* Sage affiliates in London and India will assist institutional subscribers abroad with regard to orders, claims, and inquiries for both subscriptions and single issues.

Printed on recycled, acid-free paper

THE ANNALS
© 2000 *by* The American Academy *of* Political *and* Social Science

Editorial Office: 3937 Chestnut Street, Philadelphia, PA 19104.

For information about membership* (individuals only) and subscriptions (institutions), address:

SAGE PUBLICATIONS, INC.
2455 Teller Road
Thousand Oaks, CA 91320

Sage Production Staff: MARIA NOTARANGELO, KATE PETERSON, and ROSE TYLAK

From India and South Asia, write to:	*From Europe, the Middle East, and Africa, write to:*
SAGE PUBLICATIONS INDIA Pvt. Ltd	SAGE PUBLICATIONS LTD
P.O. Box 4215	6 Bonhill Street
New Delhi 110 048	London EC2A 4PU
INDIA	UNITED KINGDOM

*Please note that members of The Academy receive THE ANNALS with their membership.
International Standard Serial Number ISSN 0002-7162
International Standard Book Number ISBN 0-7619-2337-3 (Vol. 572, 2000 paper)
International Standard Book Number ISBN 0-7619-2336-5 (Vol. 572, 2000 cloth)
Manufactured in the United States of America. First printing, November 2000.

The articles appearing in THE ANNALS are abstracted or indexed in *Academic Abstracts, Academic Search, America: History and Life, Asia Pacific Database, Book Review Index, CAB Abstracts Database, Central Asia: Abstracts & Index, Communication Abstracts, Corporate ResourceNET, Criminal Justice Abstracts, Current Citations Express, Current Contents: Social & Behavioral Sciences, e-JEL, EconLit, Expanded Academic Index, Guide to Social Science & Religion in Periodical Literature, Health Business FullTEXT, HealthSTAR FullTEXT, Historical Abstracts, International Bibliography of the Social Sciences, International Political Science Abstracts, ISI Basic Social Sciences Index, Journal of Economic Literature on CD, LEXIS-NEXIS, MasterFILE FullTEXT, Middle East: Abstracts & Index, North Africa: Abstracts & Index, PAIS International, Periodical Abstracts, Political Science Abstracts, Sage Public Administration Abstracts, Social Science Source, Social Sciences Citation Index, Social Sciences Index Full Text, Social Services Abstracts, Social Work Abstracts, Sociological Abstracts, Southeast Asia: Abstracts & Index, Standard Periodical Directory (SPD), TOPICsearch, Wilson OmniFile V,* and *Wilson Social Sciences Index/Abstracts,* and are available on microfilm from University Microfilms, Ann Arbor, Michigan.

Information about membership rates, institutional subscriptions, and back issue prices may be found on the facing page.

Advertising. Current rates and specifications may be obtained by writing to THE ANNALS Advertising and Promotion Manager at the Thousand Oaks office (address above).

Claims. Claims for undelivered copies must be made no later than six months following month of publication. The publisher will supply missing copies when losses have been sustained in transit and when the reserve stock will permit.

Change of Address. Six weeks advance notice must be given when notifying of change of address to ensure proper identification. Please specify name of journal. **POSTMASTER:** Send address changes to: THE ANNALS of the American Academy of Political and Social Science, c/o Sage Publications, Inc., 2455 Teller Road, Thousand Oaks, CA 91320.

THE ANNALS

of The American Academy *of* Political *and* Social Science

ALAN W. HESTON, *Editor*
NEIL A. WEINER, *Assistant Editor*

─────────── FORTHCOMING ───────────

See page 2 for information on Academy membership and
purchase of single volumes of **The Annals.**

CONTENTS

SCHOOL VOUCHERS

BOOK DEPARTMENT CONTENTS

SOCIOLOGY

ECONOMICS

FOREWORD

The Annenberg Public Policy Center was established by publisher and philanthropist Walter Annenberg in 1994 to create a community of scholars within the University of Pennsylvania that would address public policy issues at the local, state, and federal levels. Consistent with the mission of the Annenberg School for Communication, the Center has four ongoing foci: Information and Society; Media and the Developing Mind; Media and the Dialogue of Democracy; and Health Communication. Each year, as well, a special area of scholarly and social interest is addressed. The Center supports research and sponsors lectures and conferences in these areas. This series of publications disseminates the work of the Center.

KATHLEEN HALL JAMIESON

PREFACE

It is a truism that the issues politicians discuss in campaigns deserve study, but what about the issues they do not discuss? What the novelist Thomas Pynchon called, in another context, "the contours of our ignorance" can have profound consequences for the direction of public policy. In 1988, for example, both political parties found it convenient to avoid talking about the looming crisis in the nation's savings and loans. Yet the S&L rescue became the first order of business for the Bush administration, and the bailout's cost and complexity came to dominate his presidency. In 1992, the budget deficit similarly looked unlikely to generate meaningful campaign debate, until Ross Perot made this his mission. The question of what gets on a presidential campaign's radar screen, what does not, and why is central to understanding how effectively campaigns function as tools of self-government.

This issue of *The Annals* examines dimensions of these questions through articles originally commissioned for two conferences at the National Press Club in Washington, D.C., held in the spring of 2000. These sessions were cosponsored by the Annenberg Public Policy Center of the University of Pennsylvania, and the American Academy of Political and Social Science.

To lay the groundwork, Jamieson, Hagen, Orr, Sillaman, Morse, Kirn, Dutwin, Kenski, Waldman, and Johnston share the findings of Annenberg's extensive research on this year's presidential primaries, showing that voter knowledge and understanding are directly related to the content of campaigns.

If campaigns do indeed matter, what do they leave out and why? Sherman, Earls, Katz, and Madden analyze the extent to which the challenges of urban poverty receive little attention. Annenberg's school voucher forum then illustrates a mode of discussion often missing from campaigns: the search for pragmatic compromises that move an issue forward instead of polarizing voters for political advantage. Feldman, Alexander, Coons, Keegan, and the other participants may not finally agree on the answers, but their search for a meaningful middle ground offers fresh insights seldom heard on the stump.

Journalists share their perspective on campaign omissions, with Dionne stressing the burdens facing campaign reporters; Krauthammer, foreign policy; and Miller, questions of wage and wealth inequality. A distinguished roster of Academy Fellows then examines issues of campaign content through the prism of many disciplines and interests. Austin notes the frequent tendency to compartmentalize issues that are interrelated; Lipset advocates the establishment of national education standards; Marty laments the misuse of religion in politics; Schwartz considers the role of religion in a world rule of law that would prevent dangerous global conflict; Wilkins highlights the seemingly unutterable question of racial integration as a goal; Williamson cites the need to consider second- and third-best solutions when utopian fixes are plainly impractical.

If these articles together amount to a catalogue of complaints about the quality of America's presidential debate, perhaps that is to be expected. Views on what candidates ought to discuss will always lie in the eyes of the beholder. What these authors share, however, is the conviction that campaign discourse matters and that defining the campaign agenda is central to democracy. So long as candidates seek to win 50 percent of the vote plus one, while citizens struggle to find expression of and answers for their concerns, the question "Whose campaign is it anyway?" will be with us.

KATHLEEN HALL JAMIESON
MATTHEW MILLER

ANNALS, *AAPSS*, **572**, November 2000

What Did the Leading Candidates Say, and Did It Matter?

By KATHLEEN HALL JAMIESON
MICHAEL G. HAGEN, DAN ORR,
LESLEY SILLAMAN, SUZANNE MORSE,
and KIM KIRN

ABSTRACT: The Annenberg 2000 study of the primaries found that voters learned the issue distinctions stressed by the candidates and that these distinctions influenced votes. The study also found that those in heavily contested primaries learned more than did voters in states with less contact with the candidates and their campaigns.

Kathleen Hall Jamieson is professor of communication and dean of the Annenberg School for Communication and director of the Annenberg Public Policy Center at the University of Pennsylvania. She is the author or coauthor of ten books including Everything You Think You Know About Politics—and Why You're Wrong; Dirty Politics: Deception, Distraction and Democracy; Beyond the Double Bind: Women and Leadership; Packaging the Presidency; *and* Spiral of Cynicism: The Press and the Public Good. *Michael G. Hagen is a senior research investigator in the Annenberg 2000 study. Dan Orr, Lesley Sillaman, Suzanne Morse, and Kim Kirn are graduate students in the Annenberg School, specializing in political communication.*

I N the book *Everything You Think You Know About Politics—and Why You're Wrong* (Jamieson 2000), researchers from the Annenberg School for Communication of the University of Pennsylvania argue that voters learn from campaigns and that campaigns matter. They matter because, during campaigns, the public comes to learn important information about the candidates and about their priorities. Campaigns also matter because, contrary to conventional wisdom, presidential candidates who are elected make an aggressive effort to keep most of their promises most of the time. As a result, the issues that they advance as the most serious in a campaign are the ones on which they are most likely to act once they are elected. It is therefore consequential that some issues and not others are the focus of a campaign. As a result, we learn about those that are the focus, and the candidates commit to address them if elected. When issues are not addressed, the likelihood that they will be addressed once a candidate becomes president drops pretty dramatically.

We will argue that the focal issues were different within and between parties, that the electorate learned about those issues on which the candidates focused, and that that learning shaped some voting decisions. To make that case, we will report the results of our content analysis of every claim made by a presidential contender in a televised debate during the 2000 primaries as well as every statement in a presidential candidate's televised ads.

We picked those two forms of discourse on the assumption that, although they certainly matter, most people do not actually hear candidates' speeches. We use ads and debates as a rough indicator of the candidates' priorities and of the information about the campaign to which voters were likely to have been exposed.

We also will present results from our rolling cross-sectional survey of 30,000 voters. We began surveying in mid-November 1999. This survey report concludes just after Super Tuesday. By the time we finish in early 2001, we will have talked with 100,000 voters. We are trying to find out what they learn, how they learn it, why they vote, and the impact of all of this on their sense of governance.

The survey is in the field every day. On each day, we are talking to at least 50 voters. On some days, we are talking to as many as 500. That, of course, poses a problem when we are expected to report a standard error. When we are looking at a rolling average across seven days, the error is about plus or minus 3 percent. When we are looking at all 30,000 voters, it is minuscule.

We analyzed all the claims that candidates made in 13 Republican debates and 8 Democratic debates and also in 92 campaign advertisements. Each claim was coded into 1 of 35 issue categories.

RESULTS

We found that the parties differed in their emphasis on issues, with

Republicans more likely to focus on taxes and foreign policy, and Democratic candidates more likely to focus on health care. The Republicans were also more likely to spend time attacking Gore than the Democratic candidates were to spend time attacking any of the Republican candidates.

Within a party, we found that the candidates also had different issue priorities. George W. Bush's first issue was taxes, and, while John McCain discussed taxes, he emphasized it fourth. McCain's first issue was campaign finance, which Bush placed fourth on his agenda. Bill Bradley and Al Gore also placed different priorities on campaign finance, with Bradley discussing it first and Gore emphasizing it fourth.

Taxes constituted the issue discussed most frequently by Governor Bush, accounting for 13 percent of his claims in debates and 31 percent in ads. The most frequent claim by Governor Bush on this issue was that tax cuts encourage economic growth. He also referred to his own record, claiming that he had enacted the largest tax cut in the history of the state of Texas. He made a more specific claim about this cut, saying it created more than $3 billion in tax relief for taxpayers in his state.

John McCain emphasized campaign finance as his top issue. The claim he made most often was that when he is president, there will be a controlling authority regarding campaign finance. This referred to a statement that Gore had made about there being no controlling legal authority in 1996. McCain also said that we need to get government out of

the hands of the special interests. Third, he argued that the real scandal in Washington was the debasement of every institution of government by the Clinton-Gore administration.

Al Gore's most frequently occurring category was race relations. Within that category, his top three claims were, first, "I support affirmative action"; second, "We need to enforce civil rights laws"; and third, "I would issue an executive order to ban racial profiling."

Bill Bradley was more thematic than the other candidates. He devoted comparable attention to his top three issues, speaking about both campaign finance and race relations 12 percent of the time, and health care 11 percent of the time. His top claims concerning campaign finance were that the people had lost faith in government because of big money or, alternatively, that money was corrupting democracy. He also supported the banning of soft money and argued that special-interest lobbyists and the rich control Washington, D.C.

In the area of race relations, he argued for a need to promote racial healing, attacked Gore over his past support for tax-exempt status for racially segregated schools, and argued against racial profiling. On the topic of health care, he rebutted what he viewed as Gore's mischaracterization of his per person expenditures on Medicaid, supported universal access to affordable quality health care, and offered a prescription drug benefit for senior citizens.

When we consider responses to survey questions about specific issues addressed in the campaign, we learn that citizens did in fact learn things about where the candidates stood on the issues they emphasized. For instance, Senator Bradley's support for a universal health care plan was something that substantial numbers of the residents of Super Tuesday states, among others, learned over the first two months of 2000. A large number of people learned about Vice President Gore's opposition to school vouchers over the same period.

On the Republican side, some learned about Governor Bush's opposition to a total ban on soft money, and many learned about Senator McCain's support for such a ban. The information that people picked up over the course of the campaign made a difference in the votes they cast in primaries.

The South Carolina primary is illustrative. In that state, a substantial number were persuaded over the course of the two weeks between the New Hampshire primary and the South Carolina primary that Governor Bush would cut taxes more than Senator McCain would. Those who regarded taxes as a serious problem moved toward Governor Bush over that period, while those who regarded taxes as a less serious problem remained loyal to Senator McCain. In South Carolina, Governor Bush's campaign was able to control the agenda, and that control was consequential.

In sum, consistent with the argument that we made in *Everything You Think You Know About Politics— and Why You're Wrong* (Jamieson 2000), campaigns do matter.

Whether a campaign happens in a voter's own state or not, whether it is a contested primary or not, makes a difference in what a voter learns.

That effect is unsurprising on the face of it. What is surprising to us is that, given the intense campaigning in Iowa, the effect did not appear there. This raises the possibility that caucuses behave differently from primaries in the amount of learning that they are able to engender in audiences. This conclusion also implies that by front-loading the primaries this year in adaptation to the needs of the party and the candidates who do not want to be contesting on the eve of their conventions, a disservice may have been done to voters in states that did not have a contested primary.

HAVES AND HAVE-NOTS

Our profile is of a nation of haves and have-nots. The haves, who were voters in the contested primary states, minus Iowa, learned. They learned in all of our categories of knowledge. Those in the noncontested states did not learn much. As we enter the general election, essentially two different potential electorates exist: one is more or less up to speed on the basic issue distinctions, and the other has not learned a great deal yet about the important policy priorities of the two major parties' presumed nominees. In short, campaigns matter, communication matters, and it matters when voters do not get either. By front-loading the primaries and by featuring one so-called national primary on Super Tuesday, we signaled some people that they were in the process, and we signaled others that they were out of it.

We also saw through our content analysis that the candidates' issue agendas differed within and between parties and that in the contested primary states, minus the Iowa caucus, people learned those issue distinctions. In other words, learning not only occurred, but it occurred on the topics that the candidates featured. As important, we have evidence that learning shaped voting.

Reference

Jamieson, Kathleen Hall. 2000. *Everything You Think You Know About Politics—and Why You're Wrong.* New York: Basic Books, New Republic Books.

ANNALS, *AAPSS*, **572**, November 2000

Knowledge in the
2000 Primary Elections

By DAVID DUTWIN

ABSTRACT: The research reported in this article set out to explore the variation in political knowledge over time during the 2000 presidential primaries. Knowledge is broken down into three distinct types: candidate awareness, biography, and policy. Results show that citizens did learn substantive amounts of information during the campaign and that learning and overall levels of knowledge were most pronounced in respondents who lived in a state where a primary was held and was competitive.

David Dutwin is a Ph.D. student at the Annenberg School for Communication at the University of Pennsylvania. His research is concentrated on public opinion research, with a specific focus on political communication.

D EMOCRACY is predicated on frequent and fair elections in which citizens exercise an informed choice of candidate preference (Dahl 1989, 1998). Whether citizens are informed, however, has been a hotly contested question because people vary greatly in what they know about politics, and overall the citizenry's level of political knowledge is quite low (Delli Carpini and Keeter 1996).

To cast an informed vote, a citizen must first be able to identify the candidates and, minimally, be able to provide some overall assessment of each candidate. In assessing qualification for high office, a citizen might also want to know what major offices a candidate has held in the past as well as other pertinent biographical information. Finally, we expect citizens to know enough about the policy positions of the candidates to forecast what they will do if elected.

The present article uses data from the Annenberg Public Policy Center's 2000 Presidential Survey. By the end of 2000, over 100,000 interviews will have been conducted on Americans' political knowledge, media use, and opinions about candidates and issues. The results in this article are based on interviews completed 8 November 1999 through 6 March 2000 with random samples of adults, 18 years of age or older, living in telephone households. The survey contains a number of distinct samples, each generated using random digit dialing, including a national sample, a sample of residents living in states that held their primaries on Super Tuesday, and separate samples for Iowa, New Hampshire, South Carolina, and Michigan.

Under the direction of Princeton Survey Research Associates, the survey uses a rolling cross-sectional design, with interviewing conducted continuously throughout the campaign season. The number of interviews conducted per day ranges from a low of 50 to a high of 500.

AWARENESS OF CANDIDATES

To assess candidate awareness, we asked respondents whether they could rate each candidate on overall favorability on a scale of zero to 100 or whether instead they were unaware of the candidate and unable to provide a favorability rating. The responses indicated that, over the course of the campaign, citizens significantly increased their awareness of the four major candidates. In addition, the rate of learning was shown to be generally constant across samples, although New Hampshire respondents had significantly higher awareness rates overall.

Report

Not surprisingly, around 93 percent of respondents in the national sample were able to identify Texas governor George W. Bush and Vice President Al Gore as presidential candidates. This proportion was stable in most samples and throughout the course of the campaign. The proportion of individuals able to mention the two primary challengers, former senator Bill Bradley and Senator John McCain, nationally was below 45 percent at the beginning of our survey in mid-November. As expected, of the three types of

FIGURE 1
NAME RECOGNITION OF BRADLEY, BUSH, GORE, AND McCAIN

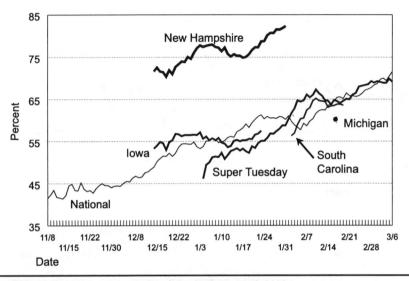

SOURCE: Reprinted, by permission, from Jamieson et al. 2000.
NOTE: Data points are 8- to 10-day moving averages, all respondents.

political knowledge, candidate awareness showed the most improvement over time. The proportion of respondents aware of the four frontrunning candidates nationally moved from below 45 percent in mid-November to around 70 percent by the first week of March (see Figure 1). Learning was generally constant across samples. That is, awareness of the candidates improved at basically the same rate for residents of New Hampshire, South Carolina, Iowa, and other states.

At first glance, there is cause for both optimism and concern. The good news, of course, is that Americans steadily learned about the candidates and at a respectable rate. However, the fact remains that, by the week before the Super Tuesday primary, which was on 7 March, only 70 percent of respondents nationally were aware of the four major candidates. In the final weeks before Super Tuesday, over 90 percent of respondents living in a Super Tuesday state and who identified themselves as Republicans were aware of John McCain's candidacy; in contrast, only 70 percent of Republican Iowans were aware of McCain the week before their caucus. This discrepancy in awareness reveals the effect of campaigning, as McCain did not campaign in the state of Iowa. In contrast, nearly 90 percent of Iowa Democrats said they were aware of former senator Bill Bradley, who did campaign in that state.

FIGURE 2
BIOGRAPHICAL KNOWLEDGE REGARDING REPUBLICAN CANDIDATES

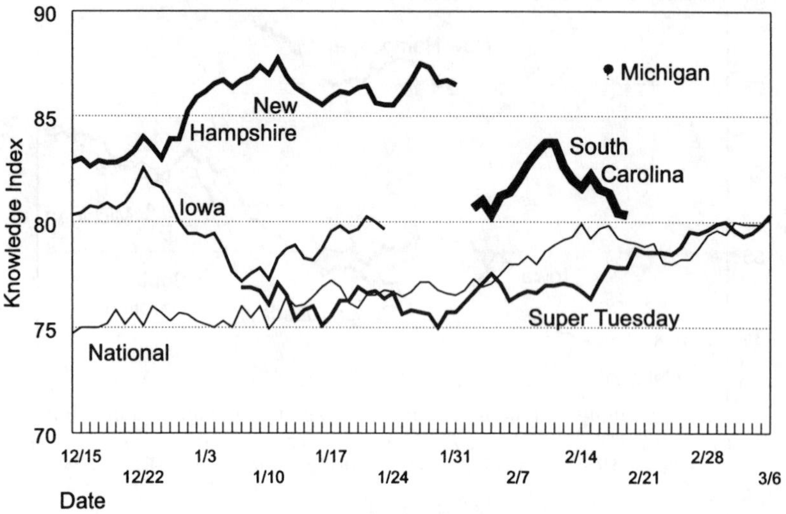

SOURCE: Reprinted, by permission, from Jamieson et al. 2000.
NOTE: Data points are 8- to 10-day moving averages, all respondents.

BIOGRAPHICAL KNOWLEDGE

Throughout the survey, respondents were asked three biographical questions about the two front-running candidates of each party.[1] Concerning the Democrats, we asked which of the candidates was a former senator, the son of a former senator, and a former professional basketball player. Concerning the Republicans, we asked which was a governor, a senator, and a former Vietnam prisoner of war.

The responses to the questions demonstrate that primaries matter: respondents in South Carolina, New Hampshire, and Michigan, where primaries were held, scored significantly higher on these measures of biographical knowledge than did respondents from states where primaries were not held. The survey results show also that, nationally, significant learning occurred during the weeks leading up to the Michigan and South Carolina primaries.

Report

Once again, the evidence suggests that primaries matter: New Hampshire respondents made significant improvement on these measures of biographical knowledge leading up to the New Hampshire primary (see Figures 2 and 3). On average, South Carolina and Michigan respondents scored much higher than respondents from all the other states in the country. The majority of learning took place in New Hampshire.

FIGURE 3
BIOGRAPHICAL KNOWLEDGE REGARDING DEMOCRATIC CANDIDATES

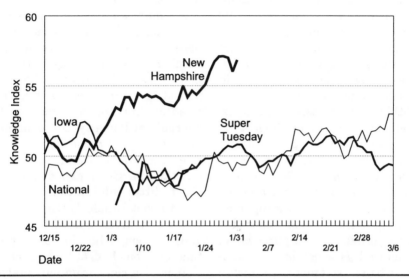

NOTE: Data points are 8- to 10-day moving averages, all respondents.

However, respondents in Super Tuesday states as well as in the national sample learned about the candidates' biographies.

POLICY KNOWLEDGE

A number of questions on policy knowledge were inserted and deleted throughout the course of the survey. The percentages here represent responses to four questions that were asked on every day of the survey. These questions were on the following topics: for the Democrats, universal health care and tax cuts; and for the Republicans, gun background checks and soft money.

The responses to the four questions indicated that overall levels of policy knowledge were low. The responses to these questions also indicated that primaries matter: citizens learned about John McCain's policy positions beginning the week before the New Hampshire primary and continuing until Super Tuesday.

Report

Measuring policy knowledge throughout the course of political campaigns presents a number of difficulties. First, the candidates' positions may change over time. Second, the degree to which candidates' positions are reported in the press can vary over time. Given these two factors, the central question is not whether respondents knew the detailed and nuanced policy positions of every candidate but, rather, whether they learned what they reasonably could have learned given the information provided. Based on our content analysis of the candidates' claims in 21 debates and 92 televised ads, as well as an analysis of the major newspaper stories about the campaigns, we were able to accurately assess what citizens could have learned and when.

With regard to the Democrats, respondents were asked which of the candidates, if any, supported a universal health care plan as well as the Reagan tax cut plan of 1981. Respondents were also asked which of the Republican candidates supported instant gun checks and opposed a waiting period prior to purchase of guns as well as which of them supported a ban on soft money campaign contributions. Senator Bradley did support a universal health care plan, which was, in fact, the focal point of his campaign. Vice President Gore, on the other hand, supported the goal of universal health care but using an incremental approach. While there was little mention of Gore's position in his remarks during debates and in his ads, Bradley enunciated his position over 35 times in debates and 15 times in nine of his televised ads. Furthermore, Bradley received significant coverage on this issue by attacking Gore for "abandoning" universal health care. Gore mentioned his position only four times in advertisements and garnered little newspaper coverage on this issue. It is reasonable, then, to expect citizens to have learned Bradley's position. Bradley's assertion that Gore had "abandoned" universal health care in conjunction with the minimal coverage given to Gore's position made it

likely that citizens would have difficulty learning where Gore stood on universal health care.

A similar scenario was played out on the other three issues mentioned here. The Gore campaign made a number of charges early in the primary season that Bradley had supported the 1981 Reagan tax cuts. Bradley did not respond to this charge until nearly three months after it was first reported in October. Even then, he only indirectly rebutted the charge in two debates. In short, little information was provided about Bradley's true position. He, in fact, voted against tax cuts in 1981 (although he did vote for the final omnibus budget that year).

It is also clear from our analysis that it would have been difficult for citizens to have learned the policy positions for all of the Republican candidates. For example, both businessman Steve Forbes and Texas governor George W. Bush came out in support of a soft money ban, but only for corporations and unions. However, Forbes's position was never mentioned in ads or debates and was picked up only once in a major newspaper. Bush's position received little coverage, and Bush himself mentioned his position in only one ad and only four times in debates. In contrast, the centerpiece of McCain's campaign was campaign finance reform. He advanced his position to ban all soft money on 29 separate occasions in debates, and he received dense coverage in the press. Finally, although McCain's position on gun checks and waiting periods was clear and concise and had been reported by the press since mid-December,

FIGURE 4
POLICY KNOWLEDGE REGARDING REPUBLICAN CANDIDATES

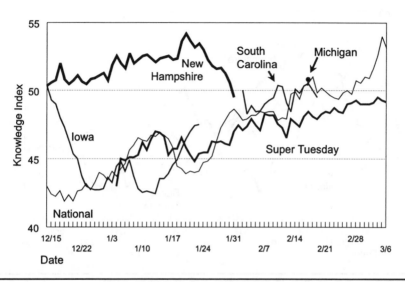

NOTE: Data points are 8- to 10-day moving averages, all respondents.

Forbes and Bush stated only that they supported "enforcement of current laws."

Our analysis, then, set out to ascertain the degree to which respondents learned the policy positions of the candidates that were frequently mentioned in ads and debates and in news. Specifically, we looked at respondents' knowledge about the 1981 Reagan tax cuts, universal health care, soft money, and instant gun checks (see Figures 4 and 5).

Our results show little evidence of learning over time about the Democrats' policy positions on Reagan's tax cuts and on universal health care. Since the Democratic contest was not competitive after New Hampshire, voters may have seen little need to learn such positions. On the other hand, respondents did learn about the Republicans'

positions on soft money and instant gun checks. Once again, New Hampshire, South Carolina, and Michigan respondents performed better on average than the national or Super Tuesday samples. Nonetheless, respondents in the Super Tuesday and national samples did learn significantly over the course of the primary season.

CONCLUSION

Although surveys have consistently shown that citizens generally exhibit a wide range and low average level of knowledge about politics, evidence from our survey suggests that citizens did learn about the candidates and that such learning was time dependent. In short, learning occurred in the weeks leading up to

FIGURE 5
POLICY KNOWLEDGE REGARDING DEMOCRATIC CANDIDATES

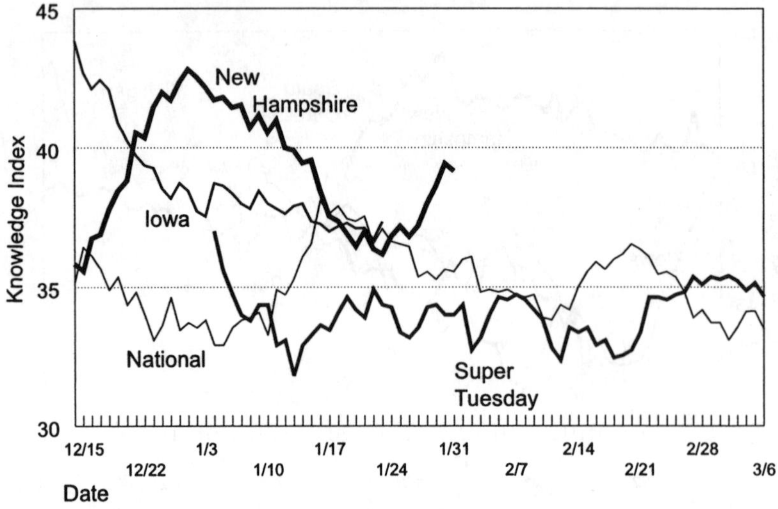

NOTE: Data points are 8- to 10-day moving averages, all respondents.

competitive primaries. When there was no immediate incentive to learn, as with the Democratic race leading up to Super Tuesday or the Republican race in Iowa, overall levels of knowledge were low and did not exhibit improvement over time. However, when primaries were competitive, as was the case with the Democratic contest in New Hampshire and the Republican races in New Hampshire, South Carolina, Michigan, and the Super Tuesday states, voters made significant strides in what they knew about the candidates.

Note

1. The following analysis of biographical and policy knowledge uses items that were coded as "1" for correct and "0" for incorrect, with the exception of respondents who answered "Forbes" or "don't know." Because businessman Steve Forbes dropped out of the race on 14 February, the option of providing Forbes as a response alternative was dropped. In order to provide longitudinal analysis, then, "Forbes" was effectively eliminated as a response alternative for responses prior to 14 February by randomly assigning those who answered "Forbes" to other response alternatives. Additionally, those who answered "don't know" were randomly assigned other alternatives to control for the variation over time of the proportion of respondents who arrive at the correct answer by guessing (see Mondak 2000).

References

Dahl, R. A. 1989. *Dilemmas of Pluralist Democracy: Autonomy vs. Control.* New Haven, CT: Yale University Press.

———. 1998. *On Democracy.* New Haven, CT: Yale University Press.

Delli Carpini, M. X. and S. Keeter. 1996. *What Americans Know About Politics and Why It Matters.* New Haven, CT: Yale University Press.

Jamieson, Kathleen Hall, Richard Johnston, Michael Hagan, David Dutwin, Kate Kenski, Kimberly Kirn, Suzanne Morse, Daniel Orr, Erika Prosper, Lesley Sillaman, and Paul Waldman. 2000. *The Primary Cam-* *paign: What Did the Candidates Say, What Did the Public Learn, and Did It Matter?* Philadelphia: Annenberg Public Policy Center.

Mondak, J. J. 2000. Reconsidering the Measurement of Political Knowledge. *Political Analysis* 8:57-82.

ANNALS, *AAPSS*, **572**, November 2000

Women and Political Knowledge During the 2000 Primaries

By KATE KENSKI

ABSTRACT: Prior research on political knowledge has found repeatedly that women do not perform as well as men on political affairs questions. The present study analyzed survey responses collected between 14 December 1999 and 8 March 2000 on political knowledge items about the issue positions and backgrounds of candidates Bradley, Gore, and McCain. Even when several sociodemographic variables were controlled for, gender was a significant predictor of political knowledge. Not only were women more likely than men to say they did not know the answer to a question, but they were also more likely to answer incorrectly when giving a substantive response.

Kate Kenski is a doctoral candidate at the Annenberg School for Communication at the University of Pennsylvania. Her research interests include political communication, public opinion, health communication, and research methods.

S INCE 1980, women have voted at the same rate as men or at a higher rate (Delli Carpini and Fuchs 1993). Why then do scholars consistently find that women correctly answer fewer questions about political affairs than do men (Bennett and Bennett 1989)? This finding is especially perplexing given that the status of women has changed substantially in the last 50 years. Educational attainment is now comparable between the sexes. There is a greater female presence in the labor force. The number of women seeking political office has risen. Nevertheless, gender differences in political knowledge persist (Delli Carpini and Keeter 1991).

STATISTICALLY SIGNIFICANT GENDER DIFFERENCES

To ascertain if sex differences in political knowledge were present in the 2000 presidential primary campaign period, a political knowledge scale was composed of eight knowledge items that asked respondents about the issue positions and backgrounds of candidates Gore, Bradley, McCain, and Bush. Using a national sample of respondents interviewed between 14 December 1999 and 8 March 2000, statistical analyses were performed to determine the factors that predict political knowledge. Three outcomes were analyzed: (1) answering questions correctly; (2) answering the questions but selecting incorrect answers; and (3) stating that one does not know the answers.

Prior research by Kenski and Jamieson (2000) on the 1996 general election demonstrated that while there were sex differences in answering questions correctly and stating that one did not know the answer, there were no significant differences in selecting an incorrect answer. Men were more likely to get answers correct, and women were more likely to say that they did not know the answers to the questions. In the 2000 presidential campaign, however, women were also more likely to answer the items incorrectly. These gender differences did not disappear when several sociodemographic and media variables were controlled for. Our independent variables included gender, age, race, marital status, having children, education, income, watching network news, watching cable news, watching local news, reading a newspaper, listening to political talk radio, talking about politics with family or friends, political interest, and party identification. Gender was the third-strongest predictor of political knowledge. Education and talking about politics with family or friends were the first- and second-strongest predictors respectively. While gender is a statistically significant predictor of political knowledge, the actual difference in correct answers between males and females is not substantively large.

CONCLUSION

The perplexing finding that women do not perform as well as men on political knowledge still persists in the year 2000. While this difference is small in magnitude, it is nevertheless puzzling. Prior research by Kenski and Jamieson (2000) on the 1996 general election demonstrated that while men answered political knowledge questions correctly more often than women and women said that they did not know the answers more often than men, there were no significant gender differences in selecting the incorrect answer. In the 2000 presidential primary season, however, women were more likely to select the incorrect answer.

References

Bennett, Linda L. M. and Stephen Earl Bennett. 1989. Enduring Gender Differences in Political Interest: The Impact of Socialization and Political Dispositions. *American Politics Quarterly* 17(1):105-22.

Delli Carpini, Michael X. and Ester R. Fuchs. 1993. The Year of the Woman? Candidate, Voters, and the 1992 Election. *Political Science Quarterly* 108(1):29-36.

Delli Carpini, Michael X. and Scott Keeter. 1991. Stability and Change in the U.S. Public's Knowledge of Politics. *Public Opinion Quarterly* 55:583-612.

Kenski, Kate and Kathleen Hall Jamieson. 2000. Do Men Know More About Politics Than Women? In *Everything You Think You Know About Politics—and Why You're Wrong*, by Kathleen Hall Jamieson. New York: Basic Books, New Republic Books.

Political Discussion in Primary States

By PAUL WALDMAN

ABSTRACT: Residents of Iowa and New Hampshire are exposed to a much more intense primary campaign than those in the rest of the country. One would therefore expect that those living in these two states would be more engaged with the primary election than residents of other states. Survey data indicate that while this proves to be true of those in New Hampshire, it does not appear to be the case in Iowa. While New Hampshire residents talked about politics more frequently than those in other states—and with greater frequency as their primary approached—Iowa residents discussed politics less often than those in states with primaries on Super Tuesday. The same result was obtained examining only survey respondents who rated themselves very likely to vote in their primary or caucus.

Paul Waldman is a research fellow at the Annenberg School for Communication, University of Pennsylvania.

NOTE: This article is reprinted from Kathleen Hall Jamieson, Richard Johnston, Michael Hagen, David Dutwin, Kate Kenski, Kimberly Kirn, Suzanne Morse, Daniel Orr, Erika Prosper, Lesley Sillaman, and Paul Waldman, *The Primary Campaign: What Did the Candidates Say, What Did the Public Learn, and Did It Matter?* (Philadelphia: Annenberg Public Policy Center, 2000). Reprinted by permission.

ONE of the key measures of citizens' involvement in political affairs is the frequency with which they discuss politics with their family, friends, and associates. In order to capture this element of political engagement, a survey of residents of New Hampshire, Iowa, and states holding primaries on Super Tuesday asked respondents how many days in the previous week they had talked about politics.

One would expect that voters in New Hampshire and Iowa would be substantially more attentive to presidential primary campaigns than their counterparts in other states. After all, the campaigns pay an extraordinary amount of attention to them, and they can reasonably expect that their behavior will have a greater impact on the outcome of the primary election contest than that of voters in Nevada or Oklahoma. Compared with voters in Super Tuesday states—a group that was too large and geographically spread out to experience much "retail" campaigning—voters in New Hampshire and Iowa had a great deal of exposure to the candidates and their messages (see Figure 1). While the candidates spent slightly more money in New Hampshire than they did in Iowa, both states were flooded with television and radio advertising.

RESULTS

When we examine the level of political discussion, we see that voters in New Hampshire talked to each other about politics substantially more than Iowans or Super Tuesday voters (see Figure 2). About a month before the primary, levels of discussion in New Hampshire began to rise. The last two weeks saw another, steeper climb, as voters reported engaging in political discussions nearly every other day.

Iowans talked about politics less than their counterparts in New Hampshire and less than even Super Tuesday voters. Where Iowans did not increase their levels of discussion until the last 10 days before the caucuses, political discussion in Super Tuesday states climbed slowly over the month before the primary.

One explanation for the fact that respondents in New Hampshire talked more than those in Iowa would be that more of the New Hampshire respondents see themselves as likely voters. After all, approximately 44 percent of New Hampshire residents voted in the primary, whereas only 10 percent of Iowans made it to a caucus. The low turnout in Iowa is usually attributed to the fact that, despite the intensity of Iowa campaigns, voting in a caucus involves a commitment of time and energy that most people are unwilling to make. However, if we examine only those most likely to vote, we see an identical pattern—Iowans talked about politics less often than people in New Hampshire or in Super Tuesday states.

We asked respondents whether they planned to vote in their primary or caucus, and if they said yes, we asked them to rate, on a scale of 1 to 10, the likelihood they would vote. Figure 3 shows only those who responded with a 10. Even among respondents claiming that they were certain to vote, New Hampshire

FIGURE 1
**EXPOSURE TO THE CAMPAIGN, AVERAGE WEEK:
NEW HAMPSHIRE, IOWA, SUPER TUESDAY STATES**

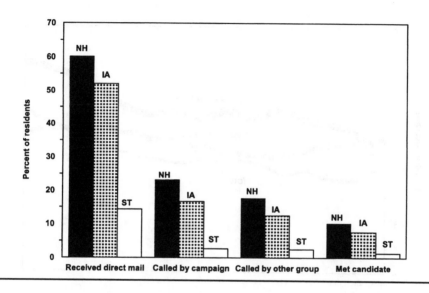

FIGURE 2
POLITICAL DISCUSSION: NEW HAMPSHIRE, IOWA, SUPER TUESDAY STATES

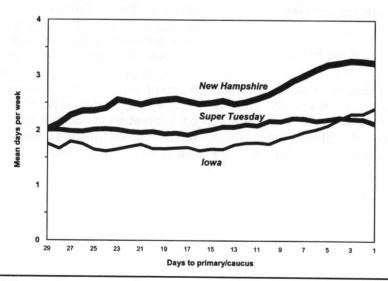

NOTE: Seven-day moving average.

FIGURE 3
POLITICAL DISCUSSION BY THOSE INTENDING TO VOTE IN PRIMARY/CAUCUS

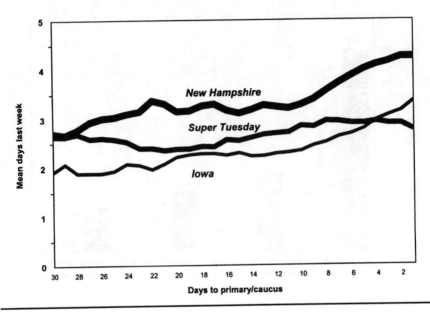

NOTE: Seven-day moving average.

residents seemed to be talking about politics substantially more.

CONCLUSION

The increases in political discussion as a primary or caucus approached indicate that, as one would expect, political engagement is responsive to the intensity of a campaign and the proximity of an election. The differences between residents of New Hampshire and Iowa demonstrate that voters in similar communication environments may engage the political process to different degrees. This engagement is not simply a function of an individual's intention to vote but may be a product of the political culture in which he or she resides.

Dynamics of the 2000 Republican Primaries

By MICHAEL G. HAGEN, RICHARD JOHNSTON,
KATHLEEN HALL JAMIESON, DAVID DUTWIN,
and KATE KENSKI

ABSTRACT: The 2000 presidential primaries were among the liveliest in recent memory. This article is the authors' first account of the changing fortunes of the candidates from the Iowa caucuses through Super Tuesday. It is based upon the nomination phase of the Annenberg 2000 Election Surveys, a collection of nearly 32,000 interviews conducted from November through March, nationwide and in special-purpose state and regional studies, on a broad range of political science and communications questions. The analysis of dynamics is facilitated by the survey's rolling cross-section design, in which the day of interview is itself a product of random selection. This account emphasizes the interplay between substantive and strategic contributions to the votes cast at different points in the campaign, between evaluations of the candidates as people and policymakers, on the one hand, and judgments about the candidates' chances of winning a party's nomination and the general election, on the other. The pervasive influence of information is demonstrated. The knowledge voters managed to acquire through the campaign informed both kinds of considerations. The weight voters gave such considerations depends on the store of information they managed to accumulate about the candidates.

Michael G. Hagen is a postdoctoral fellow at the Annenberg Public Policy Center of the University of Pennsylvania.

Richard Johnston is a visiting scholar at the Annenberg School for Communication and professor of political science at the University of British Columbia.

Kathleen Hall Jamieson is professor of communication, dean of the Annenberg School, and director of the Annenberg Public Policy Center.

David Dutwin is a Ph.D. candidate at the Annenberg School.

Kate Kenski is a Ph.D. candidate at the Annenberg School.

B EFORE the Iowa caucuses, George W. Bush was treated by press and pundits alike as the presumptive Republican nominee, a perception fueled by unprecedented endorsements from party regulars, including almost all of the incumbents in the House and Senate and virtually every governor. Helpful as well was the family name. Then there was the money: Bush entered the primaries with $70 million in the bank and, by disavowing federal matching funds and their concomitant spending cap, he signaled a limitless willingness to spend in the primaries. This put even his most serious potential rival, war hero and senator John McCain, at a serious disadvantage.

On most questions of policy, McCain and Bush hardly differed. Each is a moderate conservative. Each favors the North American Free Trade Agreement (NAFTA) and freer trade with China. Each opposes abortion except in the case of rape, incest, or threat to the life of the mother, but neither would make abortion a litmus test for Supreme Court appointments. On the eve of the campaign, each was presumably well regarded by the Christian Coalition, the National Right to Life committee, and the National Rifle Association. Their only dramatic policy differences were over campaign finance reform and the extent to which the federal budget surplus should be spent on tax cuts rather than Medicare and Social Security.

Even so, McCain threatened—or seemed to threaten for a time—to overcome the Bush juggernaut. Bush won the Iowa caucuses, which McCain did not contest, but McCain won the New Hampshire primary decisively. Bush came back to win in South Carolina, but McCain took the next primary, in Michigan. Only when Bush won the great majority of the convention delegates at stake in the Super Tuesday primaries was McCain's challenge effectively ended.

What fueled McCain's rise, and what stopped it? These questions reopen the academic study of primary campaign dynamics, begun in the 1980s but largely dormant since. We revisit it with survey data from the Annenberg 2000 Election Surveys, designed expressly to be sensitive to campaign events in real time.[1] This is an early report, based on our preliminary analysis of that voluminous collection of interviews.

We begin with the time path of McCain vote intentions, then proceed to a discussion of possible factors in the choice: substantive knowledge of the candidates, the course and bases of judgment on them, and perceptions of their chances of winning the nomination. In particular, we look at the role of issues in judgments of McCain and Bush, at media use in the gathering of knowledge, and at the role of campaign events and media use in the updating of perceived chances. Our closest focus is on the decisive event, the Super Tuesday primaries. We conclude by bringing the factors together in a simple model of candidate choice.

THE COURSE OF VOTE INTENTIONS

John McCain had established most of his New Hampshire beach-

FIGURE 1
McCAIN SHARE OF VOTE INTENTIONS, BY ELECTORATE: PERCENTAGE
OF RESPONDENTS INTENDING TO VOTE IN REPUBLICAN PRIMARIES

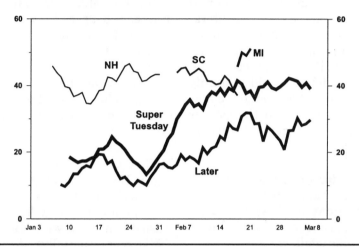

NOTE: "Later" smoothed with 11-day prior moving average, all others with 7-day prior moving averages.

head by the start of 2000, and he began his rise elsewhere just before the end of January. Figure 1 shows this by tracking vote intentions among prospective Republican primary voters by day and by electorate.[2] By our reading, John McCain's share in New Hampshire hovered around 40 percent by the start of the year. He may have fallen back in the first few weeks, but around 18 January he crossed the 40 percent threshold, never again to fall below it. Elsewhere in the country, he struggled to sustain a share in the mid-teens, indeed was falling back. But his fortunes evidently turned up on 28 January not just in Super Tuesday states but elsewhere as well. Most striking is his Super Tuesday surge. We suspect that had we been interviewing in South Carolina at the time, we would have seen a similarly striking surge in that state. In any case, by the time our South Carolina oversample began, McCain's vote-intention share in the state rivaled the actual share he had just drawn in New Hampshire. Thereupon his South Carolina share gradually dropped, such that it ultimately converged with the Super Tuesday reading.[3] Of Michigan we can say little other than that our modest oversample in that state faithfully recorded John McCain's strength.

What is clear about the last three weeks of the de facto campaign is that the McCain surge was already stalling before the South Carolina primary. By the same token, he did not appear to lose any ground after South Carolina. McCain may have fallen back slightly in the later states, but in the critical and intensely campaigned Super Tuesday states, he just stalled.

What can we say about the sources of the surge and the stall? The literature on factors in primary dynamics is small and is now getting a bit old. But Bartels (1988) proposed an elementary model that will certainly start us down the road to understanding. He conceived the vote as the product of three interacting factors:

— the voter's basic evaluation of the candidate, a compound of judgment on his character, issue reasoning, and demographic similarity;
— how much a voter knows about the candidate, where knowledge is a precondition for support but also, potentially, a source of reasons to resist the candidate's appeal; and
— the voter's estimation of the candidate's likelihood of securing the nomination, his viability.[4]

In the sections that follow, we look at each factor in some detail, with special focus on how each factor moves through time. Once we get each factor located, we bring them together in an accounting of McCain's surge. This also enables us to consider some alternative scenarios.

EVALUATIONS OF THE CANDIDATES

The heart of the matter is how prospective voters evaluate each candidate, and evaluations of the candidates themselves were a strikingly dynamic element of the Republican contest, influenced heavily by what the candidates said and what the public learned.

Our indicator of evaluation is the difference between the ratings given to John McCain and George W. Bush on a scale from "favorable" to "unfavorable."[5] The time paths of those ratings among the members of our various subsamples who intended to vote in a Republican primary appear in Figure 2.

In New Hampshire, where McCain concentrated his campaigning in 1999, his average evaluation was decidedly higher than Bush's throughout January. The reverse was true in states with primaries on 7 March or (especially) later: despite some ups and downs in Super Tuesday states, perhaps reflecting McCain's performance in debates, McCain's ratings consistently fell below Bush's during the first month of the year.

The biggest evaluative shift of the campaign occurred in Super Tuesday states and began three days before the New Hampshire primary, as we also saw (see Figure 1) with McCain's share of vote intentions. Bush's advantage in ratings eroded swiftly in the Super Tuesday states, in rather sharp contrast to states with later primaries, and 10 days after New Hampshire, McCain's average rating surpassed Bush's. The evaluations of people intending to vote in the South Carolina Republican primary were strikingly similar to those in Super Tuesday states in early to mid-February; we have too few respondents in South Carolina prior to February to be certain that they followed the same path as those in

FIGURE 2
**McCAIN-BUSH RATINGS DIFFERENCE, BY ELECTORATE:
RESPONDENTS INTENDING TO VOTE IN REPUBLICAN PRIMARIES**

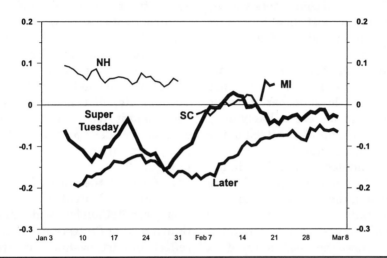

NOTE: "Later" smoothed with 11-day prior moving average, all others with 7-day prior moving averages.

Super Tuesday states, but again we suspect they did. The same may well be true of Michiganders, although they seem to have become even a bit more positive toward McCain than people in Super Tuesday states by the third week of February. By then, the latter had moved back toward Bush in their evaluations, and they favored Bush by a small margin for the remainder of the campaign. Although they became less pro-Bush during February, residents of the states with later Republican primaries nevertheless favored Bush throughout, and, on the eve of Super Tuesday, they continued to give Bush a wider margin than did those in Super Tuesday states.

Comparing the trajectories of the various electorates with a rough timeline of the campaign's events

yields some suggestions about the influences of information on primary voters. We can investigate those influences more rigorously, increasing our confidence in our conclusions, by extending our analysis in two ways. The first, which we will not pursue here but will in subsequent work, relies on content analysis of news coverage, advertising, debates, and other sources of information in order to characterize the events of the campaign, experienced as most people experience them. The second strategy involves identifying factors that shape the influence of information, either by regulating exposure to new information—the media habits of individuals, for example—or by determining reactions to new information— as do, for instance, the political predispositions of individuals. Here we can report the results of some initial exploration of the effects of predispositions on evaluations of the two main Republican contenders and, by implication at least, how those predispositions shaped reactions to new information.[6]

Early in the campaign, information alone was a boon to McCain's candidacy, at least in part because the uninformed were unlikely even to know of it. This shows itself in the relationship of education to ratings of the candidates. Before New Hampshire, other demographic factors being equal, the more educated residents of Super Tuesday states were markedly more inclined toward McCain than the less educated. A portion, but only a portion, of that difference can be explained by differences in political orientations and policy preferences associated with education. Much of the remainder probably reflects the association between education and familiarity with McCain. As the race heated up and information about McCain filtered through to the less educated, differences between educational groups faded. By the last two weeks before the Super Tuesday primaries, the effect of education had been cut nearly in half and was statistically insignificant. Virtually all of the remaining effect was due to general or specific political attitudes.

The other demographic characteristic with a strong connection to candidate evaluations is religious affiliation. Religion may be influential in any Republican campaign, of course, but the candidates' explicit remarks about religious beliefs and religious groups made religion a particularly volatile element of the 2000 campaign. In this campaign, the most important cleavage in candidate evaluations along religious lines divides Protestants who consider themselves "evangelical or born-again Christians" and Protestants who do not. Evangelical Christians make up about one-third of the Super Tuesday Republican sample and a clear majority (58 percent) of its Protestants.[7] The divergent paths of those two groups are depicted graphically in Figure 3.

Right from the start of the year, evangelical Protestants favored Bush over McCain by a wider margin than did other Protestants. This may reflect, in part, events that already had transpired: asked in a debate in Des Moines on 13 December to name the philosopher or thinker with whom he most identified, Bush responded, "Christ, because he changed my heart," sparking a burst of commentary in the press about the proper connection between religion and politics. The difference between evangelical and other Protestants held roughly constant as the two groups moved in parallel toward Bush until a couple of days before the New Hampshire primary. During the last few days of January, the gap between the groups widened, as Bush's advantage among those who think of themselves as born-again continued to grow, but his advantage among other Protestants did not.

After New Hampshire, both groups' ratings began to move back toward McCain, but the evangelicals moved neither as fast nor as far. By mid-February, nonevangelical Protestants rated McCain slightly higher

FIGURE 3
McCAIN-BUSH RATINGS DIFFERENCE, BY RELIGIOUS
AFFILIATION: SUPER TUESDAY REPUBLICAN VOTERS

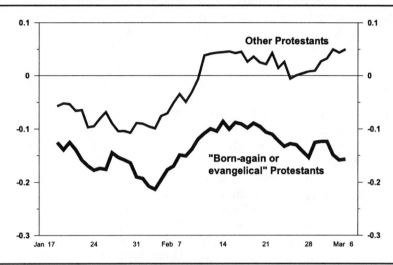

NOTE: Smoothed with 14-day prior moving averages.

than Bush, while evangelicals rated Bush considerably higher than McCain. It was during this period that the Bush campaign's appeal to evangelicals in South Carolina and McCain's ensuing denunciation of Pat Robertson and the religious Right became a national news story. The two groups of Protestants diverged further after the Michigan primary, as evangelicals' preference for Bush and nonevangelicals' preference for McCain both grew. During the last two weeks before Super Tuesday, other things being equal, the ratings of evangelical Protestants were 17 points more pro-Bush than those of other Protestants. The ratings of Catholics, of people of other denominations, and of people without religious affiliations on the eve of Super Tuesday were indistinguishable from those of nonevangel-

ical Protestants, once other demographic characteristics have been taken into account. And only evangelical Protestants gave Bush higher ratings than McCain; each of the other groups rated McCain slightly more favorably than Bush. Although we have yet to work out many of the details of the story, it seems clear that evangelical Protestants played a key role in blocking McCain's upward surge.

Other demographic factors influenced evaluations of the candidates little or not at all. The older and wealthier among those intending to vote in the Super Tuesday primaries viewed McCain a bit more favorably, other things being equal. Members of union households were more favorable toward McCain early in the campaign, but that difference disappeared after the New Hampshire primary. People in households that included a veteran or someone currently serving in the military liked McCain relative to Bush somewhat more than did other people during the middle period of the campaign. The evaluations of men and women did not differ significantly during any period.

Partisan and ideological orientations did influence evaluations of the Republican candidates strongly, and their influence grew stronger as the campaign progressed. Strongly committed Republicans gave Bush a wider edge than did weaker Republicans, independents, and Democrats before the New Hampshire primary, and the differences between the groups increased in the wake of New Hampshire and held steady through Super Tuesday. The differences were, in large measure, not related to differences in policy preferences; only a small portion of the effect of party identification is explained by positions on issues. The independent effects of ideological self-identification do not emerge powerfully until after the Michigan primary, but between Michigan and Super Tuesday the influence of ideology exceeded the influence of partisanship, even after controlling for preferences on specific policies. Self-identified liberals and moderates planning to vote in the Super Tuesday Republican primaries evaluated McCain much more favorably and Bush much less favorably than did conservatives.

Among the specific policies, three stand out. A belief that "the number of criminals not punished enough" is an extremely serious problem was associated with more pro-Bush ratings before New Hampshire and after Michigan. Between those events, respondents who wanted to restrict access to abortion and who opposed limits on soft money were markedly pro-Bush. These last two topics, at least, certainly were widely and frequently discussed during the campaign.

We find few differences in ratings of the candidates associated with economic policy preferences. In this respect, our results mirror those reported by Andrew Kohut (2000) shortly after Super Tuesday. But our data suggest that the two main Republican candidates did draw their support from distinctive and distinguishable social and political groups. George W. Bush was the candidate of conservative, committed Republicans, of those devoted to evangelical Protestantism and opposed to abortion. John McCain was the candidate of independent-minded, moderate Republicans and some Democrats, those who would like to limit the influence of money in politics and maintain the status quo on abortion. It was the campaign, at least in part, that allowed both candidates to reach and mobilize their respective coalitions.

SOURCES OF KNOWLEDGE

The American public learned from the 2000 Republican campaign, even during the brief period from the start of the year to the decisive primaries on Super Tuesday. Our measure of knowledge includes five items focused largely on information peculiar to this campaign and

FIGURE 4
KNOWLEDGE OF McCAIN BY ELECTORATE: REPUBLICAN VOTERS

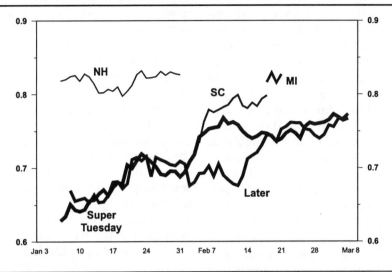

NOTE: "Later" smoothed with 11-day prior moving average, all others with 7-day prior moving averages.

information about John McCain.[8] Three of the items come from a longer battery of questions about the Republican candidates: who supports a ban on soft money campaign contributions; who is a U.S. senator; and who was a prisoner of war in Vietnam. Added to this is a measure of name recognition constructed from a respondent's willingness to rate McCain on the 100-point scale from favorable to unfavorable. Finally, we have included the interviewer's rating of "how knowledgeable the respondent is about politics."[9]

According to Figure 4, New Hampshirites intending to vote in the Republican primary knew far more about the Republican choice than did those outside New Hampshire at the start of the year. McCain had spent a great deal of time in the state during 1999, after all, and the other candidates had invested heavily in the state as well. Knowledge in New Hampshire grew no more during the month before the primary, but residents of states with primaries on Super Tuesday or afterward learned steadily, if not spectacularly, during the first three weeks of January. Learning leveled off in those states during the last week of January, and, in states with primaries after Super Tuesday, knowledge did not resume its rise until mid-February. In the Super Tuesday states, however, knowledge rose quite sharply following the New Hampshire primary. Knowledge also rose in South Carolina, and, with their primary looming, South Carolinians learned more in early February than did people in Super Tuesday states. Such a deadline effect no doubt also applied in Michigan, although other factors will have to be considered to explain why knowledge in Michigan nearly reached the level of knowledge in New Hampshire. The rate of learning in states with Super Tuesday or later primaries slowed after the South Carolina primary, and knowledge among those intending to vote in those states never approximated the level in New Hampshire.

If knowledge of the Republican candidates spread quite dynamically during the early months of 2000, standard measures of interest in politics, media exposure, and cognitive capacities do not go far toward identifying the people most likely to learn.[10] At every point in the campaign, knowledge was much more heavily influenced by one's educational background and general interest in politics than by exposure to news. Among the items assessing exposure to mass media, only newspaper reading promoted learning significantly and consistently. Even so, the knowledge difference between those who reported reading a paper every day during the previous week and those who reported reading none at all was never more than one-third the difference between the most and least educated or one-quarter the difference between the most and least interested in public affairs. Our survey question about political discussion is a bit of a hybrid, combining exposure (to the extent the responses reflect occasions on which individuals heard others talk about politics) and interest (to the extent they indicate voluntary participation in conversation about politics). It is also the most dynamic measure of campaign interest available to us for all three

periods: the fraction of Super Tuesday residents reporting political discussion in the previous week rose from two-thirds before New Hampshire to three-fourths after Michigan. As its incidence increased, however, the influence of participation in discussion was cut in half; the rate of learning among people not engaged in discussion was greater than among people who did talk about politics. In short, the campaign seems both to have caught the interest of some people and to have taught some a bit about the choice before them. The oddity in our analysis to this point is that the latter seems not to have depended upon the former.

THE VIABILITY OF JOHN McCAIN'S CANDIDACY

Why should viability matter to the vote? Bartels (1988, 108 ff) identified two avenues of effect[11] that seem relevant here: bandwagons and strategic voting. The first involves going with the winner, or climbing "on the bandwagon" of someone who seems about to become a winner (see Straffin 1977). The logic of the bandwagon effect makes most sense where a prospective supporter can expect something in return, as once was true of delegates at or in the run up to conventions. But Bartels argues for it in the mass primary setting.

In strategic voting, expectations play a gate-keeping role in choice. Where the field features more than two candidates, a voter should choose a candidate he or she prefers to at least one other candidate. But the actual choice may be of a candidate

FIGURE 5
McCAIN VIABILITY BY ELECTORATE: REPUBLICAN VOTERS

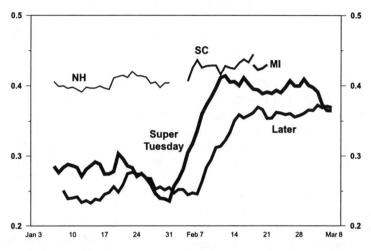

NOTE: "Later" smoothed with 11-day prior moving average, all others with 7-day prior moving averages.

other than the most preferred one if the chosen candidate is more viable. Strategic voting in this sense is focused on blocking the nomination of the least-preferred candidate. Normally, we would expect strategic calculations to figure prominently in the choice.[12] In 2000, the issue is clouded by the fact that the Republican race was only nominally a multicandidate one. Apart from McCain and Bush, only Forbes was well financed, and few believed that his support was likely to grow much. The question seemed to be, Admitting that only McCain might attract many new supporters, how much potential did he really have?

Viability is measured by a question asking the respondent to estimate each candidate's chances of winning the Republican nomination on a scale from zero to 100, where zero means "no chance," 50 means an "even chance," and 100 means "a certain win."[13]

In a sense, perceptions of the viability of John McCain's candidacy look like a caricature of his vote (see Figure 5). Perceptions were highest where he campaigned most intensely, but they surged dramatically elsewhere once the primary process emitted a clear signal. Wherever it appeared, the perception of McCain's chances reached a plateau between .40 and .45. By early January, New Hampshire residents estimated McCain's chances about where Super Tuesday residents did by mid-February. In February, residents of South Carolina and Michigan rated him slightly more highly than did Super Tuesday respondents. For most of that month, Super Tuesday respondents rated him more highly than respondents in later-primary states did.

The pattern is not one of mere projection from the state onto the nation. South Carolinians in February rated McCain's chances more highly in February than New Hampshirites did in January. Presumably, they digested the message from New Hampshire. Also, South Carolinians did not downgrade his national chances, even though his share in their own state was sliding. And they rated his chances about as highly as Michigan residents did, notwithstanding the support difference between the states. In short, voters responded to information from outside the state. Super Tuesday respondents reevaluated the McCain candidacy virtually overnight in the wake of the New Hampshire result. In a matter of days, his mean viability rating jumped over .15 points on a scale of zero to 1. It subsequently drifted down a bit, then back up a bit, and finally dropped modestly but unmistakably at the end. These ebbs and flows suggest that voters updated their perceptions in light of the South Carolina, Michigan, Virginia, and Washington results. Although the impact of South Carolina and Michigan is obscured somewhat by our smoothing procedure, the final drop is quite clear.[14]

Experiencing a real campaign seems to hasten response to external information. South Carolinians reached their expectational apogee ahead of Super Tuesday residents. The Super Tuesday surge nonetheless started the day after New Hampshire. Residents of later-primary states did not even begin to reevaluate McCain's chances until almost a week later. The post-Virginia, post-Washington drop that stands out in the Super Tuesday series finds no parallel in the sample from the later primaries.

For all the evidence of reality testing, it is still worth asking how much of this is wish fulfillment. Expressed perception of a candidate's chances may indicate little more than how much the respondent likes the candidate. This could even be true of the apparent dynamics. Although there is no mistaking the preciseness of the timing of shifts in Figure 5, room may still remain for impact from, say, reevaluation of the candidate himself. But the additional analysis that we have been able to do to this point strongly suggests that the public's reading of the race largely and directly reflected the outcomes of the primaries, especially New Hampshire, rather than McCain's growing popularity.

DYNAMICS OF THE CHOICE

In February, everything turned up for John McCain—knowledge of him, his popularity relative to George Bush, and his perceived chances of winning the nomination. Which among these were the truly active ingredients, or how much did each contribute? Answering this question requires us to take some of the information considered in close detail in earlier sections and assess its effects through a multivariate statistical model. Figure 6 depicts some of the main results from that analysis.[15]

The weakest net impact is that of gains in knowledge about John

FIGURE 6
COMPONENTS OF THE McCAIN SURGE: SUPER TUESDAY REPUBLICAN VOTERS

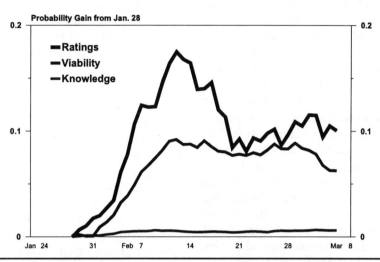

NOTE: Entries are predicted probabilities holding other factors constant, normalized to January 28.

McCain. Knowledge did surge in Super Tuesday states, but the knowledge effects are weak and offsetting. Knowledge does interact powerfully with evaluation, but remember that while McCain did markedly improve his evaluations relative to Bush, at best his roughly matched Bush's. Most of the time, he was less popular than Bush, and this remained true at the end, notwithstanding his overall improvement.

In contrast, the impact of his evaluative surge was huge; but then the surge dissipated somewhat. The evaluative surge alone would have taken McCain's share upward 15-20 points. But McCain fell back relative to Bush, and this would have taken his share back down more than 5 points.

The impact of McCain's perceived viability surge was smaller in the short run than his surge from evaluation but more sustained. Expectations for McCain surged about 20 points, by our measure, and stayed at an elevated level for most of February. The impact of this surge may have been mitigated by knowledge of McCain. Even so, the expectational surge by itself put McCain's vote share nearly 10 points ahead of his January standing. The bad news from Virginia and Washington shaved some off this, however.

Why did McCain's share of the vote not rise more? Why, in the end, did he lose? An obvious possibility is that the Bush campaign's aggressive counterattack stopped McCain in his tracks. The course of McCain-Bush rating differences gives a tantalizing hint that this happened. McCain pulled ahead of Bush a week and a half after New Hampshire, only to be pushed back. (Note that both observations also apply to South Carolina.) This reversal looks like more than mere exhaustion, or equilibration, of an impulse. If this reversal did not register at the bottom line, the vote, it may still indicate a successful intervention that stalled further growth. So far as we have pushed analysis, however, we cannot distinguish active intervention from a simpler model that says McCain grew as much as he reasonably could, full stop. Perhaps he launched his surge by staking issue claims that were too far from the Republican mainstream to carry him much beyond the favorable ground of New Hampshire.[16] Perhaps the real barrier was money.

The fact that perceptions of his nomination chances, of his viability, dropped after Virginia and Washington may be less important than that, once they reached their post–New Hampshire apogee, they rose no further. Prospective voters certainly saw him as better positioned in February than in January. But even in February he was still perceived as a long way behind Bush. What would further reevaluation have required? Michigan was a clear success, but all it did, if anything, was neutralize the South Carolina reverse. Perhaps Super Tuesday voters saw the Michigan result as essentially unrepresentative, a conjunction of permissive rules and no Democratic contest. These were also the rules in South Carolina, of course, which only worsened the interpretive implication of that result. But then, was the South Carolina result objectively that bad? What may matter is that more was expected of McCain in that state, and early returns to our South Carolina study suggest that this expectation had some warrant. The secrets of Super Tuesday, if there are any, may be buried in South Carolina.

DISCUSSION

In this article, we have barely scratched the surface of the Annenberg 2000 data on the nominating campaign. We have said nothing at all about the Democratic campaign, for instance, and therefore made no mention of the 3000 interviews done in Iowa before the caucuses or of more than half the interviews done elsewhere. Though less spectacular in their own right during this election cycle, we suspect that before we are through the Democrats will occupy a good deal of our attention, in part because the convergences and divergences between McCain's challenge to Bush and Bradley's challenge to Gore are striking and in part because McCain's appeal across party lines will be part of the Republican story.

Our account of the rise but ultimate defeat of John McCain is incomplete in several respects. While narrowing our focus principally to the primaries that gave the nomination to George W. Bush, we have emphasized the influence of voters in New Hampshire in their role as signalers of McCain's potential appeal and the influence of voters in South Carolina (and perhaps in Virginia and Washington) as signalers of its limits. To this point, we have relatively little to say, though, about the causes of the outcomes in those earlier primaries.

Why did McCain do so well and Bush so poorly in New Hampshire? Was it the tactics of the candidate, the campaign, and its allies that saved the day for Bush in South Carolina, or would it have been all but impossible for McCain to win there under any circumstances? These are among the questions we will take up in future work.

In the present article, we have begun to sketch, we believe, a persuasive account of McCain's emergence as a serious threat to a front-runner who once looked invincible. Whatever its explanation, the New Hampshire result obviously figures heavily—certainly as an indication to residents of other states (and to journalists) that McCain might have been able to win and probably also that McCain had qualities that made him worth considering. Those who intended to vote in later primaries took notice. The message played well with moderates and independents and defenders of abortion rights; it played poorly with conservatives, staunch Republicans, and opponents of abortion. As important as revised perceptions of McCain's chances were, we find that McCain's initial ascent was propelled even more powerfully by the change in what the Super Tuesday electorate thought of him.

Our account of the demise of the McCain campaign to this point is less satisfying. If McCain's share of vote intentions in Super Tuesday states had reached a plurality in mid-February and then fallen back, we could explain it in terms of the decline in his popularity after South Carolina and in his perceived chances after Virginia and Washington. In fact, though, McCain never attracted a plurality of the vote in Super Tuesday states, and his share did not decline in late February. We are thus far uncertain, therefore, how to characterize the apparent equilibrium the McCain campaign reached. Had his campaign simply reached its limits, having amassed the support of all who could reasonably be expected to come on board? Was the Bush counterattack instrumental in blocking further Bush losses? We have only begun to approach such questions.

Notes

1. The Annenberg 2000 Election Study is a continuous monitoring of the electorate, comprising national samples and oversamples of key primary and caucus states. Fieldwork is managed by Princeton Survey Research Associates and carried out by Schulman, Ronca, & Bucuvalas, Inc., and Princeton Data Services. All analyses and graphics reported here employ preprimary interviews only, distributed for each sample as a rolling cross-section: sample release is such that the day of interview is a product of random selection much as for initial selection to the sample.

2. The lines in Figure 1 are smoothed relative to the noise induced by sampling error. For the larger daily samples, we average values for 7 consecutive days. For the smallest, we pool 11 days.

3. McCain's actual share in South Carolina was 42 percent, about the same as he later received in all Super Tuesday states together.

4. In 2000, a recurring theme was the candidate's electability (as distinct from viability), his chances of winning the general election. We intend to explore this further, but space constraints and the complexity of the topic preclude doing so here.

5. The original scales ranged from zero to 100. Respondents unable to rate a candidate were assigned a score of 50 on his scale. The scale was then compressed to the range of –1 to

1, where zero means that the respondent gave the two candidates the same score.

6. For this analysis, we regressed the difference between evaluations of McCain and Bush on an array of demographic characteristics, then on the demographics plus party identification and ideological self-identification, then on those first two groups plus attitudes on a dozen matters of public policy. We modeled our batteries of policy items on those devised by Merrill Shanks and his collaborators (Shanks and Strand 1998) for their Survey of Governmental Objectives. To highlight the evolution of the candidates' coalitions and the importance of the information the campaign conveyed, we have divided the primaries into three periods: from the start of the Annenberg survey, 8 November, until the New Hampshire primary, 1 February; from New Hampshire until the Michigan primary, 22 February; and from Michigan through Super Tuesday, 7 March. Once again, analysis is confined to Super Tuesday respondents who intend to vote in a Republican primary.

7. These figures vary greatly across Super Tuesday states, of course. Massachusetts and Connecticut have the smallest percentages (under 15 percent), while in Missouri, Ohio, and Georgia, evangelical Protestants constitute nearly one-half (in Georgia, more than one-half) of the prospective Republicans in our sample.

8. We might have preferred to include in our measure questions about Bush as well. Despite our best efforts, however, we have been unable thus far to identify questions about Bush from our surveys on which the public seems to have learned much. Much of the blame may reside in our own choices about items to include in the survey, of course. But we suspect that it may reflect as well some of the oddities of the Bush campaign and of the candidate himself. The Bush name was well known long before the campaign began, although whether it was the candidate's name or his father's that was well known remains an open question. Beyond his name and his bank balance, however, Bush's campaign seems to have taken pains to reveal as little about the candidate as possible, certainly prior to the New Hampshire primary (cf. Mayer 2000) and to some degree even after. Whoever is respon-

sible, we will need to consider alternative measures of knowledge as our project progresses.

9. Further details about the index's construction appear in Hagen et al. 2000.

10. To investigate the influences of these factors, we regressed our measure of knowledge on a measure of attention to government and public affairs; self-reported exposure to network, local, and cable television news, newspapers, and political discussion during the previous week; and educational attainment. To facilitate comparisons between them, each independent variable is scored from zero to 1. To be sensitive to changes during the campaign in the sources of information, we again have divided the primaries into three periods: before New Hampshire, New Hampshire through Michigan, and Michigan through Super Tuesday. The analysis again is limited to respondents who expressed an intention to vote in the Republican primaries in Super Tuesday states.

11. Bartels (1988) identified a total of four processes. One sees some voters as cue takers, letting other voters take the lead in evaluating candidates. A prospective voter who is generally uninformed about the candidates might take the candidate's popularity with others as an indicator of his or her basic fitness for office. Models of cue giving and taking tend to emphasize cues originating with well-informed elites. The best recent example is Lupia and McCubbins 1998. That collectivities, through polls, could help individuals interpret candidates or propositions was first proposed formally by McKelvey and Ordeshook (1986). Bartels also argued that viability might feed contagion, which he took some pains to distinguish from cue taking. He admits that the two are essentially impossible to distinguish and carry the same implication for estimation, which is that one impact of viability would be on the candidate ratings discussed earlier. Bartels found this impact to be weak, however, and Brady and Johnston (1987, 179-80) found it to be essentially nonexistent.

12. It does in Bartels 1988, for instance.

13. In the analysis, we divide the raw score by the sum of the ratings given to McCain and to Bush. In the survey protocol, no mention was made of the total field of candidates, just of the candidates to be rated, candidate by can-

didate. Before 12 January, we asked about Bush, Forbes, and McCain. Thereafter, we asked only about Bush and McCain. Dividing the McCain rating by the Bush-McCain total should neutralize any artifact from this shift, and Figure 5 reveals no telltale movement around the date in question. Dividing through by the Bush-McCain total also neutralizes some interpersonal differences in scaling.

14. Inspection of the raw daily tracking suggests that McCain perceptions were sliding before the South Carolina setback, possibly as Super Tuesday voters digested coverage of that state. The Michigan result appears to have arrested that slide and, so to speak, corrected it. McCain's disappointing results in Virginia and Washington on 29 February caused a drop of .05 to .10, which the smoothed tracking never completely registered before time ran out.

15. For details about the analysis summarized here, see Hagen et al. 2000.

16. But then recall that, as we stated right at the top, on most questions McCain is hardly out of his party's mainstream.

References

Bartels, Larry M. 1988. *Presidential Primaries and the Dynamics of Public Choice*. Princeton, NJ: Princeton University Press.

Brady, Henry E. and Richard Johnston. 1987. What's the Primary Message: Horse Race or Issue Journalism? In *Media and Momentum: The New Hampshire Primary and Nomination Politics*, ed. Garry R. Orren and Nelson W. Polsby. Chatham, NJ: Chatham House.

Hagen, Michael G., Richard Johnston, Kathleen Hall Jamieson, David Dutwin, and Kate Kenski. 2000. Dynamics of the 2000 Presidential Primaries. Paper presented at the annual meeting of the American Association for Public Opinion Research, 17-19 May, Portland, OR.

Kohut, Andrew. 2000. What "McCain Voter"? *New York Times*, 12 Mar.

Lupia, Arthur and Mathew D. McCubbins. 1998. *The Democratic Dilemma*. New York: Cambridge University Press.

Mayer, William G. 2000. Turning a Candidate into a Lightweight. *New York Times*, 4 Feb.

McKelvey, Richard D. and Peter C. Ordeshook. 1986. Information, Electoral Equilibria, and the Democratic Ideal. *Journal of Politics* 48:909-37.

Shanks, J. Merrill and Douglas A. Strand. 1998. Understanding Issue Voting in Presidential Elections: Results from the 1996 Survey of Governmental Objectives. Paper presented at the annual meeting of the American Association for Public Opinion Research, 14-17 May, St. Louis.

Straffin, Philip D., Jr. 1977. The Bandwagon Curve. *American Journal of Political Science* 21(4):695-709.

ANNALS, *AAPSS*, **572**, November 2000

The Hole in the Doughnut:
Center Cities and Sprawl

Of all the issues left out of the presidential campaign of 2000, none is more basic than the geographic distribution of our population by social class. This issue is fundamental to a wide range of more visible problems. Traffic jams, sprawl, air pollution, obesity, water shortages, the decaying infrastructure of our sewers, bridges, and water supplies, gun control, health care, deforestation, education, the price of gasoline and home heating oil, infant mortality, and a host of other troubles are linked, by good evidence, to geographic segregation by race and class. Scouring census records over the past century or more, some scholars suggest that our nation now features more geographic segregation by race and class than at any other time in our history.

The absence of debate over this issue is striking on two dimensions. One is the moral or ideological dimension. Despite the traditional philosophical differences of the two major parties on this issue, neither side has chosen to either defend or attack rising geographic segregation. As suburban votes increasingly determine the outcomes of presidential campaigns, perhaps it is no surprise that no one dares to attack a foundation of suburban life. Yet the silence on the matter is deafening.

The other dimension is purely pragmatic. Given the concentration of federal and state expenditures for health, public safety, and welfare on the small percentage of the population isolated in impoverished inner-city areas, there is a possibility for enormous reductions in tax burdens from solving the problems of those areas. Those problems appear strongly linked to concentration. Whether the problems can be solved by dispersion or diversification of social class in those areas remains to be seen. But if crime is an indication, there is a good possibility to cut the national crime rates in half by succeeding in the inner cities first.

The next three articles take different approaches to this issue left out of the campaign. Each author was asked to describe why his or her aspect of the issue was important, what the major choices were for dealing with it, and why it had not been given more attention in the presidential campaign so far.

In the first article, Harvard public health professor Felton Earls considers the plight of urban areas where the majority of families live below the poverty line. His article draws on a major long-term study of human development in 343 Chicago neighborhoods. This evidence shows the massive and far-reaching effects of concentrated poverty on national ills of all kinds. Considering the alternatives of deconcentration versus revitalization of these areas, Earls explores the limitations of both approaches. He gives special attention to the difficulty of discourse around issues of race and class, which hurts efforts to link programs for nature conservancy to human conservancy. As long as we cannot discuss these issues openly, he concludes, we are unlikely to see our presidential candidates trying to lead the discussion.

Brookings Institution fellow Bruce Katz takes up the solutions that could help revive inner-city poverty areas as well as reduce rural sprawl. Katz portrays a striking contrast in locations of growth and stasis. While the centers of Ohio's seven largest cities gained just 636 new jobs in the years 1994-97, Katz tells us, the suburbs of those same seven cities gained 186,410 new jobs—a growth ratio of almost 300 to 1. The concentrations of welfare cases, of course, go in the opposite direction. Baltimore's 13 percent of all Marylanders includes 56 percent of Maryland's welfare recipients, a poverty ratio of over 4 to 1. Katz's analysis shows how appropriate these issues are for a presidential campaign. Not only do federal policies fail to address these issues, he argues, but they create positive incentives for what others call the "hole in the doughnut": the hollowing out of the economic life in center cities of our metropolitan areas. The proposals on the table in several states are all ripe for national debate. These include metropolitan government of specific functions like transportation and waste management, land use reforms for managed growth, public purchase of large tracts of land in outer and inner metropolitan areas, redirection of infrastructure funds to older, established areas, and public disclosure of the spatial allocation of governmental funds.

Janice Madden completes the analysis with the most pragmatic claim of all. Without vibrant and flourishing cities, her evidence suggests, the competitiveness of the U.S. economy will decline in the face of globalization. She not only shows how cities are the wellspring of new ideas for economic growth—including the development of many new products—but she also shows that concentrated poverty in cities hurts the growth of entire metropolitan areas. Her evidence suggests that government services become far more expensive under conditions of concentrated poverty and could serve the same people less expensively with greater dispersion of poverty. She concludes by joining Felton Earls and Bruce Katz in a clear attribution of these problems to federal policies, many of which date back to the New Deal.

Whatever the right solutions to these problems might be, we cannot adopt them without debate. The complexity of cause and effect in the connection between growth, land use, and social class is enormous. Yet this connection lies at the heart of all domestic problems, in an election year dominated by

domestic policy issues. Many people seem ready to listen. The question, as of
the date of this writing, is whether any candidate is willing to talk.

LAWRENCE W. SHERMAN

*Lawrence W. Sherman is the Albert M. Greenfield Professor of Human Relations at
the University of Pennsylvania, director of the university's Fels Center of Government,
and president of the International Society of Criminology.*

ANNALS, *AAPSS*, **572**, November 2000

Urban Poverty: Scientific and Ethical Considerations

By FELTON EARLS

ABSTRACT: Concentrated urban poverty in the United States is addressed from a dual perspective. The first viewpoint is derived from the social science literature. To advance the existing base of knowledge, reference is made to a specific research program, the Project on Human Development in Chicago Neighborhoods. This effort is currently in mid-course of a decade-long study of children from all major racial/ethnic, social class, and neighborhood groups in the city and is demonstrating the negative impacts on children's behavioral and social development of being raised in zones of concentrated poverty. The second perspective views urban poverty in the context of widening income disparity and through the lens of the economic and social rights accorded to citizens of a democracy. Political leadership is urgently needed to challenge this level of disparity and to acknowledge concentrated urban poverty as an insidious violation of human rights, particularly those of African American children.

Felton Earls is professor of child psychiatry at Harvard Medical School and principal investigator of the Project on Human Development in Chicago Neighborhoods. He is a fellow of the American Academy of Arts and Sciences and a member of the Institute of Medicine at the National Academy of Science. He serves on the Board of Directors of Physicians for Human Rights and is a member of the Committee on Human Rights at the National Academy of Sciences.

I N this article, I consider the plight of urban neighborhoods where families living below the poverty line represent the majority of the residents. My understanding of and response to these geographic areas and the children and families residing in them has been much enriched by research conducted by my colleagues and me in the city of Chicago over the past decade. But it would be remiss not to mention at the outset that my perspective has also been cultivated by work I have done outside the United States, in wealthy countries as well as resource-poor nations.

In wealthy countries, such as Sweden, it has been important to acknowledge how relative deprivation and issues of social equity are dealt with. In many developing societies, such as Tanzania, the issues have to do with survivorship and the quality of life under conditions of absolute poverty. There are also countries that may be more similar to the United States, like Brazil and South Africa, where wealth and poverty coexist. This international perspective provides a context in which U.S. domestic concerns are understood in a broader scope and thus makes available a more complete range of solutions than would be the case if the United States alone were the focus. While I appreciate this to be a controversial point of view, I hasten to add that, from my point of view as a physician whose primary interest has been the health of children, national interests have little persuasive power in relation to the transnational dynamics of drug abuse, violence, and infectious disease. These are conditions that disproportion-

ately affect the poor worldwide. Further, in our increasingly globalized world, they are conditions that spring not from within nation-states but involve intricate forms of international trade and communication that are becoming increasingly more complex and orthodox.

In this article, several questions related to concentrated poverty as it exists in urban areas of the United States are addressed. Although the focus is on large cities, I realize that the concept of concentrated poverty aptly applies to many Native American reservations, to rural areas throughout the country, and to an increasing number of suburban communities. The questions are the following: (1) why is this an important problem? (2) what are the major sources of controversy surrounding it? (3) what strategies are we using to address it? and (4) why is it not a more central issue in the presidential campaign of the year 2000? Since my responses are framed from the perspective of a social scientist, it is necessary to begin with an overview of my research.

THE PROJECT

The Project on Human Development in Chicago Neighborhoods was designed over a period of several years with the expectation that, in the course of a single large-scale study, an understanding of the behavioral and social problems experienced by children growing up in cities would be substantially advanced (Tonry, Ohlin, and Farrington 1991; Earls 1991). The research was located in Chicago on the basis that a single large urban setting could provide a broad range of locales stratified by race, ethnicity, and social class. Both advantages and disadvantages have been derived from this decision. An advantage is that the multiple administrative systems (schools, police, child care, and so forth) that regulate and support urban life can be examined in more depth than is typically done in studies that cover many jurisdictions. Another advantage is that a single site permits greater intensity of measurement and thus greater interpretability of results. With multiple and repeated measures of the same units, one gets to know the character of the neighborhoods and a more detailed picture of the way people live their lives (Holton 1999). The project has also had the good fortune of having generated several ethnographic studies completed by graduate students during the same period when the survey work was conducted, permitting even more intimate encounters with the setting and residents. We have also formed networks of youths and adults who have served as collaborators, critiquing our measures and providing detailed accounts of daily life (Earls and Carlson forthcoming). As Richard Wright (1945) wrote over a half century ago, "Chicago is a *known* city; perhaps more is known about it, how it is run, how it kills, how it loves, steals, helps, gives, cheats, and crushes than any city in the world" (xviii). This known quality continues to attract the world of social science. The results of our work at the end of this century and the beginning of a new one stand on the shoulders of eminent scholars, community activists, and politicians.

A disadvantage of the design is the limitation of the geographic sampling frame to the city limits of Chicago, rather than covering the entire metropolitan area. To the extent that the neighborhoods within the city boundaries function as subunits of the larger metropolitan area, inferences about the course of local changes may be misspecified. Nonetheless, the study achieved a diverse sampling frame of neighborhoods despite its focus on the city. Areas of concentrated poverty were captured, but so were many areas of concentrated affluence. Not surprisingly, the areas of concentrated affluence were predominantly European American and the areas of concentrated poverty primarily African American and Hispanic American in composition. There are also many working- and middle-class neighborhoods as well as neighborhoods characterized by populations of mixed ethnic and racial backgrounds.

The research design incorporates both multilevel and longitudinal features. The multilevel aspect examines the influences of neighborhoods, family, and individual differences simultaneously. The longitudinal component examines the impact of multiple determinants of problem behavior in individuals as well as protective factors that inhibit or deflect their occurrence.

To date, the analysis has been devoted to measuring neighborhood social processes that are postulated to be important in regulating the lives of children (Sampson 1999). Given the extensive data collected from 343 neighborhoods in the city, this effort is contributing to both theory and methodological development in urban sociology (Raudenbush and Sampson 1999). The study has succeeded in demonstrating that the expectation that neighbors can be counted on to intervene in the lives of children constitutes a condition that reduces levels of violence in neighborhoods (Sampson, Raudenbush, and Earls 1997). While this feature of social organization operates in conjunction with structural conditions such as residential stability, density of poor families, and immigrant concentration, it is important to note that demographic indicators of wealth, poverty, race, and ethnicity alone are not sufficient to explain variations in violence. The capacity to measure social cohesion, trust, and mutual support and the willingness of neighbors to act collectively breaks new ground by providing access to a proximal mechanism through which neighborhoods may affect how parents, peer groups, and children themselves behave.

Ongoing analyses are expanding the range of outcomes examined from crime and violence to physical health and mental health conditions such as low birth weight, asthma, depression, suicide, post-traumatic stress disorder, and substance abuse. The main hypothesis views the features of civic engagement and the security of interpersonal relationships that differentially characterize urban neighborhoods as determinants of well-being across this entire range of outcomes. An example of analysis that we are currently pursuing

regards the difference between black and white women with respect to the proportion of low-birth-weight infants delivered. The interest is in the extent to which a woman's residence in a stressful neighborhood independently predicts a lower birth weight for her offspring. The findings show that the higher rate of low birth weight among the infants of black women is the result of a "weathering" effect. The cumulative stress of living in an environment of poverty and social depreciation appears to produce a phenomenon in which birth weight decreases with the age of the black mother rather than increasing as it does for white women (Rich-Edwards et al. forthcoming).

In examining the distribution of resources across the many types of neighborhoods in Chicago, and in interviewing families intensively and repeatedly from each type, little imagination is needed to appreciate the stark contrast between areas of concentrated poverty and all other areas. This concern for the clustering of poor people regards the extent to which such neighborhoods undermine the capacity of residents to achieve a level of social organization necessary to protect the lives of children. While there are a variety of reasons why low levels of adult supervision and monitoring of children might be present, the problem is the extent to which structural conditions of high-density poverty—as reflected in physical blight and poor housing, depleted services, single-parent family structures, and strapped institutions—overwhelm the capacity to achieve common purposes and the social power to take action in pursuit of these concerted goals (Sampson, Morenoff, and Earls 1999).

THE SIGNIFICANCE OF CONCENTRATED POVERTY

What are the ways in which poor neighborhoods aim to overcome some of the structural impediments associated with economic and social disadvantages? What policies exist that encourage or inhibit such an effort? These questions evoke both scientific and ethical responses. It is well established that concentrated poverty is associated with high crime, violence, and poor health. Its importance to public health and to the fear of crime constitutes problems that seriously diminish the quality of life not just for residents of high-poverty areas but for others who share the same regional resources and infrastructure. Perhaps the most tragic aspect of this phenomenon is the waste of human potential that is a consequence of growing up in such areas. Indeed, this is a predicament that compromises the foundation of a modern democracy. When it is further realized that the problem is deeply mired in a history of racism and racist policies, the full extent of its ethical dimensions is captured. Although the absolute number of persons living in such conditions does not exceed more than 2-3 percent of the entire American population, the costs to the society are great, and they are evident and measurable in a host of ways, ranging from the imprisonment of a large number of young males to the loss of vital urban centers.

There is also the political reality that the long-fought effort to achieve civil rights for African Americans has not solved the problem of economic and social equity. The fact that intense poverty in cities is highly stratified by race makes it appear intractable. But, on a closer examination, the exclusion and lack of voice of the poor is as central to the problem as the depreciation of the poor in the mainstream of American society.

It should also be stated that the spread of urbanization, and thus urban poverty, is a global phenomenon. Although Chicago provides a setting in which to conduct rigorous research on the impact of urban environments on human development, it has been important to examine the same types of issues in other domestic and international locations for at least two reasons. First, the patterns of migration, concentration, and dispersion of poor families may reveal common determinants. Second, the policies and actions taken to alleviate this condition may suggest what the best practices are (Blanc 1994). Though much less systematic in method than the Chicago research, my more informal observations and consultations with agencies such as UNICEF has generated a much more interesting and complete understanding of urban poverty than would have been the case had this mission not been pursued. Much of the focus of this work has been on the conditions that force some poor children to work or live on the streets (Earls and Carlson 1999). In the course of this work, our notion of citizenship has been embellished, and the demand for research and researchers to aim toward more genuinely participatory frameworks has advanced. Recognizing poor, African American parents and children as full-fledged citizens of the oldest democracy in the world has urged me toward a new appreciation for the ethical basis on which a legitimate social science is made possible (Earls 1999).

THE CONTROVERSIES

The term "concentrated poverty," like the terms "ghetto" and "underclass neighborhood," carries a certain kind of stigma that is worth addressing. What subtle meanings or implications does the label "concentrated poverty" carry? Is it any different from "ghetto," "underclass," and so forth? The meaning turns out not to be subtle at all. In a national culture that prides itself on "rugged individualism," those who remain poor are losers in a struggle for self-determination and material success. The fact that African Americans, representing the great majority of persons and families that are geographically segregated and very poor, carry the enduring burden of being historically considered as subhumans, slaves, and secondary citizens, depending on the century, serves to isolate a group in a way that reduces societal attention to and interest in the particular reasons why their circumstances remain unimproved. The penchant to believe that people themselves are responsible for the state of their welfare and well-being weakens the incentive to consider persons in this predicament as

full-fledged citizens. This alone makes the issue of inequality less relevant, less evident, and less axiomatic than it might be had the persons so affected not carried the legacy of exclusion that characterizes African Americans. It is in this sense that the term "concentrated poverty" is problematic. The solution is not to disregard the term but to understand why concentrated poverty exists and to find effective remedies. In a modern state, this means summoning the best of social science.

Quillian (1999) provides an insightful review of the major scientific distinctions involved in interpreting the changing character and persistence of concentrated poverty. The contours of the argument regard the extent to which the phenomenon is a consequence of the out-migration of the most aspiring and able African American residents to white and middle-class neighborhoods versus the extent to which policies and attitudes of the larger society toward the African American poor remain fundamentally racist and exclusionary. Quillian concludes that both explanations are true. The out-migration hypothesis advanced initially by Wilson (1987) takes the post-civil-rights decade as a basis for postulating that persons left behind were deficient in motivation and skill and thus were not in a position to take advantage of new economic opportunities. On the contrary, Massey and Denton (1993) advance the argument that entrenched racism is the operating mechanism throughout society that results in the absence of political will to address the needs of people living in high-poverty areas. At more psychological and moral levels, it might appear that there exists an attitude of resignation about this problem, as if it were already established that not much can be done to change such people or raise their standard of living (Jarkowsky 1997).

As Quillian (1999) notes, these differences between social scientists do not represent a controversy as much as a difference in the specific contexts studied and in the ways of interpreting the evidence. For example, Wilson (1987) was correct in noting the out-migration of middle-class blacks to white suburbs for the particular Chicago neighborhoods that he observed. Indeed, the increasing location of jobs in the suburbs combined with improved transportation has been an inducement for African Americans to move to such areas. But it is also the case that some white communities are more defended than others against the acceptance of African Americans (Suttles 1968), so that the choice of where to move is constrained. On the other hand, our analysis of the spatial typology of Chicago neighborhoods shows that some African American middle-class residents have remained in the city. Because these neighborhoods are contiguous with areas of concentrated poverty, however, they are rendered more vulnerable than white middle-class areas in human development terms (Sampson, Morenoff, and Earls 1999). This result derived from survey data is confirmed by ethnographic study (Patillo-McCoy 1999). Whatever level of communal protection and support is afforded by growing up in such neighborhoods, it is threatened by the fact that fewer material resources, poorly functioning institutions, and scarce services are shared by these groups. For children, attending the same schools and being exposed to similar peer influences represent potent developmental factors that can undermine the capacity of families to raise highly motivated teenagers.

Although the scientific debate does not generate competing claims, reflecting for the most part inherent limitations of a particular method or location studied, the manner in which such differences influence the making of public policy makes them appear mutually exclusive, if not frankly antagonistic to one another. The two extremes in the debate attribute persistent poverty either to bad genes or to a human rights violation. More temperate positions might argue that concentrated poverty affects all people in ways that may not, at first blush, seem so obvious. It reduces the quality of life in the city through fear of crime and through the spread of drug abuse and some types of communicable diseases. Ultimately, the economic viability of a place is threatened.

Based on the Chicago experience, it is useful to take cognizance of the fact that a new set of demographic and geographical changes are taking place that might not have been predicted during the time when Wilson (1987) and Massey and Denton (1993) were conducting their research. These changes are resulting in increasing gentrification of urban areas that could have been thought of as beyond reclamation just a decade ago. As examples, areas surrounding the Cabrini-Green and Henry Horner public housing complexes in Chicago are undergoing rapid change, with the objective that mixed-income housing will produce racially and economically diverse neighborhoods. A combination of factors would appear to be fueling this phenomenon, among them a booming economy and improvements in community safety. Yet there may be countervailing factors, such as the uncertain impact of welfare reform on family life and the unplanned dispersion of former residents of public housing across the metropolitan area. How these newer urban dynamics will play out against the legacy of racism and revised public policies will be extremely important to monitor over the next decade.

STRATEGIES TO ADDRESS CONCENTRATED POVERTY

Two general approaches have been used to address the predicament of concentrated poverty. The first is to deconcentrate the poverty in these geographical areas by encouraging residents to disperse. The second is to provide the resources required to make such places more habitable.

Efforts to deconcentrate the poor have their origin in the lawsuit initiated by Dorothy Gatreaux, a resident of public housing in Chicago. After a long and protracted court battle that eventually reached the Supreme Court, a decision was made to require the U.S. Department of Housing and Urban Development (HUD) to desegregate pubic housing by developing a program that

granted tenants rent subsidy vouchers. Over a period of years beginning in the late 1970s, Rosenbaum and Popkin (1991) documented the benefits of relocating families from central-city public housing units to middle-income, low-crime, predominantly white suburban neighborhoods. While the results are promising, they lack scientific rigor because of the highly selective nature of the families involved in the transfers. For this reason, HUD, as part of its HOPE VI program, moved to design a more formal experiment in which families were randomly assigned to either an intensive intervention aimed to support their relocation to low-crime areas or to control groups in which they would either remain in public housing or be given vouchers to assist them in finding housing on the open market. This project, Moving to Opportunity, is currently in a late stage of evaluation.

The alternative to deconcentration is to revitalize blighted urban neighborhoods that have high proportions of poor families into more habitable locales that attract residents from a more diverse class and racial/ethnic status. In fact, both deconcentration of the poor and gentrification are happening. Gentrification of urban neighborhoods has been taking place for over a decade in Chicago, and in the past few years the Chicago Housing Authority's Plan for Transformation has entered a definitive phase of demolishing 52 high-rise buildings. The interests and values that lead some middle-class married or single adults to want to build a life in the city rather than the suburbs is a subject worth knowing much more about. The Gatreaux experience is useful for getting an idea of what attracts poor families to suburban areas. But we know too little about how these different motivations unfold in population and demographic terms. Rapid assessment of these trends might be very useful to urban planning.

A persistent concern is that the economic forces driving gentrification will be intolerant of genuine income mixing. As public housing buildings are removed, land values in these central-city areas are rising, and neighborhood revitalization in several areas is flourishing. In this context, poor families face two options. Both are challenging. The first is to resist the wholesale reclamation of neighborhoods by developers and families moving to areas formerly occupied by public housing dwellers. It is feasible, and perhaps ironic, to envision that class action suits might ensue with the opposite intent of the Gatreaux case, that is, to protect the rights of public housing tenants to remain attached to central-city neighborhoods as they are transformed. The other alternative is to seek housing in new areas. As former tenants enter the market, however, it is likely that some communities will resist their presence more than others, with the result that anti-discrimination claims of quite a different nature will surface.

Systematic and sustained efforts at long-term regional planning are needed to overcome the problems of concentrated poverty. An attractive example is the Chicago Metropolis 2020 of the Commercial Club of Chicago (1999). By underscoring the interdependence of the city and suburbs, it aims to improve the quality of life in the metropolitan region by focusing on six sectors: education, economic development, governance, land use and housing, transportation, and taxation. Three strategies are recommended:

1. Compact development schemes, in which open spaces are protected, public transportation is expanded and improved, and employer-assisted affordable housing is created near centers of employment, should be fostered as an antidote to urban sprawl, which has proven to be wasteful and damaging.

2. Healthy communities should be forged through support of community development corporations, faith community initiatives, banks that extend low-cost loans and extension of credit, and fair-housing groups.

3. Low-income housing tax credit should be expanded.

These are rational, constrained responses that reflect a charitable or, perhaps better yet, philanthropic attitude. They stop far short of moral outrage and, in a reasoned way, argue that the solution requires time and considerable political will to solve. But there is quite a different response that reflects a sense of urgency and consternation: the claim that reparations are due to African Americans. The higher rates of mortality, decreased quality of life, and higher proportion of low-birth-weight infants among African Americans compared to whites are some of the health-related indices that reflect a historical process of exploitation and exclusion and could be used to advance the claims for reparations.

THE TOLERANCE OF CONCENTRATED POVERTY IN AN AFFLUENT SOCIETY

In response to the question of how society chooses to ignore what was then known as the "Negro problem," Richard Wright (1945) wrote,

The answer is, directly and bluntly: American whites and blacks both possess deep-seated resistances against the Negro problem being presented, even verbally, in all its hideous fullness, in all of the totality of its meaning. The many and various commissions, councils, leagues, committees, and organizations of an interracial nature have consistently diluted the problem, blurred it, injected foggy moral or sentimental notions into it. This fact is as true of the churches as of the trade unions, as true of Negro organizations as of white, as true of the political Left as of the political Right; as true of white individuals as of black. (xxviii)

One noticeable characteristic of the current presidential campaign is its almost complete focus on domestic policies. In an era when the American economy is doing exceptionally well, this interest in domestic well-being might be considered an ideal time to raise the issue of concentrated poverty. Yet, because poverty can too easily appear to be the failure of individual initiative, there is the penchant to move it down on the political agenda. Just as is the case for persons in institutions such as prisons and nursing homes, people living in geographical areas of concentrated poverty do not appear on the radar screens of many Americans. It is the responsibility of the candidates to raise the issue in relation to the creation of a stable economy, the need for common security, and the demand to fulfill the promises of democracy. The failure to do so is not just a failure to come to grips with a persistent deficiency of government; it raises an ethical concern over the limits of what is tolerable. The serious level of income inequality alone raises issues of the extent to which social justice and economic rights are realized in the United States. To what extent is the nation ready to guarantee all its citizens an adequate standard of living given our collective resources? And in the context of increasing wealth, do we dare ask if our resources are adequate to substantially improve the economic and social status of 2 percent of the American population?

A parallel could be drawn between interest in the social and natural environments. The environmental movement has succeeded in activating both government and civil society to develop strategies to conserve healthy ecosystems for animals and plants. Unfortunately, there is no articulation for bipartisan support for the conservation of human beings in the current presidential campaign. If one framed the issue of concentrated poverty and aggravated disadvantage in the concepts and language of international law, one would say that progress in reaching civil and political rights (also termed negative rights) for all American citizens now must be coordinated with efforts to achieve economic and social rights (or positive rights) for all

(Morrison-Rodriguez 1999). Is the United States ready to eliminate this form of injustice? One candidate did address the issue with a sense of resolve in the early phases of his campaign, but by the time the primaries were under way, his campaign had lost steam and rapidly withered.

FINAL THOUGHTS

The Chicago neighborhood project seeks to make a contribution that will serve as a basis for improving the quality of life for children in cities around the world. At an early stage of development, the project stated a point of view that aimed to move social science beyond its purely academic interests to become more engaged in seeking solutions to problems such as the concentration of poverty and race relations (Earls 1994). The idea was that the hypotheses, methods, and products of science should become integrated with democratic principles and practices. In parallel with the main study, a separate but linked effort has been made to work with small groups of citizens as collaborators (Earls and Carlson forthcoming). While this allows the work to become more transparent and intelligible to an ordinary citizen, it is also important to state that it has not constituted a threat to the scientific rigor of the project. The benefits of receiving genuine feedback on the quality of the measures coupled with the knowledge that our results are interesting and useful far outweigh the disadvantages associated with a loss of scientific objectivity. Moreover, we have had no reason to believe that these participatory modes have distorted or changed in any fashion the social and behavioral phenomena under study.

A final insight derived from the Chicago experience needs to be presented with regard to the societal tolerance of concentrated poverty among African Americans. It has to do with the situation of new immigrants from Latin America. A second "Great Migration" has dominated the life of the city over the past two decades; it comprises Mexicans mostly from rural regions of Mexico, who come directly to Chicago (Cervantes 1996). Unfortunately, there have not been satisfactory estimates of the numbers of immigrants settling in the city because a large proportion arrive with an illegal status. It might be speculated, nonetheless, that the numbers are as large as, if not larger than, the 1 million blacks who migrated from the rural South to Chicago in the middle of the twentieth century.

The character of poor immigrant communities is to be distinguished from that of poor African American neighborhoods. The motivation to work hard despite low wages, to educate one's children, to gain citizenship, and to own a house—in short, to fill in the contours of the American dream—remain a positive force in Mexican neighborhoods. At the same time, there is a character of resignation, frustration, and hopelessness in African American neighborhoods that often lie side by side with areas of concentrated immigrants. The problem this contrast raises is that as long as the larger society can point to poor people who still believe in the ethic of "pulling oneself up by one's bootstraps," the plight of African Americans can be justifiably sidelined. Meantime, the realities of inheriting a debilitating history remain inadequately addressed. This neglect further toughens racist attitudes. A paradox exists that thus far is only partially understood. As Mexicans become acculturated to American society (that is, as they become Mexican Americans), they appear to lose certain advantages that might have been retained during the process of immigration (Hayes-Bautista et al. 1994; Mendoza 1994). The protective factors that shield them are reflected in greater longevity and relatively lower rates of low-weight births and infant mortality than predicted by their income and educational status. But these protective influences diminish with successive generations; the mortality and morbidity rates begin to converge toward those of African Americans (Cervantes, Keith, and Wychak 1999).

Social science has advanced considerably over the past few decades and has the potential to advance society in ways that strengthen democracy, promote social justice, and support the negative and positive rights of all citizens. This is no more an idealistic statement than to say that economics research aims to improve understanding of and support for a market economy. Let not democracy suffer from a social science that fails to recognize its vitality as well as its limitations and shortcomings.

References

Blanc, Cristina. 1994. *Urban Children in Distress: Global Predicaments and Innovative Strategies.* New York: Gordon Breach.

Cervantes, Arturo. 1996. Latinos in the U.S. and Chicago: The History, Demographics, and Prospects of a Growing Population. *Chicago Project News* 2(3):1-4. Also available at http://phdcn.harvard.edu.

Cervantes, Arturo, Louis Keith, and Grace Wychak. 1999. Adverse Birth Outcomes Among Native-Born and Immigrant Women: Replicating National Evidence Regarding Mexicans at the Local Level. *Maternal and Child Health Journal* 3:99-109.

Commercial Club of Chicago. 1999. Chicago Metropolis 2020. Executive Summary.

Earls, Felton. 1991. Not Fear, nor Quarantine, but Science: Preparation for a Decade of Research to Advance Knowledge About the Control of Violence. *Journal of Adolescent Health* 12:619-29.

———. 1994. Connecting Social Science to the World: The Project on Human Development in Chicago Neighborhoods. Harvard Medical School. Brochure. Also available at http://phdcn.harvard.edu.

———. 1999. Frontiers of Research on Children, Youth and Families. *Journal of Community Psychology* 27:517-24.

Earls, Felton and Maya Carlson. 1999. Children at the Margins of Society. In *Homeless and Working Children Around the World: Exploring Developmental Issues*, ed. M. Raffaeli and R. W. Larsen. San Francisco: Jossey-Bass.

———. Forthcoming. Adolescents as Collaborators: In Search of Well-Being. In *Youth in Cities*, ed. Marta Tienda and

William Julius Wilson. New York: Cambridge University Press.

Hayes-Bautista, David, L. Beazconde-Garbanati, W. O. Schink, and M. Hayes-Bautista. 1994. Latino Health in California, 1985-1990: Implications for Family Practice. *Family Medicine* 9:556-62.

Holton, John. 1999. Notes from the Field. *Chicago Project News* 5(1):1-5. Also available at http://phdccn.harvard.edu.

Jarkowsky, Paul A. 1997. *Poverty and Place: Ghettos, Barrios, and the American City.* New York: Russell Sage Foundation.

Massey, Douglas S. and Nancy A. Denton. 1993. *American Apartheid: Segregation and the Making of the Underclass.* Cambridge, MA: Harvard University Press.

Mendoza, Fernando. 1994. The Health of Latino Children in the United States. *Future of Children* 3:43-72.

Morrison-Rodriguez, Barbara. 1999. Twenty-Six Steps to Article 27: The Example of African-American Children in South Carolina. In *Implementing the U.N. Convention on the Rights of the Child: A Standard of Living Adequate for Development*, ed. A. B. Andrews and N. H. Kaufman. Westport, CT: Praeger.

Patillo-McCoy, Mary. 1999. *Black Picket Fences: Privilege and Peril Among the Black Middle Class.* Chicago: University of Chicago Press.

Quillian, Lincoln. 1999. Migration Patterns and the Growth of High Poverty Neighborhoods, 1970-1990. *American Journal of Sociology* 105:1-37.

Raudenbush, Stephen W. and Robert J. Sampson. 1999. Ecometrics: Toward a Science of Assessing Ecological Settings with Application to the Systematic Social Observation of Neighborhoods. *Sociological Methodology* 29:1-41.

Rich-Edwards, J., S. Buka, R. T. Brennan, and F. Earls. Forthcoming. Diverging Associations of Maternal Age with Low Birth Weight for African-American and White Mothers. Harvard Medical School. *American Journal of Public Health.*

Rosenbaum, J. and S. Popkin. 1991. Black Pioneers: Do Their Moves to Suburbs Increase Economic Opportunity for Mothers and Children. *Housing Policy Debate* 2:1179-1214.

Sampson, Robert. 1999. What Communities Supply. In *Urban Social Problems and Community Development*, ed. R. F. Ferguson and W. T. Dickens. Washington, DC: Brookings Institution Press.

Sampson, Robert, Jeffrey Morenoff, and Felton Earls. 1999. Beyond Social Capital: Spatial Dynamics of Collective Efficacy for Children. *American Sociological Review* 64:633-60.

Sampson, Robert, Stephen Raudenbush, and Felton Earls. 1997. Neighborhoods and Violent Crime: A Multilevel Study of Collective Efficacy. *Science* 277:918-24.

Suttles, Gerald. 1968. *The Social Order of the Slum: Ethnicity and Territory in the Inner City.* Chicago: University of Chicago Press.

Tonry, Michael, Lloyd Ohlin, and David Farrington. 1991. *Human Development and Criminal Behavior: New Ways of Advancing Knowledge.* New York: Springer-Verlag.

Wilson, William Julius. 1987. *The Truly Disadvantaged: The Inner City, the Underclass, and Public Policy.* Chicago: University of Chicago Press.

Wright, Richard. 1945. Introduction. In *Black Metropolis: A Study of Negro Life in a Northern City*, by St. Clair Drake and Horace R. Cayton. New York: Harcourt, Brace.

The Federal Role
in Curbing Sprawl

By BRUCE KATZ

ABSTRACT: This article contends that the federal government has a significant role to play in curbing metropolitan sprawl and promoting reinvestment in cities and older suburbs. It outlines the dominant growth trends under way in U.S. metropolitan areas (that is, the rapid decentralization of employment centers and residential areas) and discusses the implications of these trends for the economy, the environment, social welfare, and general quality of life. It also shows how a new metropolitan agenda is emerging in the states to address such issues as metropolitan governance, land use, infrastructure spending, and job access. Finally, the article calls on the presidential candidates to discuss ways in which federal action can help metropolitan areas grow differently—by providing directives and incentives for metropolitan governance, enacting policies that facilitate smart growth, and helping regions understand their challenges.

The founding director of the Brookings Institution Center on Urban and Metropolitan Policy, Bruce Katz has previously served as chief of staff to Henry G. Cisneros, former secretary of housing and urban development, and was the staff director of the U.S. Senate Subcommittee on Housing and Urban Affairs. He is a magna cum laude and Phi Beta Kappa graduate of Brown University, attended the London School of Economics, and received his juris doctorate from Yale Law School. He has written op-eds and articles for a wide range of major national and regional newspapers and is a frequent commentator on urban and metropolitan issues.

I N the past few years, widespread frustration with sprawling development patterns has precipitated an explosion of metropolitan thinking and action across the United States. A new policy language—"smart growth," "livable communities," "metropolitanism," "sustainable development"—has emerged to describe efforts to curb sprawl, promote urban reinvestment, and balance growth. Such language has now become common among political, civic, and corporate leaders as well as developers and other participants in the real estate industry.

The involvement of governors and state legislatures has been particularly noteworthy. Since 1997, states have made considerable progress on several fronts, including metropolitan governance, growth management, land use acquisition, infrastructure policy, and information disclosure. The metropolitan reforms taking hold in state legislatures are ambitious and reflect a sharp departure from the general ethos that has dominated growth discussions in most parts of the country.

This article argues that the federal government (and the presidential candidates in the year 2000) should also support efforts to curb sprawl. Current federal spending, tax, and regulatory policies distort metropolitan growth patterns and need to be reformed if serious alternatives to sprawl are going to be possible. The consequences of sprawl also undermine core national priorities such as protecting the environment, revitalizing older communities, and helping low-income families gain access to employment and educational opportunities. The federal government, in short, must engage fully if metropolitan areas are to move beyond sprawl.

HOW METROPOLITAN AMERICA GROWS

America's cities and metropolitan areas are experiencing similar patterns of growth and development— explosive sprawl where farmland once reigned, matched by decline or slower growth in the central cities and older suburbs. Suburban areas, some of which were small towns a few decades ago, are capturing the lion's share of population and employment growth. The rate of population growth for suburbs was more than twice that of central cities—4.2 percent versus 9.6 percent—from 1990 to 1997 (Rusk 1998, 14). From 1989 to 1996, 7.4 million upper- and middle-income households left cities for suburbs, while only 3.7 million moved from suburb to city (Kasarda et al. 1995, 341-42).

More and more people are living, working, shopping, and paying taxes at the farthest edges of metropolitan areas. The cities of Baltimore, St. Louis, Philadelphia, and Washington, D.C., for example, lost population throughout the 1990s as their metropolitan areas expanded. Even cities that are growing are not keeping pace with the ferocious rate of growth in their suburbs. Denver gained about 35,000 people in the 1990s (after having lost residents in the decade before), but the surrounding counties that compose the Denver metropolitan area are now home to an additional 340,000 people—

almost 10 times the population gain of the city. In Atlanta, Dallas, and Houston, central-city growth is far outmatched by growth in outlying counties.

The suburbs also dominate employment growth. A study of 92 metropolitan areas found only 17 places where city job growth outpaced suburban job growth during the middle of the 1990s (Hill and Brennan 1999). The bulk of the cities did gain jobs, but at a slower pace than their suburban neighbors. For example, from 1994 to 1997, the central business districts in Ohio's seven major cities experienced a net increase of only 636 jobs. Their suburbs, by contrast, gained 186,410 new jobs (Hill and Brennan 1998). In the greater Washington, D.C., area, the city's share of regional employment dropped precipitously in the 1990s: from one-third in 1990 to one-fourth in 1998. The suburbs outside the Capital Beltway are now home to half of all regional jobs, up from 38.7 percent in 1990 (Brookings Institution 1999).

Meanwhile, the poor have been left behind in the cities. Urban poverty rates are twice as high as suburban poverty rates, and the implementation of welfare reform appears to be a special problem for cities. While welfare caseloads are shrinking in most cities, with some exceptions they are not shrinking as quickly as they are in the states and in the nation as a whole. A city's share of a state's welfare population often far outstrips its share of the state population as a whole. Philadelphia County, for example, is home to 12 percent of all Pennsylvanians

but 48 percent of all Pennsylvanians on welfare. Baltimore has 13 percent of Maryland's population but 56 percent of its welfare recipients. This hardly adds up to an urban renaissance (Katz and Allen 1999).

Metropolitan growth patterns are also transforming the suburbs. Older suburbs, mostly developed after World War II, are starting to look more and more like the central cities. Poverty rates are increasing, schools are struggling, commercial corridors are declining, and property values are stagnating or falling. In the Atlanta metropolitan area, for example, 86 percent of the children in the central-city public school system qualify for free or reduced-cost lunch (an indicator of low income). Yet the proportion of poor children is also extremely high in the older suburbs of DeKalb County (60 percent) and Clayton County (53 percent) (Brookings Institution 2000). The city-versus-suburb idea makes no sense in trying to describe these places, because their differences from the cities are less important than their similarities.

Another group of suburbs is grappling with the consequences of rapid growth. These suburbs are choking on development, and in many cases the local governments cannot keep providing the services that residents need or demand. Traffic congestion has become a major concern, as have environmental degradation and the loss of open space. Loudoun County, a boom suburb in northern Virginia, epitomizes this kind of place. The overall population of Loudoun, the fourth-fastest-growing county in the nation, increased by 67 percent from

1990 to 1998; the school population increased by 78 percent during the same period. The county school board predicts that it will have to build 22 new schools by 2005 to accommodate an abundance of new students (Brookings Institution 1999). Suburbs like Loudoun simply cannot maintain their standards: there are too many new people who need too much new, expensive infrastructure—not just schools but also sewer and water lines, libraries, fire stations, and roads.

The patterns of extensive growth in some communities and significantly less growth in others are inextricably linked. Poor neighborhoods with high costs, inadequate services, and badly performing schools push out families with resources, who move to the edges of the region. As these families leave, so do jobs, services, and businesses. This flight further weakens already struggling neighborhoods, accelerates the decentralization of the region's economy, and puts more pressure on other fast-growing jurisdictions.

Major federal and state spending programs, tax expenditures, and regulatory and administrative policies fundamentally shape these growth patterns in metropolitan areas. Federal and state policies, taken together, set "rules of the development game" that tend to facilitate the decentralization of the economy and the concentration of urban poverty (see Katz 1999, 310-14; see also Nivola 1999). Federal and state transportation policies generally support the expansion of road capacity at the fringe of metropolitan areas and beyond, enabling people and

businesses to live miles from urban centers but still benefit from metropolitan life. Tax and regulatory policies have given added impetus to people's choices to move farther and farther out. The deductibility of mortgage interest and property taxes from state and federal income taxes appears spatially neutral but in practice favors suburban communities, particularly those with higher-income residents. Major environmental policies have made the redevelopment of urban land prohibitively expensive and cumbersome, increasing the attraction of suburban land.

Other federal policies have concentrated poverty rather than enhancing access to opportunity (Katz 1999, 315-16). Devolving responsibility for workforce and housing voucher programs to thousands of local public housing authorities and workforce investment boards has made it difficult for low-income families to know about suburban housing vacancies or job openings. Until recently, federal public housing catered almost exclusively to the very poor by housing them in special units concentrated in isolated neighborhoods. More than half of public housing residents still live in high-poverty neighborhoods; only 7 percent live in low-poverty neighborhoods, defined as neighborhoods where less than 10 percent of residents are poor.

THE NEW
METROPOLITAN AGENDA

An emerging awareness of the costs of sprawl—and the role of government policies in facilitating sprawl—is transforming metropolitan area politics around the country (see Katz 1999, 316-24). Elected officials from cities and inner suburbs; downtown corporate, philanthropic, and civic interests; minority and low-income community representatives; environmentalists; slow-growth advocates in the new suburbs; farmers and rural activists; and religious leaders are realizing that uncoordinated suburban expansion brings needless costs. With this in mind, they are working on a new metropolitan agenda. In Chicago, the Commercial Club, an organization of top regional business leaders, has released the Chicago Metropolis 2020 report, an ambitious plan for meeting that area's myriad challenges in the coming decades. In Ohio, elected officials from inner suburbs around Cleveland are joining forces with farm preservation constituencies to push state growth management reforms. In Maryland, a coalition of environmentalists (the Chesapeake Bay Foundation), business leaders (the Greater Baltimore Committee), and urban advocates (the Enterprise Foundation and the Citizens Housing and Planning Association) is leading statewide efforts to curb suburban sprawl and promote reinvestment in older, established communities.

The new metropolitan coalitions are making a difference on transportation and land use issues. Leaders in Chattanooga, Portland, and St. Louis are choosing to repair existing infrastructure, invest in mass transit, and preserve open space rather than to build more roads. In virtual

revolt over congested roads, overcrowded schools, and loss of open space, citizens of outer suburban communities in northern Virginia and Seattle have pushed county governments to increase developer fees, scale back existing plans for residential growth, and buy land to preserve open space. Often, however, these coalitions find that power over land use, welfare, housing, tax policy, and local governance is exercised in state capitals and Washington, D.C.

Several states have recognized the power of a new "metropolitics" (Orfield 1997) and are pursuing five sets of complementary policies to support it. First, they have authorized new forms of metropolitan governance to handle transportation, environmental protection, waste management, cultural amenities, and economic development. Second, they have embraced land use reforms to manage growth at the metropolitan fringe. Third, they are increasingly spending state funds to buy tracts of land threatened by sprawl as well as reclaiming urban land for productive use. Fourth, they have begun to steer infrastructure investment and other resources to older, established areas. Finally, they are starting to disclose the spatial allocation of state funds. Each of these reforms is discussed next.

Metropolitan governance

States are extending metropolitan governance over activities that naturally cross borders and benefit residents of an entire region, including transportation, land use planning, and economic development. The most ambitious efforts are under way in Oregon and Minnesota. These states have created multipurpose regional entities in Portland and the Twin Cities to carry out certain operational and planning functions. In 1978, Oregon created the Greater Portland Metropolitan Service District, an elected body that oversees regional transportation and land use planning, including the development and preservation of the urban growth boundary. It also operates the mass transit system, various parks, and cultural facilities. In the early 1990s, Minnesota placed all regional sewer, transit, and land use planning in the Twin Cities area under a single entity, the Metropolitan Council. The state's action transformed a planning agency with a $40 million annual budget into a regional authority with a $600 million annual budget.

In 1999, Georgia became the most recent state to experiment with metropolitan governance. In response to federal enforcement of the Clean Air Act, the state established the Georgia Regional Transportation Authority, a new regional transportation authority in the Atlanta metropolitan area with sweeping powers over land use, transportation, and development.

Land use reforms and growth management

Since the early 1970s, 11 states—Delaware, Florida, Georgia, Maine, Maryland, New Jersey, Oregon, Rhode Island, Tennessee, Vermont, and Washington—have enacted state land use laws to direct local governments in the management of growth. Oregon has the most comprehensive growth management effort in the United States. In 1973, the state enacted the Land Conservation and Development Act to contain urban sprawl and preserve forests and farmland. The act requires that urban growth boundaries be drawn around all cities throughout the state, and it mandates comprehensive land use planning at both the local and metropolitan levels. The act also requires that all city, county, and metropolitan plans be consistent with state planning goals and authorizes the State Land Conservation and Development Commission to enforce compliance with the consistency requirement.

The appetite for growth management will probably expand in the next few years. In 1998, Tennessee passed a law requiring counties to adopt land use plans that designate growth boundaries for existing municipalities and set aside rural preservation and "planned growth" areas. Land use reforms are picking up steam in Arizona, Pennsylvania, Ohio, and Michigan. Maryland and New Jersey, where growth management laws are already on the books, are expanding state intervention.

Land acquisition

In recent years, an increasing number of state governments have been spending money to conserve land threatened by development and to clean up land in older communities. In 1998, ballot initiatives asked voters to approve bond measures or tax increases to preserve open space or acquire parks and wildlife habitats in Alabama, Arizona, Florida, Georgia, Michigan, Minnesota, New

Jersey, New Mexico, Oregon, and Rhode Island. All passed except Georgia's and New Mexico's. New Jersey amended its constitution so that $1 billion over 10 years will go to open-space conservation efforts. Taken together, the voters in 1998 approved 72 percent of the ballot measures to preserve open space and promote conservation, entailing a commitment to spend $7.5 billion, directly or indirectly, to implement these measures.

The voters' actions have continued through 1999 and 2000. In 1999, for example, the Pennsylvania legislature enacted the five-year, $650 million Growing Greener initiative to preserve farmland, protect open space, restore watersheds, and help communities address land use. In early 2000, California voters approved a $2.1 billion park bond and a $1.9 billion water bond. Nearly half of this new money will go to preserve open space in urbanized areas. It is expected that a number of states will have referenda on land-related issues in the November 2000 elections.

Infrastructure spending

Maryland and New Jersey are in the vanguard of the smart-growth movement, which includes the efforts of states to target direct spending and tax incentives to communities where infrastructure is already in place. In 1997, Maryland enacted laws to steer state road, sewer, and school moneys away from farms and open spaces to "priority funding areas." Some of these areas are designated in the law—Baltimore and certain areas within the Baltimore and Washington beltways, for example. Counties may designate other areas if they meet certain guidelines. In 1998, New Jersey expanded on Maryland's approach; Governor Christine Todd Whitman ordered state agencies to give preference to projects in areas where infrastructure was already in place.

Smart-growth policies do not stop development or repeal the operation of market forces; they simply control where the government chooses to spend its resources. According to Ronald Kreitner, Maryland's former state planning director, smart-growth policies repeal an "insidious form of entitlement—the idea that state government has an open-ended obligation, regardless of where you choose to build a house or open a business, to be there to build roads, schools, sewers."

Information disclosure

A few states have begun to disclose the spatial allocation of state economic development funds and other investments. Curbing sprawl is often not the primary objective of these disclosure efforts; rather, disclosure advocates are generally trying to ensure that state resources are spent in a prudent and efficient manner. Yet smart-growth advocates can benefit substantially from these disclosure efforts. Anecdotes abound of states' providing major corporate employers with incentives to locate their facilities in exurban areas, thereby subsidizing sprawling development far from existing labor markets and older economies. Disclosure can be used to curb such instances of sprawl.

Minnesota's disclosure law should be studied for replication. The Minnesota Subsidy Accountability Law mandates an annual reporting procedure for tracking economic development grants, loans, and tax increment financing. Each local, regional, or state agency that provides the subsidies must report both the goals and the results. A similar law has been enacted in Massachusetts.

WHAT ROLE CAN THE FEDERAL GOVERNMENT PLAY?

States have the primary responsibility in efforts to rejuvenate metropolitan areas and reduce the costs of sprawl because they set the rules for land use, state and municipal taxes, transportation, and governance. But the federal government will also play a major part in determining the success or failure of efforts to advance the metropolitan agenda described in this article because many current federal policies facilitate sprawl and concentrate poverty, and new policies can promote metropolitan solutions to urban and suburban problems (see Katz 1999, 324-27; see also Katz and Bradley 1999).

Metropolitan governance

The federal government should take a number of actions to provide support for greater metropolitan governance. First, it should extend the level of metropolitan administration that has been a part of federal transportation law since 1991. In many metropolitan areas, city bus routes continue to stop literally at the border of the central city, greatly impeding the ability of urban workers to access suburban jobs. Express bus services from labor markets in central cities to job centers in suburbs are the exception. Federal action should be taken to create transit systems that meet the real needs of firms and workers in economies that are rapidly decentralizing. The federal government could, for example, require the integration of metropolitan transit systems as a condition of receiving federal funds. As an interim step, federal agencies should review whether the balkanization of metropolitan transit systems violates federal civil rights laws. Federal incentives could also help grow the small job-access demonstration projects in the Department of Transportation into initiatives that more directly address the commuting challenges faced by low-income workers.

Second, metropolitan-wide administration should be promoted in areas like housing, workforce, and economic development. Action in the housing arena is particularly important, given the role of housing in shaping growth patterns. Housing is perhaps the most difficult of the regional challenges because of the persistent pattern of racial and ethnic discrimination in the marketplace. Yet government programs and policies have also impeded housing mobility and choice. The federal voucher program—now serving over 1.6 million families with rental subsidies—is administered by some 4400 separate public housing bureaucracies operating in parochial jurisdictions. This hyperfragmentation of governance makes it difficult for low-income recipients to understand, let alone exercise choice in, a metropolitan housing market. The federal government should shift governance of the housing voucher program to the metropolitan level. Competitions should be held in dozens of metropolitan areas to determine what kind of entity—public, for-profit, nonprofit, or a combination thereof—is best suited to administer the program.

Finally, where metropolitan governance is impracticable, the federal government could encourage metropolitan collaboration. Recently, the federal government has started to provide additional services—transportation, job training, housing, child care—to people moving from welfare to work. As local governments compete for scarce federal resources, the federal government could give preference to applicants that demonstrate metropolitan collaboration. Preferences of this sort could also apply to block grant programs.

Land use reforms

State and local governments have the principal responsibility in determining patterns of land use. Yet the federal government can play two constructive roles in this area. First, the federal government should provide resources for the preservation of open space in metropolitan areas and the reclamation of urban land for productive use. The Clinton administration's Better America Bonds proposal, modeled on some of the state programs that were approved in 1998, is an excellent start. The proposal would use tax expenditures to leverage $9.5 billion in state and local bonds for the preservation of open space and the cleanup of brownfields. The proposal could be improved by targeting additional resources to states and other jurisdictions that are practicing smart-growth policies in areas such as transportation, housing, and economic development.

Second, the federal government should enforce environmental laws like the Clean Air Act and the Endangered Species Act. The recent advances made in the Atlanta and Seattle metropolitan areas are in large part due to the federal government's judicious use of its regulatory powers in the environmental arena.

Promoting smart growth

The federal government should promote smart growth by leveling the playing field between older and new communities. The propensity of federal programs to subsidize the development of new communities should be ended in favor of policies that reinvest in existing communities, both cities and suburbs.

Federal transportation funds should be used in metropolitan areas almost exclusively for the repair and maintenance of existing highways and for the expansion of alternative transportation strategies that relieve congestion and promote more balanced growth patterns. Federal funds should be used to build new highways in metropolitan and adjoining areas only in exceptional circumstances.

The federal government also needs to put highway and transit spending on a more equal footing than currently allowed. Some 19 states have constitutional provisions requiring that the state gasoline tax be spent exclusively on roads and bridges. In Georgia, for example, the state constitution prohibits the use of funds generated by the state's gasoline tax for anything but road construction. Thus the Metropolitan Atlanta Rapid Transit Authority is the only metropolitan transit system that receives no funding from its state government. Such constitutional barriers also disadvantage transit and alternative transportation projects in the receipt of federal funds. Since federal funds require a state match, transit is forced to compete with nontransportation priorities for general state revenues.

The reallocation of transportation resources will serve two related purposes. It will weed the subsidy out of sprawl and compel exurban retail, commercial, and residential projects to stand on their own merits. It will also enable the financing of major infrastructure repair projects in cities and older suburbs that have been neglected for decades.

The federal government should use the tax code to invest smartly. Federal homeownership tax incentives, for example, should be expanded to boost homeownership in areas where homeownership rates lag far behind the national average (Retsinas 1999). By lowering the costs of homeownership, such incentives would enhance the ability of working families to build equity and contribute to the stability of neighborhoods. Such incentives would also expand the incentives for the production of affordable housing, either through new building or through renovation of existing homes.

Information disclosure

Finally, the federal government has an important role to play as a provider of demographic, market, and programmatic information. First, the federal government should provide metropolitan areas with a clear spatial analysis of how federal resources are allocated. The Department of Commerce, for example, should show the extent to which individual jurisdictions in major metropolitan areas benefit from federal procurement decisions. The Department of Transportation should, likewise, annually display the spatial distribution of federal transportation dollars in states and metropolitan areas. Disclosure of federal spending patterns is not an onerous burden; in fact, it will subject federal bureaucracies to the same standards that now govern private institutions like banks and thrifts. The Home Mortgage Disclosure Act requires every depository institution to disclose its lending patterns by race, location, and income. If the federal government can require banks to disclose where they lend, why can't the federal government require bureaucracies to disclose where they spend?

Second, the federal government should make available information about the performance of metropolitan markets. The Department of Labor, for example, could track the pace of employment decentralization by place and by sector. The federal government already mandates the collection of the pertinent data; what is missing is a sustained effort to interpret the information and make it available in an accessible form.

CONCLUSION

The substantive rationale for a federal metropolitan agenda to curb sprawl, promote urban reinvestment, and enhance access to opportunity is strong. Calling for discussion of such an agenda in the 2000 election is also not an academic exercise. Polls from around the country illustrate the fundamental frustration of the electorate with the negative consequences of sprawling development patterns.

To his credit, Vice President Al Gore has discussed the challenges associated with sprawl since the fall of 1998 and has promoted federal initiatives like Better America Bonds as part of his livable-communities agenda. Yet federal efforts need not conform to traditional partisan or ideological lines. At the state level, Republican governors (for example, New Jersey's Christine Todd Whitman, Pennsylvania's Tom Ridge) as well as Democratic governors (for example, Maryland's Parris Glendening, Georgia's Roy Barnes) are leading their state reform efforts. These leaders recognize the common ground between the cities and a good portion of the suburbs on growth and development issues.

The federal government can help shape a new kind of growth—more fiscally responsible, more environmentally sensitive, more socially inclusive—in metropolitan America. Yet that will require a change in federal policies that facilitate sprawl and economic decentralization. It will also require providing a variety of supports to states and metropolitan coalitions that are trying to take sensible action. Federal reform is both empirically grounded and politically feasible. It is also long past due.

References

Brookings Institution Center on Urban and Metropolitan Policy. 1999. A Region Divided: The State of Metropolitan Growth in Greater Washington, D.C. Report, July.

——. 2000. Moving Beyond Sprawl: The Challenge for Metropolitan Atlanta. Report, Mar.

Hill, Edward W. and John Brennan. 1998. Where Is the Renaissance? Paper prepared for the Conference on the Interdependence of Central Cities and Suburbs, Sept., Chicago.

——. 1999. Where the Jobs Are. Brookings Institution Center on Urban and Metropolitan Policy, Washington, DC. Survey.

Kasarda, John D., Stephen J. Appold, Stuart H. Sweeney, and Elaine Sieff. 1995. Central-City and Suburban Migration Patterns: Is a Turnaround on the Horizon? *Housing Policy Debate* 8(2):307-58.

Katz, Bruce. 1999. Beyond City Limits: A New Metropolitan Agenda. In *Setting National Priorities*, ed. Henry Aaron and Robert Reischauer. Washington, DC: Brookings Institution Press.

Katz, Bruce and Kate Allen. 1999. The State of Welfare Caseloads in America's Cities: 1999. Brookings Institution Center on Urban and Metropolitan Policy, Washington, DC. Survey.

Katz, Bruce and Jennifer Bradley. 1999. Divided We Sprawl. *Atlantic Monthly* Dec.:26-42.

Nivola, Pietro. 1999. *Laws of the Landscape: How Policies Shape Urban Cities in Europe and America.* Washington, DC: Brookings Institution Press.

Orfield, Myron. 1997. *Metropolitics: A Regional Agenda for Community and Stability.* Washington, DC: Brookings Institution Press.

Retsinas, Nicolas. 1999. Towards a Targeted Homeownership Tax Credit. Discussion paper 99:1. Brookings Institution Center on Urban and Metropolitan Policy, Washington, DC.

Rusk, David. 1998. The Exploding Metropolis: Why Growth Management Makes Sense. *Brookings Review* 16(Fall):13-15.

ANNALS, *AAPSS*, **572**, November 2000

Jobs, Cities, and Suburbs in the Global Economy

By JANICE FANNING MADDEN

ABSTRACT: Intra-metropolitan shifts in the location of higher-income people increase the concentration of the poor in cities. These movements threaten the economic productivity of cities, endangering national prosperity. If we cannot utilize fully the capital, buildings, and environments that are unique to cities because of problems that arise from the concentration of the poor, then we have diminished the nation's "economic portfolio." Jobs decrease not only for city residents but for people throughout the nation, regardless of whether they live in or near a city. The author examines evidence for the premise that cities are essential to the productivity of the U.S. economy. She also examines how cities affect their suburbs. Some national policies are identified that encourage higher-income metropolitan residents to live in new suburbs. The policies include the home mortgage and property deductions from income taxes and the cost to city residents of poverty and other income redistribution programs.

Janice F. Madden is professor of regional science, sociology, and real estate at the Fels Center of Government at the University of Pennsylvania. She has written four books: The Economics of Sex Discrimination *(1972, reprinted 1975);* Post-Industrial Philadelphia *(1990);* Work, Wages, and Poverty *(1991); and* Changes in Income Inequality Within U.S. Metropolitan Areas *(2000).*

O UR largest central cities, particularly the older ones with an infrastructure and many buildings that were designed and built for a pre-automobile and manufacturing-intensive era, have experienced increases in their poverty rates, relative both to their own histories and to the levels currently experienced in their suburbs. These rising poverty rates are due to the income-selective suburbanization of metropolitan residents. Upper- and middle-income residents have been moving to the suburbs while the poor are remaining in the city.

The changing intra-metropolitan location of higher-income people—that is, the decreases in the share of higher-income people living in central cities or their older suburbs—has increased the pace of new construction of housing and infrastructure at the outer reaches of metropolitan areas. Outer suburbs are experiencing increased congestion. Many suburban residents are expressing concerns about their quality of life.

In articles included elsewhere in this volume, Bruce Katz and Felton Earls discuss how the movements of the higher-income populations from the central city and inner suburbs affect the quality of life for both central-city and suburban residents and also raise issues of equity and fairness. These concerns alone provide sufficient reason for candidates for public office to consider whether, and how, the rate of suburbanization might be changed. I turn, however, to a different concern about the patterns of suburbanization: the effects of suburbanization on the long-term growth and competitiveness of the entire U.S. economy.

Intra-metropolitan shifts in the location of higher-income people, which increase the concentration of the poor in our largest central cities, threaten the economic productivity and competitiveness of these cities and endanger our national prosperity, which relies on the productive capacities of these cities. Actions that reduce the efficiency of the American economy decrease jobs not only for city residents but also for people throughout the nation, regardless of whether they live in or near a city or not. If we cannot utilize fully the capital, the buildings, and the special production environments that are unique to larger cities because of social problems that arise from the concentration and isolation of the poor, then we have lost a vital component of the nation's "economic portfolio." The inability to exploit fully the nation's productive capacity ultimately leads to a loss of good jobs for Americans, regardless of where they live.

In the following section, I examine the reasoning and the evidence supporting the premise that cities are essential to the productivity and the international competitiveness of the U.S. economy. The third section examines the effects of cities on their suburbs. The fourth section discusses the policy issues and some specific national policies that matter, and the final section summarizes the discussion.

CITIES ARE ESSENTIAL COMPONENTS OF THE NEW ECONOMY

The extraordinary recent growth in income and employment in the United States has been attributed, especially in the last few decades, to innovation and invention. Cities play an important role in an economy that is based on invention and innovation (the so-called new economy) rather than on mass production of goods. Cities provide an environment that uniquely encourages creativity, allows ideas to become products more rapidly, and builds the skills of workers.

Innovation and invention in the economy

To the extent that there is a new economy, it can be described as one in which creativity has become more important than the production of goods. The growing importance of innovation and invention to the U.S. economy is illustrated by the increase in patent applications. Kortum and Lerner (1997) show that, between 1990 and 1996, annual patent applications from U.S. residents grew to over 120,000 from the rather random fluctuations between 40,000 and 80,000 throughout the remainder of the century.

The change in the structure of the labor force also supports the premise that ideas and creativity have increased in importance relative to the mass production of goods. In 1900, 8 of 10 workers produced goods and services; by 1998, this number had decreased by half, to 4 of 10. Over the same period, the share of workers most likely to be involved in invention and innovation (that is, engineers, architects, writers, designers, artists, entertainers, and scientists) grew fivefold, from less than 1 in 100 to over 5 in 100 (Nakamura 2000).

Creation and transport of ideas

Interactions between people who think differently generate ideas. The high spatial concentrations of people and jobs that occur in our larger central cities provide unique environments for the interactions that generate ideas. Larger cities, because they are efficient producers of new ideas, are crucial components of the growth and expansion of the U.S. economy.

In the past, when goods were expensive to transport, cities were essential to mass production because they were transportation hubs. We no longer need cities as hubs for the transport of manufactured goods or raw materials. Now, we need them as the hubs for the creation and transport of ideas. Sir Alfred Marshall, writing in 1890, described cities as "having ideas in the air." Jane Jacobs (1961), writing 70 years later, explained how cities encourage the unplanned combination of ideas. Dense, city environments allow a diversity of people to interact, and, in that way, they are an incubator for innovation and invention.

Although some futurists have argued that technological innovations in telecommunications will replace the need for face-to-face encounters, experience suggests otherwise. It seems more likely that personal contact and advances in

telecommunications are comple-
ments to one another than they are
substitutes. Innovations in telecommunications have made proximity
less important in transmitting data
or information, but the increasing
availability of data has made the
more complex, uncertain, and vague
knowledge of how to put data
together more valuable. The trans-
mission of knowledge, which
requires context, is best done face to
face and with repeated and frequent
interaction. Cities provide the opportunity for these interactions. This is
why people in cities, with great
opportunities for personal contact,
use the telephone and other communication devices more than do other
Americans (Imagawa 1997).

Spatial concentrations of people
have become less important for production in many divisions of many
industries—that is, production
among manufacturers—so that
fewer plants or offices have their productivity increased when they locate
within a large central city or metropolitan area. Nonetheless, high-density or city environments are increasingly important to U.S. productivity
because they are critical to the inno-
vating sectors that have accounted
for much of the growth in the U.S.
economy over the past decade. The
proportion of the workforce engaged
in creative activity does not measure
the relative importance of innovation
to economic growth; similarly, the
importance of cities to the economy
cannot be measured by changes in
total employment within cities
versus suburbs or within metropolitan areas versus non-metropolitan
areas.

Statements about the importance
of cities to the generation of ideas and
creativity are more easily made than
documented, however. It is substantially more difficult to measure or
quantify the production of an idea
than of goods and services. While in-
direct evidence supports the connection between cities and ideas, the evidence is probably not sufficient to
convince a doubter. Recent evidence
on the connections includes the
following:

1.   Virtually all new products are
developed in cities and almost half in
the four large cities of New York City,
Los Angeles, Boston, and San Francisco (Audretsch and Feldman 1996).

2.   Firms located in cities that include other firms with greater diversity in their innovation activities but
that also have a common science base
introduce more new products in a
given year (Feldman and Audretsch
1999).

3.   New patents are 5-10 times
more likely to cite previous patents
from the same state, even after elimi-
nating those that are from the same
firm (Jaffe, Trajtenberg, and Henderson 1993). The locational ties are
more important for patents originating in private firms than for patents
from universities.

4.   A study of firms that were
large employers in 1956 showed that
those located in more industrially diversified environments—that is, city
environments—experienced greater
subsequent growth in employment
(Glaesar et al. 1992). Furthermore,
small firms, after considering their
investments in research and development, account for a disproportion-

ate share of new product innovations (Acs and Audretsch 1990). Such firms rely on the knowledge they acquire through their neighbors, including other firms and research institutions, and from their workers (Audretsch 1998). Large cities provide small firms with greater numbers and diversity of neighbors and workers.

5. Since the middle of the nineteenth century, cities whose workforces contained more business professionals—the potential generators, recipients, and implementers of ideas—grew more rapidly (Simon and Nardinelli 1996).

Quicker transformation of ideas into products and services

In addition to creating a fertile environment for creativity, larger central cities also contribute to growth in the new economy by providing a variety of intermediate services that are critical to turning ideas into products and services (Krugman 1993). For example, they provide highly specialized producer services in subspecialties of accounting, advertising, financing, legal services, repair, and so forth. In Manhattan, there are more specialized lawyers, investment bankers, chefs, and musicians than in smaller cities. Furthermore, because these services are in one location, the costs of coordinating the complex set of activities required to bring new ideas and products to the marketplace are lower (Becker and Murphy 1992).

Similarly, larger cities offer firms labor forces that are more diversified

in skills than the labor forces in more rural or other less densely settled environments. The importance of the specialization of labor to economic efficiency and growth has been recognized since Adam Smith wrote of pin factories in 1776. A recent study by Dumais, Ellison, and Glaeser (1997) supports the importance of specialization of the workforce to firms. They find that the extent to which firms require the same labor force skills is the best predictor of whether they locate together. Cities, with more diversity of skills in their population, provide a way for even small firms to hire workers with highly specialized skills.

Unique training and learning opportunities for workers

Cities, especially larger ones, provide better learning or training experiences for workers. These opportunities for skill enhancement translate into more productive or more highly skilled workers in cities.

The evidence for the higher productivity of city workers comes from data on wages. Employers can pay higher salaries to workers only if they are producing more. Glaeser and Mare (1994) find that workers in metropolitan areas with large central cities earn 10 percent more than other metropolitan workers and over a third more than those not in metropolitan areas. Furthermore, they find that the wage advantage increases with time in the city, indicating that it is experiences in the city itself that increase worker productivity.

CENTRAL CITIES MATTER
TO THEIR SUBURBS

Because the health of our larger cities affects economic conditions in the nation, it is not surprising that they have even greater effects on the health of their own suburbs. It is within the metropolitan area that a paradox, affected by both local and national policies, is evident. Ideas, critical components for economic growth, are created in environments that are diverse and dense, that is, cities that have diverse people and large numbers of people per square mile. As people become richer, however, they prefer residences in less densely populated neighborhoods that include people like themselves, that is, neighborhoods that are neither dense nor diverse. Dense and diverse environments (large cities) make us prosperous, but prosperity leads us to move to sparse and homogeneous residential environments (suburbs) that make it more difficult for the cities to generate creativity. In this section, I discuss some of the evidence on the relationships between central cities and suburbs within a metropolitan area.

Effect of central-city economic conditions on suburbs

Long-run changes in population (Voith 1998), employment (Linneman and Summers 1990), housing prices (Voith 1998; Goetzmann, Spiegel, and Wachter 1996), and urban distress (Bradbury, Downs, and Small 1982) of cities and their suburbs are correlated. Metropolitan areas whose central cities have more highly educated residents experienced more employment growth over several decades (Simon 1998). While most of these studies show only a correlation between these outcomes in cities and their suburbs, Voith's study provides evidence of causation, arguing that the economic conditions in the city affect those in their suburbs.

Metropolitan areas that cannot fully utilize the infrastructure and the location advantages of their large central cities have lower productivity and earnings. Voith (1998) has found that central-city income growth affects suburban growth in income and housing values when the central city is large (population in excess of half a million). He finds no effect for small central cities (population less than 300,000). Larger cities have higher densities of residents and jobs than smaller cities do. The differences in densities of jobs or people between central cities and suburbs are greater, therefore, when central cities are larger. Voith's estimates of the effects of the large city economy on the pocketbooks of their suburban residents are substantial. Suburban residents who earned $50,000 a year and owned $150,000 houses in 1980 would have experienced an additional $9560 in earnings and $15,075 in the value of their houses by 1990 if their cities had had the same increase in average income as the suburbs. These central cities actually experienced a 14 percent increase in their average income, while their suburbs' average income increased 19 percent.

FIGURE 1
CHANGES IN THE PROPORTIONS OF POOR AND NONPOOR MSA
POPULATION IN LARGE SOUTHERN AND WESTERN MSAs, 1970-90

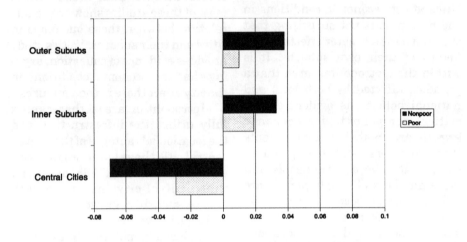

City amenities versus suburban amenities

Cities provide different sets of amenities from those provided by their suburbs. Suburbs have more spatially dispersed housing units and privately controlled outdoor space; cities have housing units closer together and a considerable amount of publicly accessible outdoor and other space such as waterfronts, museums, and pedestrian-oriented streets. If cities become unavailable for use by suburban residents and tourists because the concentration of poverty and crime has made these amenities either inaccessible or unpleasant to use, then suburban residents and potential tourists from the nation and the world, as well as city residents, will suffer.

SEPARATION OF THE POOR IN THE CITY THREATENS ECONOMIC GROWTH

While metropolitan residents have been moving to the suburbs over the last half of the century, it is the income selectivity of that movement, rather than the movement itself, which poses the greater problem. The isolation of the poor in our cities is a nationwide phenomenon that threatens all cities and our national competitiveness in the long term. The poor are left in our cities because the suburbanization of the metropolitan population differs between income groups. Figure 1 shows the changes in the proportion of the poor and nonpoor metropolitan populations of our larger cities in the West and in the South[1] living in the

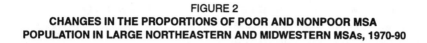

FIGURE 2
CHANGES IN THE PROPORTIONS OF POOR AND NONPOOR MSA
POPULATION IN LARGE NORTHEASTERN AND MIDWESTERN MSAs, 1970-90

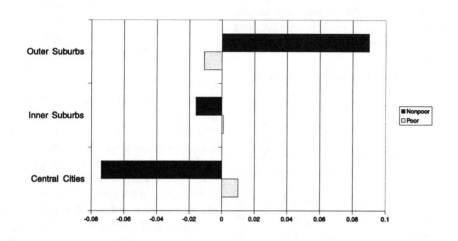

central city, the inner suburbs, and the outer suburbs between 1970 and 1990. In the large cities of the South and West, both the nonpoor and the poor are leaving the central cities for the suburbs, but the nonpoor are doing so at a faster rate, creating increasing concentrations of the poor in the cities. Figure 2 shows the same changes for our larger cities in the Midwest and in the Northeast.[2] In the older, historically industrial cities of the Northeast and Midwest, the nonpoor are leaving the central cities and the inner, older suburbs for the outer, newer suburbs, creating increasing concentrations of the poor in the cities and older suburbs.

The suburbanization of our large metropolitan areas is a problem for two reasons. First, the suburbanization of richer residents of metro-

politan statistical areas (MSAs) creates large concentrations of the poor in the cities, and those concentrations make poverty more difficult to alleviate. Second, federal and state policies encourage suburbanization, particularly of higher-income households, beyond the levels that would occur in a more neutral policy environment. Segregating the poor in the city and the nonpoor in the suburbs threatens the productivity of the central city and, therefore, of the metropolitan area and the entire nation.

*Increased cost of
governmental services*

Local governments provide education, police and fire protection, and sanitation. The cost of providing those services is higher, on a per capita basis, when there is greater residential segmentation by income. Pack (1995) estimated that, in 1990, each percentage point of poverty for a city increased the annual per capita cost of police, fire, courts, and general administrative functions of the city by $28.

Furthermore, because poor residents cannot pay sufficient taxes to cover the costs of their municipal services, the city must either collect additional taxes from nonpoor residents or not provide those services to the poor. The former creates an incentive for the nonpoor to move to the suburbs; the latter affects the quality of life in the city, resulting in lower productivity and quality of life, which also encourages movement from the city.

*Income segregation
and labor force skills*

Extreme residential sorting by income lowers productivity in a metropolitan area because it becomes more difficult for firms to combine workers with a variety of skills at a single job location (Benabou 1993). The phenomenon of spatial mismatch—the situation in which, in metropolitan areas, the poor are in the central city and those who wish to hire the poor are in the suburbs—first affects the city by increasing unemployment among city residents. Mismatch ultimately limits growth in the suburbs as firms either cannot hire sufficient numbers of less skilled workers or must pay them higher wages to compensate for their longer commutes.

*Concentrated poverty
and economic productivity*

Because greater concentrations of the poor in the city mean that public services are more costly to provide, either taxes must be higher in the city or services must be lower if the city is forced to serve its poor exclusively from its own tax capacity. Either strategy—higher taxes or poorer services—drives those who can create new ideas and inventions from city locations, rendering the city and the entire economy less productive in the long term. Grants to the city or programs paid for by other levels of government are the only solution that will allow cities to be places with high densities of diverse people who generate the ideas that lead to innovation.

NATIONAL POLICIES
SUBSIDIZE SUBURBANIZATION

The federal government does not now, and is not likely in the future, to favor cities. Less densely populated areas have more senators by design, and, due to the U.S. Census undercount, which is greater in the more densely populated central cities, such areas have more congressional representatives as well. Many federal policies actively disfavor cities, especially older cities, in that they encourage suburbanization, especially of higher-income households. Bruce Katz discusses several relevant policies in detail in his article in this volume. I briefly discuss two federal policies that matter here: the home mortgage and property tax deduction from income tax, and poverty and other income redistribution programs.

Income tax deductions

The federal income tax allows homeowners who itemize their deductions to deduct their annual payments for interest on their home mortgages and their property taxes. The standard deduction is an alternative to itemizing that is more attractive to lower-income households (that is, those with deductions of lower value). As the tax rate is progressive (making the value of a $1 deduction increase with income), higher-income households get more subsidization of their housing than lower-income households do. The value of these deductions increases with the income of the taxpayer and, in that sense, these deductions subsidize the consumption of more housing by higher-income households. Voith (1999) has shown that owners of houses valued less than $80,000 get no added value from itemizing their deductions and that 57 percent of central-city residents and 37 percent of suburban residents reside in houses that are worth less than $80,000. The tax deductibility of interest on a home mortgage and of property taxes is more likely to benefit suburban residents.

Voith also points out that local governments depend on the property tax for their revenue and, as suburban residents have their property tax payments subsidized by the federal government, residents of suburban communities are able to finance schools, parks, and police and fire services at lower cost than are city residents. Furthermore, as the federal government subsidizes the cost of larger lot sizes for high-income residents, it lowers the cost to communities of imposing exclusionary regulations, such as minimum lot sizes, that further increase the income segmentation of residential communities.

Income redistribution or poverty programs

Local and state governments that pursue tax packages or programs that benefit lower-income groups at the expense of higher-income groups create incentives for those higher-income households to leave that local area or state (Peterson 1981). Any attempt to redistribute income at a subnational level creates incentives for higher-income households to move to jurisdictions that have lower taxes or more public goods and services that they can consume for their tax expenditures. These incentives are particularly strong within metropolitan areas where it is easy to commute to jobs and other activities from several jurisdictions.

As the federal government has cut back on poverty programs, thereby relinquishing more responsibility to state and local government, central cities with more of the poor are faced with an impossible dilemma. Either they ignore the needs of the poor and risk higher crime and an increasingly undereducated labor force or they try to provide services that the poor cannot pay for themselves by taxing higher-income residents. If they follow the latter strategy, the taxes, in turn, drive the higher-income residents to the suburbs, creating yet greater concentrations of the poor in the central city.

SUMMARY

Cities provide unique innovative environments for an economy whose growth and vitality depend on maintaining a rapid pace of invention and innovation. The health of our cities is tied to the health of our economy and its ability to provide well-paying jobs to citizens in cities, suburbs, and rural areas. While it may not be clear that the role of urban environments is sufficiently important in producing innovation to justify subsidization of large cities, there is absolutely no reason why cities should subsidize other locations, as they do now. Policies that subsidize the movement of higher-income persons from the city render the city less productive and threaten the ability of the economy to grow. Policies that force cities to redistribute from their higher-income citizens to their poor drive higher-income residents out and increase the concentration of poverty.

Cities cannot redistribute from their nonpoor to their poor residents. If they try to do so, they lose their nonpoor residents. The needs of the poor in the city must be met, however, so that the resources of the city can be optimally utilized in the new economy. Solutions must come from other levels of government. Given the importance of cities to the economy, these concerns should be central in any state or national political campaign.

Notes

1. The cities are Portland, San Francisco, Oakland, San Jose, Los Angeles, San Diego, Denver, Dallas, Fort Worth, Austin, Houston, Charlotte, Atlanta, Memphis, Nashville, Jacksonville, and Miami.

2. The cities are Boston, New York City, Philadelphia, Baltimore, Washington, D.C., Pittsburgh, Columbus, Cleveland, Indianapolis, Detroit, Chicago, Milwaukee, Minneapolis, St. Paul, and St. Louis.

References

Acs, Z. J. and D. B. Audretsch. 1990. The Determinants of Small-Firm Growth in United States Manufacturing. *Applied Economics* 22(2):143-53.

Audretsch, D. B. 1998. Agglomeration and the Location of Innovative Activity. *Oxford Review of Economic Policy* 14(2):18-29.

Audretsch, D. B. and M. P. Feldman. 1996. R & D Spillovers and the Geography of Innovation and Production. *American Economic Review* 86(3):630-40.

Becker, Gary and Kevin Murphy. 1992. The Division of Labor, Coordination Costs and Knowledge. *Quarterly Journal of Economics* 107(4):1137-60.

Benabou, Roland. 1993. Workings of a City: Location, Education, and Production. *Quarterly Journal of Economics* 108(3):619-52.

Bradbury, Katharine, Anthony Downs, and Kenneth A. Small. 1982. *Urban Decline and the Future of American Cities.* Washington, DC: Brookings Institution.

Dumais, G., G. Ellison, and E. Glaeser. 1997. Geographic Concentration as a Dynamic Process. Working paper no. 6270, National Bureau of Economic Research, Cambridge, MA.

Feldman, M. P. and D. B. Audretsch. 1999. Innovation in Cities: Science-Based Diversity, Specialization and Localized Competition. *European Economic Review* 43(2):409-30.

Glaesar, Edward L., H. Kallal, Jose Scheinkman, and A. Shleifer. 1992. Growth in Cities. *Journal of Political Economy* 100(6):1126-52.

Glaeser, Edward and D. Mare. 1994. Cities and Skills. Working paper no. 4728, National Bureau of Economic Research, Cambridge, MA.

Goetzmann, William N., Matthew Spiegel, and Susan Wachter. 1996. Suburbs and Cities. Working paper, Real Estate Center, University of Pennsylvania, Philadelphia.

Imagawa, T. 1997. Essays on Telecommunications, Cities and Industry in Japan. Ph.D. diss., Harvard University.

Jacobs, Jane. 1961. *The Economy of Cities*. New York: Vintage Books.

Jaffe, Adam, M. Trajtenberg, and R. Henderson. 1993. Geographic Localization of Knowledge Spillovers as Evidenced by Patent Citations. *Quarterly Journal of Economics* 108(3):577-98.

Kortum, Samuel and Josh Lerner. 1997. Stronger Protection of Technological Revolution: What Is Behind the Recent Surge in Patenting? Working paper no. 6204, National Bureau of Economic Research, Cambridge, MA.

Krugman, Paul. 1993. First Nature, Second Nature, and Metropolitan Location. *Journal of Regional Science* 33(2):129-44.

Linneman, Peter and Anita Summers. 1990. Patterns of Urban Population Decentralization in the United States 1970-1987. Working paper, Real Estate Center, University of Pennsylvania, Philadelphia.

Marshall, Alfred. 1890. *Principles of Economics*. London: Macmillan.

Nakamura, Leonard I. 2000. Economics and the New Economy: The Invisible Hand Meets Creative Destruction. *Federal Reserve Bank of Philadelphia Business Review* July-Aug.:15-30.

Pack, Janet. 1995. Poverty and Urban Expenditures. Working paper no. 215, Real Estate Center, University of Pennsylvania, Philadelphia.

Peterson, Paul E. 1981. *City Limits*. Chicago: University of Chicago Press.

Simon, C. J. 1998. Human Capital and Metropolitan Employment Growth. *Journal of Urban Economics* 43(2):223-43.

Simon, C. J. and C. Nardinelli. 1996. The Talk of the Town: Human Capital, Information, and the Growth of English Cities, 1861 to 1961. *Explorations in Economic History* 33(3):384-413.

Voith, Richard. 1998. Do Suburbs Need Cities? *Journal of Regional Science* 38(3):445-64.

———. 1999. Does the Federal Tax Treatment of Housing Affect the Pattern of Metropolitan Development? *Business Review* Mar.-Apr.:3-16.

ANNALS, *AAPSS*, **572**, November 2000

Preface

Vouchers take up much of the oxygen in today's school reform debate while serving less than 1 percent of K-12 students. Even in an age of heated rhetoric, the issue is unusually polarizing. Advocates view vouchers as an indispensable way to shake up troubled school systems; foes see them as a dangerous sideshow, an assault on the very notion of public schooling. As the issue heats up, and the fate of millions of urban schoolkids is affected by the evolving Republican and Democratic agendas, it is timely to explore whether there is a way to move beyond the traditional positions of left and right toward some grand bargain on vouchers that might help the kids most in need—and offer lessons from which reformers and policy analysts could learn.

To promote this dialogue, the Annenberg Public Policy Center of the University of Pennsylvania hosted an innovative forum entitled *School Vouchers: Breaking the Stalemate* at the National Press Club on 29 February 2000. The first of two panel discussions featured newer voices in the debate over school choice: the pro-voucher Left and the pro-equity Right. The second panel brought together prominent leaders from education, government, and the advocacy community to discuss potential bargains between traditional sides of the issue.

The following is a distillation of the conference proceedings. It is our hope that the salient points have been preserved.

MATTHEW MILLER

ANNALS, *AAPSS*, **572**, November 2000

Introduction

MATTHEW MILLER: Thanks to all of you for being here this morning. Thanks especially to Annenberg and to Pew and to the American Academy of Political and Social Science for helping us explore these issues. I'm delighted we could all be here for a discussion of one of those quiet little issues that doesn't generate much controversy and about which all reasonable people can agree. [laughter]

Obviously, the truth, of course, is that the subject that we're talking about today, school vouchers and school choice, is not an issue like that. In fact, it's something that very often can quickly degenerate into a food fight. The passions on both sides run high; the blood is quick to boil on these issues in ways that, if nothing else, make TV producers very happy.

There's an old story about TV producers on political shows, when they see a calm reasoned debate unfolding, shouting to the contestants—which is what they should be called—"Get mad, get mad." This issue is contentious enough that that kind of egging on from TV producers is not usually required.

With all due respect to those kinds of shout fests or food fights, we're going to try to do something a little bit different today. We will try to shed a little more light than heat and have a reasoned discussion with some fresh perspectives that may not always be heard on this topic, with a view to seeing whether there may be some grounds for breaking the stalemate on an issue that seems to take up so much of the oxygen in the school reform debate nationally.

I think a premise of this session this morning is that leaders on both sides of this debate usually confront each other only through televised sound bites, through dueling quotes in newspapers, forums like that. They spend much of their time huddled, understandably, with like-minded allies trying to plot and plan against the other side's moves.

What we're hoping is that this morning's discussion is a chance for some of those leaders to think out loud a little bit with you all and with each other in a way that lets them not just hear the arguments, which sometimes can be well-worn, but get some insight into why each of them thinks the way they do and how they've come to the positions they hold. I hope we can increase, at least a little, the understanding across what can sometimes be a very serious chasm.

As all of you know, the issue couldn't be more timely. The general election that we're about to head into is going to feature vouchers as a major issue. Education is topping voters' concerns in most national polls. Both of the Republican candidates (John McCain and George W. Bush) have voucher proposals—different kinds of voucher proposals but voucher proposals that are sure to spark controversy—and Al Gore, the likely Democratic nominee, will fiercely resist them. So this issue is sure to be atop the news, for those of you who are helping shape coverage of this.

At the same time, there is lots of public confusion about vouchers. This means that, especially for reporters and editorial writers and for analysts who help shape the terms of debate on this issue, there's a real role for those who wish to clarify the stakes and help dispel some of the confusion. As Kathleen Hall Jamieson would have said this morning, and I'd like to remind you on her behalf, it is not true that a voucher is a voucher is a voucher. The specific details of the voucher program's design have a huge impact on both the way the public perceives it and its likely impact on different kinds of students. Who's eligible for a voucher, how much of the tuition a voucher is going to pay for, how it's funded, who funds it, whether it comes out of money that's currently allocated to the public schools—all of these things have an enormous impact on how the public perceives it. Being pro- or anti-voucher doesn't really say very much without the details.

Our plan this morning, with our terrifically distinguished panels, is to get at these issues—we hope in a fresh way—through two themes. The first panel is going to feature some fresh voices that tend not to be heard as often in the very loud and often divisive debate—the pro-voucher Left and the pro-equity Right. The second panel will try to explore whether there is some kind of grand bargain possible between Left and Right on these issues and, if so, what the shape of that might be and, if not, where there are areas of consensus and possibilities that might lead to some bridging of the divide down the road.

Let me quickly offer you at least one man's quick guided tour to the leading charades of the traditional Left and Right on vouchers. The Left actually has more charades that it offers on vouchers, but the Right, even though it has fewer charades, makes up for it by having each one pack a bigger deceptive punch. There is an even-handedness, then, to this inventory.

ARGUMENTS FROM THE TRADITIONAL LEFT

Those on the Left who tend to be anti-voucher offer the following arguments. First they'll say that there's no evidence that vouchers work. To that I would suggest that experiments that are under way now are too small yet to provide good evidence. For all the air time and passion that the voucher debate takes up, they serve far less than 1 percent of K-12 schoolchildren today. They are tiny experiments in a few cities. One getting under way in Florida is a set of privately funded plans that still amount to just a tiny, tiny fraction of schoolkids. And then both sides come in with dueling studies purporting to prove that vouchers either did or did not improve student performance.

It seems to me at least, as a journalist trying to make sense of this stuff, that the studies seem to be based on such small samples that it's very hard to draw any conclusions one way or another. It's just too soon; the evidence is not persuasive yet.

The second argument is that vouchers drain dollars from public schools. Now this is possible, of course, but it's not necessary. Cleveland's program, for example, added an additional $10 million to fund their voucher trial. It's unfair, I would argue, in cases where new money is added to the budget for these experiments for voucher foes to then come back and protest that this money would be better used within the current system. It is unfair because one of the ways in which political compromises have been struck concerning new voucher trials is precisely to add that new money. So it's not true that vouchers have to drain money from current public schools.

The third argument is that vouchers are unconstitutional, that the use of them to attend religious schools, with Catholic schools now being the biggest sector of the private school system, means that they violate the prohibition against the establishment of religion as put forward in the Constitution. I understand that's an argument that legal scholars debate quite seriously, and many voucher advocates have concerns about it as well.

My own view is that it shouldn't be the trumping argument. No one complains at the postsecondary level, past K-12, when kids use their Pell grants to go to Notre Dame. Some argue that K-12 is different, but it seems to me that we can't be in a situation where we are constitutionally obliged to imprison kids in schools that don't work.

The fourth argument that the Left makes is that the capacity isn't there, that a voucher system will not be able to handle all the schoolchildren. To that I would answer, What's the problem then? If we think, as a practical matter, that a voucher system in a city or a state will not prompt a supply of new schools to accept students with these vouchers, then it's hard to see what the downside is to the voucher experiment. If there won't be new schools cropping up, then 98.9 percent of the kids are going to be where they are now, perhaps with more money if the voucher system included additional resources for the public schools. So it seems to me that's not a trumping argument, and it also ignores the fact that, as we've seen in so many different sectors, when a kind of market is created, there's a huge response from the supply side. Internet sales were in the pennies a few years ago. Now they're in the multi-billions of dollars. Things can happen quickly if there's a chance given to some of these experiments.

The fifth argument from the Left is, I would argue, that profit is bad, that somehow there's something venal about letting for-profit operators in a privatized system operate schools for profit. The charade here, I think, is that right now K-12 public education is a huge business, as everyone knows. Over $300 billion goes from government at all levels to K-12. That money is lusted after by textbook publishers, software companies, janitorial services, cafeteria services, you name it. Every public sector that is big—defense, health, education, and so forth—will always be a big business. There's no reason to believe, I think, that the inevitable abuses under a voucher system would be any different from the inevitable abuses we have today in any large public sector where big business is involved.

The sixth argument from the Left is that vouchers cream off the best and the brightest students and the most motivated parents from the public school system, leaving those parents and families who are less active in the public school; the public school then deteriorates without the useful influence of those highly motivated parents and kids. This argument is partly a function of the fact that the voucher experiments today are so tiny. If there were more widespread use of vouchers in one town or city, for example, it wouldn't be a matter of removing from the public school just a handful of those folks who are most motivated; in fact, vouchers would actually reach much deeper into the population of students. I think there's also little evidence right now that that creaming is occurring, even in the places where vouchers are being tested.

There is the argument made by voucher foes that private schools can pick and choose the students they want. They don't have to deal with troublemakers, difficult kids, the way the public schools do. This is true, undoubtedly. Public schools have to take all comers. But the idea that kids can be disruptive in class and ruin learning for lots of other kids is an argument for trying to figure out how to get those troublemakers out of the public school classes where they're disrupting learning. But it's not an argument against trying something different in terms of options for kids who want a choice, I think. So it's a real issue, but again, not one that should trump or that directly takes on the voucher argument.

Voucher foes argue that the regulatory regime that would eventually come with public money going to private schools would become so great that these private schools before long would end up being just as bureaucratic and stifled as public schools.

That's an argument, to be sure. Most of the analysts and experts that I've talked to on all sides of this debate think that, at the end of the day, there will be far more flexibility in terms of hiring and firing, in terms of resource allocation, in terms of curriculum design, in schools that are using vouchers as opposed to the very highly regulated public school system we have today. So there's still a difference, and it's hard sometimes not to suspect that the argument about oversight and regulation isn't a tactical attempt by voucher foes to scare off, for example, the private schools, the Catholic schools, which are very sensitive to the idea of having too much government intrusion.

Finally, there's the argument that at first blush is very powerful: that vouchers are a scheme to subsidize richer people who are already choosing private schools. They're already paying their own money to send their kids to private schools that are often quite expensive. Why would we now offer $1500, $3000, $5000 and in effect subsidize wealthier Americans who are making that choice today? At first blush, that's a powerful argument.

What I'd say in response to that is that those better-off citizens are in effect already paying twice today: they're paying local property taxes and other taxes for the school system they're not using, and they're paying for the other school that they are choosing. The more compelling argument, I think, is that if you target vouchers toward low-income populations, which is obviously one option, that issue goes away altogether. So the argument that the better-off are being subsidized is not something that's ultimately trumping.

ARGUMENTS FROM THE TRADITIONAL RIGHT

That's my brief inventory of what I call the dubious arguments from the Left. Here are the three dubious arguments that are made by the pro-voucher Right. They are big arguments, and they also can be usefully pierced.

The first argument is that vouchers invariably save us lots of money. It's very clear that a lot of voucher proponents feel that going to vouchers can save lots of money and can be accompanied by tax cuts. That's something that raises fears in the hearts of those who care about the public school system.

It is true that private schools now spend half or less on average per pupil compared to public schools. The reason that's so is that the Catholic schools spend much less than public schools, and Catholic schools supply the bulk of the private school seats we have today. Catholic schools have less administrative bureaucracy per pupil, which is a favorable comparison with the public schools. But they also pay teachers less, which does raise a question, because public school teachers are already paid very shabbily, at least in my view, so that Catholic schools are relying largely on a missionary spirit, if less on actual nuns today than they did in the past. Anyone who has reported on Catholic schools, as I have, at least in Los Angeles, knows that there is a tremendous religious spirit of service that imbues teachers in Catholic schools. I think it's hard to expect that a missionary spirit is going to be the answer to all of what ails urban education.

In addition to lower teacher salaries, Catholic schools also have far less in the way of amenities: theaters, gyms, and the like. Catholic schools aren't happy that they spend this little. I've talked to folks in these dioceses who are desperate for more money and who in fact view vouchers, as I'm sure we'll get into later, as one way to actually inject some cash into their system in a way that would help them improve the service they offer to existing students.

Catholic schools don't have to take special education students, disabled kids. They don't have to take a lot of the kids that public schools must take by law. They don't have to offer bilingual programs, transportation, and various breakfast and lunch programs, all of which increase costs. Pretty fair-minded economists who've looked at these things say that when you take away the implicit subsidies from church grounds and the lower teaching costs, and compare some of the other costs that public schools have, some of the differences go away. I think Jack Coons may share with us this morning the notion that others have that if a voucher is not set at the level of something like 80 percent of the current per pupil spending in a town, you'll end up with something that is so low as to only fill up empty Catholic school seats but not enough to actually attract new capital investment that's needed for any kind of supply response to come in the form of new schools. The idea that you can save tons of money, as Milton Friedman tends to argue, I think is wrong.

The second charade on the Right, I think, is, "The freer the market, the better the result." The debate is commonly cast in sort of TV style between the free market, on the one hand, and government, on the other. We all know in reality that that's a false dichotomy. We're always talking instead about what gradations of government regulation or what government role will be involved with what level of harnessing of private market forces, which are very powerful in terms of getting results and efficiently allocating resources.

Anyone who thinks for a minute about health insurance or insurance in general, for example, knows that free markets do not provide the best possible result. If it's left only to free markets, sick people or old people will not have health insurance. It's a problem today. It was a problem in the sixties, which is why the federal government designed Medicare. So we need to pierce the idea that's often common that the market is the only solution and yields the best result.

Finally, the last charade on the Right is the notion that the problem with urban schools is all the schools' fault, that there is something dysfunctional in these systems, and that the schools themselves are entirely to blame for what ails urban educational achievement and what ails the education system. Anyone who saw James Traub's compelling cover story in the *New York Times Magazine* not long ago knows that this simply isn't true. Anyone who's reported on urban schools or been in them knows that these kids are coming to school with enormous problems—family problems, social problems, difficulties that most middle-class families would have a hard time imagining. And to expect the schools to be the answer to all of those problems is crazy. To blame the schools for the lagging achievement of those kids is equally wrong-headed, I think. You can't report on urban schools or spend time in urban schools without developing a tremendous empathy for the teachers who are trying to make a difference in the lives of the kids there.

I know from just doing the reporting I've done both on vouchers and on teachers in general that spending time in urban schools makes you understand why the teachers who feel so under siege there view the voucher movement as a real poke in the eye. The debate is often structured to conclude that urban teachers have failed so badly that these kids just must be removed from urban schools. It's an understandable sentiment on the part of parents regarding school systems that are failing, but at the same time it's important to empathize with teachers and understand that it is not all the schools that are the problem.

ANNALS, *AAPSS*, **572**, November 2000

The Pro-Voucher Left
and the Pro-Equity Right

By JOHN E. COONS, LISA GRAHAM KEEGAN,
and T. WILLARD FAIR

MILLER: Our first distinguished panel of the morning will offer fresh voices on the voucher issue, the pro-voucher Left and the pro-equity Right. I am delighted to have this wonderful panel. I'm going to introduce the panelists in turn, ask them to make some opening remarks, and then we'll move on to debate and discussion.

John E. Coons is professor emeritus of law at the University of California, Berkeley. In the late 1960s, he spearheaded the movement for constitutional challenges to the inequities in school finance that began with the Serrano case in California. This has led to the challenge of the system in 40-some states, the overturning of it in 16 or 17 states, and I suppose Jack would be either praised or cursed by various folks in this debate for having set these things in motion. He has written numerous books on school choice, on education reform, and on law and has an interesting perspective, different from what one usually hears in terms of the voucher movement. Jack Coons, we're glad to have you.

A TRULY PUBLIC
SYSTEM OF EDUCATION

JOHN E. COONS: The problem in the United States is that we never had public education. We have education of all sorts, but none of it is public, at least if you mean by "public" that ordinary people have access to the institutions, as in the case of the library, the museum, the streets, the courts, the golf courses, the stadia, and so on.

What we have instead is a system in which people like you and me come to Falls Church or whatever the appropriate parallel suburb would be in New York City or Detroit and buy our way in. We have our voucher: it's called the deed to our house, and we buy our way in to a good school. Alternately, we live in the city, and we go to a private school. And that's fine.

Either way, we have a market all ready for us.

The poor, by contrast, have conscription. They are sent off to a school not of their choosing but according to their address. The idea that our state institutions must take all people is, of course, nonsense. They take the people who can afford to live in their neighborhood, and they don't take people who live outside. If you try to get into a school in Orinda or Beverly Hills and you live in Los Angeles, let me tell you it's not so easy. In fact, our private sector schools are, in that respect, much more open.

My assumption is that this is not necessarily a good thing, even in the eyes of people who have historically been great supporters of what they call the public sector, the public schools. They would indeed, if pressed, say that they'd like to create access to all these institutions for all kinds of people, irrespective of their wealth. That's my first assumption, that we all want to create a public system.

My second assumption, and one I'm going to talk most about, has to do with the means. The means involve subsidies in one form or another for people who can't afford to buy their way in to Beverly Hills. We've got to be careful about democratic values and the means that we choose, the scholarships or the vouchers or whatever we call these things that we're going to give to them.

So we're going to prefer the poor. How do we go about this? First of all, if you give whatever it is you give only to the poor or another target group (for example, children in spe-

cial education), you don't have much of a need for regulation. You haven't done any harm anyway. I'm oversimplifying: certainly, in Milwaukee and Cleveland and Florida, although these are targeted programs, the states and the cities in these cases have been very careful to protect the poor with various kinds of additional, perhaps even unnecessary, regulations.

If, on the other hand—and there is heuristic value to talk about it this way—you talk about a general system in which all children are ultimately to receive subsidies from the state for parental choice, then you have to think about regulation. I will offer you seven criteria for such a system, which now seem to be more or less agreed upon among those people who have thought a bit about vouchers.

First of all, any general system is going to have to empower state institutions to participate in a way that allows them to compete with the private providers in an open market. School districts, museums, cities, counties, libraries, public universities, and so on could all form their own schools, free to operate independently, in the manner of private institutions, both in management and in mission, choosing all sorts of variety. The public sector would become as open as the public sector chose to be.

Second, the private sector should not be regulated out of its own identity. Individual schools would be permitted to keep the special qualities that make them worth choosing in the first place. You can make your own list of identity-specific things.

My first has to do with curriculum: allow no more restraint on the curriculum than is currently respected by the states for private schools. In addition, leave the school free with respect to hiring and student discipline.

On the other hand, if private schools are going to take public money, they will have to—remember we're thinking about the poor—set aside spaces for participation by those who are the object of this program in the first place. There are many different ways to do this. One way is through admissions policy, and I include the public sector, too. Beverly Hills can't do what it used to do: the schools are for everybody now, including the disadvantaged.

With respect to participating private schools, if we allow them to charge tuition in addition to the voucher, we also have to be careful that we don't price the poor out. So we'll need some kind of add-on control. In Cleveland and Milwaukee and Florida, the schools are not allowed to add tuition to the voucher at all. They can't charge anybody any tuition over and above the voucher, and that's one way to do it—at least if the voucher is big enough. As Matt Miller said, the voucher must be big enough to give incentive to new providers so we don't just wind up filling up all the Catholic schools, though certainly that would be an advantage for the children in those schools. We need more providers, and thus the subsidy must be large enough to attract new entrepreneurs, public and private.

Fifth, we need to watch out for children in special education. One simple way is to set a dollar value on each child's individual educational program, as determined for the child by the bureaucracy. The family could be given 80 percent of that dollar value with which to choose its own school.

Sixth, transportation and, seventh, organized information would be important.

I've already exhausted my time without getting to the question of why the conscription of the poor is bad in the first place. Plato, after all, thought it was a marvelous thing. His republic would have conscripted everybody, including the rich. But let me present two facts that argue against conscription, and I want you to consider whether they're true and whether they're relevant.

One is the fact that educators know many different wonderful ways to teach reading, writing, arithmetic, and the rest of the basics, but those methods are all in conflict. And in a world of indeterminate methodologies, it is very hard to justify a system in which the poor get conscripted for one specific pedagogy only because the family happens to live on 38th Street and PS 99 is down the street and uses Montessori.

Second, and a much more important fact, is the value of pluralism of this country. We have a minimum consensus for the content of education: children should learn the basics, and they should learn science, and they should learn to respect the law. But that's it. Now above that, what have we got? We've got subjects on which we disagree, such as human reproduction, gender roles, and environmental questions. This diversity isn't necessarily bad. Nonetheless, it raises the serious question of whether those who can afford to do so should be allowed to choose to send their children to a school that shares the value system of their parents while the poor are conscripted for the value system hawked in the neighborhood school.

In this country, all value systems in the schools are private, whether the school is a private or state institution. There is no agreement on many issues, yet that subject matter will be taught. It will be taught either in conservative terms or in liberal terms or, God help us, in terms of something called neutrality or value clarification or some other vapid nonsense. Something will be taught, and the poor will have no choice but will be conscripted for the particular morality of the folks running their local school.

Now is that what you want? It seems to me that this is the least democratic of all imaginable polities for education. It is a perfect recipe for hostility among the poor. If you want Nazis, force people to study material that violates their family's identity.

It seems to me, finally, that all of this is about the worst thing you can do to the human family, the institution upon which we must ultimately depend for our stability. If you're a kid and you find out at age 5 that the person who has represented you for 5 years and been your one hope and your one leader and your lawyer and everything else is a wimp when it comes to the most important experience of your life—schooling—your confidence in the family and its con-

fidence in itself are shattered. This is no way to nourish society.

MILLER: Thanks, Jack. Up next is Lisa Graham Keegan. Lisa is currently serving her second term as Arizona's superintendent of public instruction, an elected position. In this capacity, she has oversight of Arizona's $4.5 billion public education efforts for K-12. She also serves on the state boards of universities, colleges, and charter schools. She's developed a real national reputation as an innovator and a creative thinker on school choice, on equity, and on how all these things might merge. She has called the property tax basis for school finance unfair and argues that conservatives need to support financial equity in exchange for choice. Lisa, welcome.

EQUITY AND ACCOUNTABILITY
IN PUBLIC EDUCATION

LISA GRAHAM KEEGAN: One of the things that fascinates me about education debates is that oftentimes we don't care what the issue is; we care who is espousing it, so we align ourselves with people and not ideals. Unfortunately, I think that happens far too often, and I appreciate this opportunity to talk about ideals. I also appreciate the opportunity to discuss this with Sandra Feldman and the American Federation of Teachers (AFT). We relied very heavily on the AFT when we went to reorganize our state standards because they were doing some of the best work in the country on academics. So there are all sorts of places where we agree, and there are all sorts of places where we disagree.

What I really want to talk about is why I think fundamental philosophy leads to school choice, but also why the Republican Party, which is my own party, and the Right have been wrong on occasion in this argument. Matt Miller hit on it briefly. Certainly Jack Coons has done more work on this than most people in the country, and we owed him a great debt of gratitude when we tackled this issue in Arizona.

Public education is an education in the interest of the children. It is paid for by the public, it ought to be equally supported no matter who you are, where you live, or what the geographic tax base is in your neighborhood, and it also ought to be accountable to the public in terms of academics. That leaves a whole lot of governance in there. Those principles can be met in any number of ways, but you need that basic infrastructure.

Before I started to study the inequalities of public education, I was in the Arizona House of Representatives and I'm sorry to say I did not realize the extent to which our own system in Arizona was quite unequal along the lines that Jack has been talking about. But I had also proposed, at that time, school choice and vouchers: partial-payment vouchers, which families would need to supplement, similar to what goes on in the private sector with some of the trust grants that are out there. I think these are marvelous and are extremely helpful, and poor families do find a way to pay the difference. But in a public system, I do not believe what we should be looking for is a way to fully support some students and partially support others based on the fact that some would choose a private school and some would choose one of the government-run schools. I think that is inherently unequal, and I have changed my mind, mostly due to study of what the system really looks like. The traditional public system is very closed. Public education is closed because it assigns children to schools by proximity. This assignment, part of the local control of schools, originated in the way local communities raised money to provide schools. If a school were needed where there hadn't been one before, then the folks in that area would generate a way to pay for it. That arrangement evolved into property taxes for a particular school or for one, two, or three schools. Under this funding mechanism, by the end of World War II there were roughly 115,000 school districts in the United States, very small school districts. Today the nation has about 15,000 school districts and twice the number of children. We have centralized greatly.

What that means is that we now have huge school districts, a property tax basis for education, and huge inequities because of the property tax basis. I think right now that fully half of the states in the nation are engaged in some sort of lawsuit over inequities in public education.

The property tax basis works in the following way. A jurisdiction taxes the properties within it for schools. If there is a lot of value in the jurisdiction, a fairly low tax can be levied, with a fairly high return for the students. The school system will function very well. But if the jurisdiction is property poor, then the taxes are quite high, with a fairly low return for the students.

Most states have gone about the business of trying to mitigate this inequality somehow. They will establish a minimum and allow residents to exceed it if they want to, if they live in a wealthy area. Some believe that although the funding is unequal, the system is fair because wealthier areas simply tax themselves more willingly, thus raising more money. But that is not what happens. The fact is that poor areas have tax rates often twice as high to raise less money per pupil.

My party, the Republican Party, has been unwilling to deal with this. As a matter of fact, my father came to my office one day when I proposed that we establish complete equity in Arizona and that we basically get rid of local property taxes that are individually assigned. In other words, we would have statewide property taxes that would be for the benefit of all students. He showed me that the top 10 wealthiest school districts were also the most Republican in the state. He said, "Enjoy this, dear. It's the last thing you'll ever do politically." I appreciate that observation; it was very helpful and uplifting.

The fact of the matter is that he was right. My party does not want to hear this. This has been very difficult for us. Nonetheless, we have succeeded in this in Arizona at the end of the day. We did succeed, and our school-funding formula is now philosophically based on students. We

have a statewide property tax. We have done away with bonding for construction of schools and replaced that with what I see as a horrible sort of centrally planned transitional program. I hope we will evolve out of that. Its basis, however, is philosophically sound; it's based on individual students.

All students merit the same financial support, and we have got to deal with this as a nation, on both sides of the aisle. Quite frankly, in this debate in Arizona, I don't think that the debate revolved around political party. Rather, it was a matter of who had a school district that they liked and who did not.

What we don't want to deal with is the fact that we have in place systems in which inherent inequalities are solidly entrenched. This situation can be fixed only by adopting the fundamental principle that every child deserves to be supported by an amount of money that is based on that child's need. Absolutely equal amounts of money do not really make sense when factors such as special education are involved. But there ought to be a formula that applies to any child regardless of where she lives, and there ought to be a tax formula that applies to all members of the citizenry, regardless of where they live and not based on the wealth of the property next to them. If a nice commercial building is sitting next to my property, my tax rates are going to be lower just by virtue of the fact that a very expensive building is next-door. I don't think the current systems make sense; we ought to do away with them.

Howard Fuller said it best at a conference a few years ago: "If money did not matter in education, the people who had it wouldn't be trying so hard to hang onto it." We love to say money doesn't matter, but you will hear that only from people who have it. So I think we have to challenge that just a little bit.

As I approached this issue in Arizona, I was advised by friends not to speak in terms of equality because advocating equality sounds so socialist. I'm not kidding. Republican or Democrat, we don't want to hear about equality. It has a nasty ring to it. But that we can't broach the topic of equal opportunity for our kids is crazy.

Most people in a community will favor equality of access. But when you then promote equal access to schools that may not be the traditional local district schools, you lose the community support. As a society, we want equality in a closed system, but that doesn't make sense. Choice, opportunity, and the ability to exercise the values that you think are important with the resources that the state backs your child with cannot, it seems to me, be separated.

Moreover, while, on the one hand, we have this difficulty in agreeing that kids have had unequal opportunity, the other side has not been willing to say that that opportunity ought to extend to a school that works for a child, whether that school is government run or not. I believe that in here somewhere lies a great compromise, one that so far we have not been able to reach.

The other thing I want to talk about briefly is the question of accountability. Our state has been particularly strong in the public charter school movement. As we have developed public charter schools in Arizona, we have been a little bit more freewheeling than other states by allowing a lot of providers in. We immediately began to see some outstanding providers. The majority of them, in fact, are quite good; we also have some schools that are not doing well and should be closed. This accountability issue is critically important. I do not believe that a pure marketplace solves the educational problem, but if there is no feedback to the public about the quality of schools, no good choices will be made.

Having the opportunity to choose any one of a number of terrible schools is not an improvement in public education. It is therefore fundamentally important to have accountability, but, lest we forget, the system that we're currently operating in does not have accountability structures in place. It is not the case that you can simply take that really sound accountability program that we've been applying to the traditional system forever and judge the quality of these new schools. Our accountability system in Arizona is quite new. For three years now, we've tested every child every year with a Stanford 9 test, and soon we'll introduce a state test as well. The beauty of an annual test is that you can measure the progress of students and not just look at absolute scores, which I think is critically important, especially in evolving school markets.

The question of accountability will continue to be critically important.

Even so, we ought not expect that we will be able to inspect new schools and private schools and immediately know how effective those schools are. We've never done it in the traditional system. The accountability measure has got to apply to the entire public system, whether the schools are privately run or government run, so that we can say to the public at large, "This is a school that works in the following way and you should choose it or you should not choose it." We can tell parents what happens in any given school. Then their choice is informed. By insisting first and foremost on equal and portable funds for all students, and by providing solid academic information, we create a system in which all students have the right to expect equal support and also equal opportunity to choose where they go to school.

MILLER: One of the wonderful things in American politics is that someone like Lisa could be a rising star in Barry Goldwater country and, on some of the equity issues, sound a lot like Ted Kennedy.

Our last distinguished panelist on our first distinguished panel is T. Willard Fair. Mr. Fair is president and chief executive officer of the Urban League of greater Miami. He's been a powerful voice in the effort to improve his community, having worked for the Urban League since 1963. One of his many interesting achievements over the years is that he most recently has, in a disagreement with the National Urban League, been a supporter of Jeb Bush's statewide voucher plan in Florida, which I'm sure he'll tell us about.

EDUCATING CHILDREN FOR SUCCESS

T. WILLARD FAIR: Good morning, and thanks very much, Matt, for making it public that I am in disagreement with Hugh Price. I hope that that does not translate into being in disagreement with the National Urban League, for I have not been able to find anyplace where the league's delegate assembly, which is the policymaking body, has adopted a resolution regarding the issue of vouchers. But it wouldn't matter if they had, for I would also be in disagreement with them.

At the Urban League in Miami, unlike Urban League affiliates elsewhere, we decided in 1980 to get out of the service-delivery business. We decided that we would spend that time attempting to prepare children in Liberty City to be competitive. We thought that we would be the leaders of what we defined as the final revolution for black Americans. We felt that, given the impact and the benefits from the legal revolution and the civil rights revolution, we could afford to spend a significant amount of our time on child development. We needed to make sure that children today were being prepared to be competitive with their counterparts in Miami, in the state, in the country, and in the world.

As we moved away from the issue of service delivery, we were forced to begin to look at things that were working and things that were not working. If we're talking about development, then we must be very clear as to how each institution begins to make a negative or positive contribution toward the development of children. At the Urban League in Miami, we're doing a variety of things, all related to preparing children to be competitive with their counterparts, be they Hispanic, be they Haitian, be they non-Hispanic or non-Haitian.

We are doing significant things in terms of drug trafficking. We've taken the drug process head-on because we understand that you cannot talk about child development in an environment where there is a value system that says that the way you make money doesn't matter, that money's the most important thing. If you're going to talk about kids staying in school, if you're going to talk about kids achieving, then you have to take temptations like drugs and drug dealing away from them as they go to and from school, as they play in the neighborhood. Some of our campaigns are very aggressive, designed to deal with the whole issue of getting rid of drug trafficking and other illegal pursuits that make educational achievement insignificant.

We have developed a lot of affordable housing whereby we have made sure that families now have enough space to accommodate their needs and desires. You really can't suggest that inner-city kids get excited about education and doing homework if their homes are extremely overcrowded. For instance, at one time, one mother had 13 children living in one bedroom. Where is any significant homework going to be done under such circumstances? Therefore part of what we've done is to recognize that there's a direct correlation between affordable housing configurations and the develop-

ment of families. We've made sure to begin to give the issue of creating affordable housing in the community a direct connection to child development.

Given our goal of child development, it is no accident that we are supporting those things that are going to challenge the public education system in Dade County to deliver quality education to all of the children in the county. Dade County is the fourth-largest school system in the country. In terms of our capacity, as it relates to language spoken and as it relates to demographics, there's no doubt in my mind that there's a tremendous challenge on behalf of those who administer and on behalf of those who are in charge of the instructional methodology for the system.

But if you look at the system in a segmented fashion, you will find that, according to all of the most recent data, all of the kids who are failing seem to be in my community, the African American community. If you look at those kids who are dropping out, disproportionately the number of kids who are dropping out are in my community. The list goes on and on, and it does not speak uniquely to Dade County. It probably speaks to what is happening in the country.

We're about the business of making sure that we participate in the discussion about what has to be done differently in the public schools in order to prepare kids to be competitive. It seems to us that it is appropriate for the Miami affiliate of the Urban League to be an active, aggressive player in the discussion of education reform. We could not sit on the sidelines and allow others to make definitive conclusions about how all children get a quality education, especially when the discussion addresses who would be the ones most likely to take advantage of vouchers. We're talking primarily about black and brown and yellow children.

As a result, it does not make any good sense to talk about breaking the stalemate if we're not going to seek out ways to aggressively involve black parents in the argument, in the debate. So part of what we've got to do in this conversation is to make sure that those who live in these communities and who share a concern about what's happening to their children participate in this conversation.

What we've attempted to do is to make sure that we make that happen. We will not allow the discussion to be one-sided as it relates to ethnicity or political ideology. We will force ourselves to make sure that we participate in that discussion and that the arguments we make are made vociferously. What we will not do is stand idly by and allow persons who look exactly like us to take positions that in our judgment are not in the best interest of all of us. So we have no qualms about taking the risk that will allow us to disassociate ourselves from Hugh Price, the president and chief executive officer of the National Urban League, to say to the NAACP that it may speak for the membership of the NAACP but not, in 2000, for all people.

All of the arguments made earlier by this panel are great, but the fact is that children in Liberty City are not learning. The fact is that if we're going to do something about that, then we've got to be part of the reform movement that makes that happen.

We can talk about the need for us not to do anything, but the reality says to us that we've got to do something. So as we listen to all of the arguments, at the end of the day we know clearly that we have got to move beyond the arguments and beyond the stalemate. We think you do that by simply making sure that the facts are given out correctly to the community.

A new participant in the school voucher discussion in our state is called OUCH. This is a group of persons who have decided to make sure that the facts are given out to the people so that the people cannot support the issue of vouchers. We've done an analysis of the persons who are behind the campaign. That's important to us because they are hiding behind the cloak of their liberalness and their blackness. If you look beyond their liberalness and their blackness, you will see that they do not support those things that are in the best interest of the children.

It's not popular or ethnically correct for blacks to be attacking each other because it violates ethnic solidarity. The concept of ethnic solidarity holds that we don't want to give anybody the impression that all of us don't think the same way about everything. In Miami, ethnic solidarity is a myth. Some of us think the correct thing about the right things and the less correct thing about other things. It is very interesting that voucher opponents have come together, while the proponents don't often do that. That is why I'm pleased that we're here today to talk about the issue of school vouchers: we often have our own individual agendas and individual directions, and we really never show the power that results from our coming together. I'm so glad you invited me because it adds some coloration to this process that is missing in the discussion nationally.

An interesting aspect of OUCH is that there's a foundation that has agreed to fund it anonymously. I find it surprising that an organization would give its money away for such an important cause and not attach its name to it as the activity goes forward. I'm trying to find out who that person or persons are so they, too, can be exposed, because we need not have anybody hiding behind the cloak of anonymity in response to those things that are important to us as we go into the twenty-first century. So I suggest to you that part of what we see as important with respect to this issue, moving beyond the stalemate, is to begin to talk about how we make sure that the truth is told. If that happens, then I think we move beyond the stalemate.

The key to the issue of school vouchers, moving beyond the stalemate, is for us to make Hugh Price, Al Sharpton, Kweisi Mfume, and others say what they know to be correct: that part of the delivery system for quality education, for the children whom they profess publicly to be concerned about, is to support and embrace the voucher movement. I read with interest the proposition that was made about a possible compromise. I wait today for them to say publicly that it's the right thing to do.

* * *

QUESTIONS AND ANSWERS

MILLER: Thank you very much. With those stimulating remarks as our kickoff, let me tee off the discussion with a couple of questions. First, Jack, one of the things that I think people don't get a sense of as much is how long-standing the pedigree is on the Left intellectually for vouchers. A lot of folks think that it's a Milton Friedman idea from the 1950s and that it's been passed on through his libertarian devotees over the years. You, I recall, have been debating these issues with Friedman since 1960—didn't you have a radio show in Chicago about this?

COONS: I did. You, I understand, have a radio show in Los Angeles.

MILLER: That is true. I didn't mean that as a slur. Jack once told me a funny story about Milton Friedman and himself. Jack has debated these issues with Friedman now for more than a century, it turns out. Jack actually got a letter from Friedman at one point because Friedman was trying to scare off one of the conservative pro-voucher funders from being involved with Jack. The letter was copied to Jack as a courtesy because the letter warned the man against involvement with Jack

Coons because he was an egalitarian, which was the worst thing someone could say, I guess, about Jack. When I asked Friedman about that one time, he said, "It's true. Jack Coons is an egalitarian, but he's a nice egalitarian."

Can you comment a little bit, Jack, on the major contours of the debate on your voucher design between your camp and Friedman's and the way it's played out, say, in California and elsewhere so folks have a concrete understanding of it?

COONS: I'll give a brief history. In the late 1960s, I exploited my former students mercilessly to produce a whole spate of books and articles and models of what we thought of as the necessary guarantees to the people for whom vouchers were really intended. These produced some interest. The late, lamented Congressman Leo Ryan called in the summer of 1978 and suggested implementing an initiative in California. He said, "We'll start as soon as I get back from my trip. I have to make a trip." Well, of course, he didn't come back. Leo died in Guyana.

But a movement went forward in California with an initiative that never got enough signatures because it didn't get enough money. Of course, it looked as if it would have great support, from both Left and Right. The Right liked the market; the Left liked the focus on the poor. But in the end, both withdrew. The unions found it unappealing in terms of its competitive aspects, and the Right found it too regulated for their taste. As I say, we've been caught between their trenches ever since. Damned by the Left, damned by the Right, and

maybe properly so. In any event, that is the history.

The rhetoric for vouchers has been largely captured since the 1970s by libertarian formulas. The libertarians, God bless them, like to talk this way. They like to talk about how the market is going to fix everything. The unions were only too glad that they did talk this way because they knew such views couldn't get more than 30 percent of the vote. As long as your rhetoric is exclusively on the free market and damn the regulation, you're not going to win anything.

At last, out of the forest has come a coalition of people like Tommy Thompson and Polly Williams and the gangs in Florida and Ohio and elsewhere to show that this really has nothing to do with either party or the self-interest of individual groups. In fact, it has a broad appeal to all people who would like to help the disadvantaged and who have interest in the family.

———

MILLER: Lisa, can I ask you a question? Every politician says we must honor the notion of local control. And yet as you point out, people don't distinguish between matters such as local control over curriculum text and the financial aspect of local control that you stressed. Do you see this becoming something that anyone at the presidential level is going to talk about? Is John McCain going to talk about this? How does the financial aspect of local control get into the mainstream debate in a way that is different from the way it is included today?

KEEGAN: Candidly, Matt, I'm not sure that it does because local control is such a wonderful term. Nobody knows what it means, but it certainly feels good to use it. So we throw it around all the time. I'm guilty of it myself. I do it with great fervor when it's necessary, and I denounce it when it's necessary. It's just one of those catch phrases.

I don't think that the financial issues of local control are going to catch fire in a presidential debate because they are counterintuitive to what everybody believes is true about public education. People believe that it is true that they are taxing themselves at the same effort level, that whatever effort they are exerting on their taxes is resulting in the same amount, if you will, of money for kids. They do not believe it is true that taxes in lower-income communities are higher. They just don't believe it. So it takes a huge educational process.

Under this marvelous debate structure where you get 30 seconds to comment on the issues of the day that are the most important to the nation, I just cannot see raising this issue and putting it out there in its fullness. A lot of people say, "That's true, there are inequities, but there is Title I money for the poor, and that more than offsets the inequities." To that I would respond that actually it does not offset them because state legislators feel that, if the local schools want to do something with their local control money, that doesn't cost anything at the state level. This sort of thinking leads to a bigger and bigger disparity.

The important issue, Matt, is that you have to be able to connect that.

There is no morally compelling vision for me in equalizing school districts to each other. I think school districts are not only unequal; they are monopolies. So even though at the margins California says it has open enrollment, a student from Los Angeles would not be allowed to just walk in and attend Beverly High.

Some of the nastiest debates I ever had to engage in were on this issue of where poor kids get to go to school, quite frankly. So I think you have to discuss the larger issue, which is what I think the candidates are attempting to do. The system ought to be based on the individual needs of students, it ought to be driven by parent choice of school, and it ought to be fair in its support of students. That's about as far as you can go. Even though the local control issue needs serious policy work at the state level, I just don't think most people are ready to hear the facts about it. Their initial reaction is, "That's not true," and it takes them a long time to see that it is true.

MILLER: In Vermont, where they have a court-ordered state equalization plan, one of the strange spectacles about the property tax in this regard is that the wealthier communities are engaged in civil disobedience now, taking to the streets because they're being asked to raise the tax themselves on their property at levels that are still lower than the levels at which the poor communities have taxed themselves for decades.

KEEGAN: Right. And we call that a Robin Hood scheme.

MILLER: Right. And this is an irony that I think isn't well understood sometimes by the press even, and others.

———

MILLER: Willard, let me ask you a question before we turn to our audience to continue the discussion. In terms of the political dynamic, what do you think it will take for minority leadership to decide to take a different public view of these issues?

FAIR: Constituents would have to begin to say to their leaders, "We think you are wrong." It's amazing that, while all the polls show that, in Liberty City and in other inner cities, the parents support vouchers, the leadership nationally would say that vouchers are bad. This is a pathology associated with the ism called racism. This ism allows individuals who think they are superior to believe that they know what's good for us. However, what they think is not good for us is, in most instances, not necessarily so. Their position on vouchers follows this rule.

The mere fact that some of us of color are standing up with Jeb Bush, for example, for the initiative makes the initiative more believable. It is no longer viewed just as another Republican gimmick being perpetrated on black people. So what's going to take it to the next level is that I've got to multiply the voices of outrage against the leadership. As soon as we stand up and say that what they're saying is incorrect, inappropriate, is not validated by any facts, other people will be freed up because part of their reluctance is that they don't want to get caught up in our fight.

You know that they should be condemned, and you're waiting for me to do it. I'm going to do it, and now I dare you not to do it.

MILLER: We had asked, by the way, Kweisi Mfume to appear. He had a scheduling conflict, and we're sorry he couldn't be with us. But to be fair to today's minority leadership, let me pose a question. So many of the voucher proposals are so tiny and affect so few kids. Just as a matter of political strategy or tactics, isn't it reasonable for them to wonder why they should split with traditional allies, like the teachers' unions and other groups that have been walking with them shoulder to shoulder on a lot of issues on a broader agenda that matters for them, for programs that seem so token and that are going to leave almost all the kids out?

FAIR: That's a very valid and real concern. But if, as a minority leader, you had said to me before making that observation that you are really concerned about children, then I'd expect you to make that valid concern public, and then I'd expect you no longer to be a critic but a creator of something that's going to do something about the children. If minority leaders are not prepared to support vouchers due to these sentimental circumstances, but they nevertheless have a commitment to and a concern about the children, they would put their plan on the table.

All I've heard is criticism. I've heard complaining; I've heard whining. I've yet to see anyone come forward and say the voucher plan is no good. We agree that something has got to be done, and this is what we propose. Just to criticize and be allowed to do that and do nothing else I think is unfair and irresponsible leadership.

———

QUESTION FROM THE AUDIENCE: We're looking for ways of creating a compromise here. We've had success with tax credits rather than vouchers. Would that be a better way to try to move forward?

KEEGAN: It seems to be in Arizona, but that doesn't mean that we've given up on also wanting to have the option for parents to take the amount of money that's allocated for their kids and go directly into a school. At this point, I am up for all options that move toward more availability of school choice for students. Incidentally, in Arizona, tuition tax credits mean that our family gets $500 a year as a direct tax credit to a scholarship organization that funds a private school. The tax credit cannot be for the benefit of my own child. The tax credit is basically just funding scholarship organizations. This creates a great deal of space, if you will, between government and private schools. That was one of its biggest selling points, quite frankly. It's given millions of dollars to scholarship organizations, which can then fund kids into private schools. So, yes, I think tuition tax credits are one opportunity.

Having said that, the tuition tax credit in Arizona was contested in court by any number of groups. The teachers' union and folks who ordinarily oppose vouchers also opposed that tax credit. We had to fight them in court; ultimately, we prevailed.

FAIR: As Matt said, a voucher is a voucher is a voucher. Clearly, what you call it is important. In Florida, we call ours an opportunity scholarship, but it still serves the same purpose as a voucher. It allows kids who have been in a school that has received an F grade for two consecutive years to apply for an opportunity scholarship and to move to another school. We think that just changing what we call it makes it much more palatable to many folks who think they ought to oppose it.

COONS: I want to register my unswerving admiration and my unswerving resistance—the admiration for Lisa Keegan, the resistance to tax credits. Tax credits are largely useful for the rich, unless they're refundable. And the Arizona system is among the most peculiar that I have met. You don't need a speech on this, but if you want to get the details, we'll try later.

———

QUESTION FROM THE AUDIENCE: What about families that would use vouchers to go to a school that teaches hate or racism?

KEEGAN: First of all, it's important for me that a parent's choice of a school for his or her child is respected. What Jack Coons said before about values being taught is absolutely true. Hateful though I might find some of what gets taught in a lot of places, I recognize that it does get taught.

I don't believe in voucher programs that would allow private schools to determine which students they will admit. Our voucher programs have always specified that there has to be a set-aside of so many spaces and that the kids are selected for admission to a school by lottery, and so forth. If a family is choosing to send their child to a school where I deem that the material being taught is contrary to my values, I guess my answer to that would be that, in fact, those values are being taught to that child regardless of where they are, in school or elsewhere. I find it greatly regrettable. I find it hateful in some instances.

But I find more hateful and more repressive the idea that my values are the ones that will absolutely be taught to your child and you will not have a choice about that. I believe, at the end of the day, that the vast majority of Americans denounce that kind of hatefulness. You will not see it in most schools, but where you do see it, a child absolutely has the opportunity to get out. And it does not just happen in private school.

FAIR: When we define the rules, we also define them in the context of the value system that's prevalent at the time. If, in our judgment as definers of the rules, we think that there is a tendency for those kinds of institutions to exist, then we will define the rules so that they cannot exist and be involved in the process. Not any hospital can be involved in an HMO. There are qualifications; there's an accountability process that says that certain standard criteria must be used.

As we talk about vouchers, we want to make sure that families who are in a position to accept the vouchers have rules specifying at least the minimum things that they must do and cannot do if they're going to be part of the process. I think we're smart enough to do that. Our history tells me that we are.

———

QUESTION FROM THE AUDIENCE: Jane Hannaway of the Urban Institute. This is a question of clarification for Jack Coons. I believe you made a statement that schools must set aside places for voucher children. Could you expand on what your thinking is on that? Is it public and private schools? What are the details?

COONS: In every voucher scheme—every scholarship scheme—you have to make some decision about who can participate and the rules of participation. The proponents have felt that if you're going to take public money for either a public charter school or a private institution, you ought to be playing by rules that are more democratic than the very undemocratic rules that now govern the public sector. That is, you can't exclude people by the fact that they live outside the boundaries or because they're poor or whatever.

Now how do you make sure? You have conflicts because, on one hand, there is the identity of the school to preserve in order to make it worth choosing; on the other hand, there is the importance of the accessibility for the people who need to get in the school. So you have two problems. One is how to regulate admission so that kids have a reasonable chance of getting in. There are various ways to do it. In the 1978 proposal in

California, there was to be random selection among all who applied. That's okay by me. Random selection of half is also okay. Over the long run, Steve Sugarman and others who have worked on these things with me have preferred a regulation that would make the school set aside 20 percent or something like that of its new spaces each year for low-income families. That isn't perfect, but it works, and it satisfies the culture of almost all of the private schools. Most private schools do this now as a matter of their own preference.

The other, very important concern is that the kids not be priced out. The schools could say, "Come on in, we love you, but by the way, we need an extra $5000 in addition to your voucher." That's a problem. It's another form of the present state system. It's the Beverly Hills system in a new dress. That problem has two solutions. One is for the voucher system to permit no add-ons; the voucher would be big enough that no add-ons are needed. The other solution is to have the voucher as big as you like (big enough to provide new schools) and you can add on but only according to the capacity of the family to pay: in other words, price control. You can imagine how Milton Friedman feels about that.

MILLER: Let's take one more question before our break. Paul Peterson from Harvard. A heckler from Harvard, I describe him.

PETERSON: I thought the analogy to trench warfare that Jack raised earlier was accurate, that there are two sides out there, one political party against another, conservatives against liberals. But there's one dynamic element in the story. There's only one force out there that's probably going to change the story, and that's black families. The reason is that if black families say that this is something that's really important to them, it's going to change the calculations of all the politicians who have lined up on one side or another. They're going to have a lot of difficulty dealing with that reality and not doing something about it.

We already see that. There is much more support in the black community, especially among families with children in schools, for vouchers than there is in the white community. There's much more in the center city than there is in suburban areas. Just yesterday we released a study that showed that it was the black kids who benefited from vouchers in Dayton, Ohio, and here in Washington, D.C. It was the black kids who benefited from the vouchers. If this finding repeats itself in other places, and if it penetrates into the consciousness of the civil rights community, then the grand bargain becomes a possibility. I don't think it becomes a possibility until we reach that point.

FAIR: He's absolutely correct. We just got a three-year grant from a foundation to make parents consumers of education. I've got a workshop next week, and I can't wait to get back to tell them I've got some new evidence that it works.

MILLER: Let me thank our distinguished panel for starting off a very stimulating discussion.

ANNALS, *AAPSS*, **572**, November 2000

Is a Grand Bargain Between Left and Right Possible?

By LAMAR ALEXANDER, CLINT BOLICK,
ANDREW ROTHERHAM, and SANDRA FELDMAN

MILLER: Welcome back. For our second panel, which is devoted to the question of whether a grand bargain between Left and Right is possible, we have very distinguished speakers. Let me introduce them all to you quickly so they can offer their remarks and we can get into debate and discussion. We've got a litigator on this panel, we've got a labor negotiator. This means we could end up with quite a vocal debate, but we're still going to try to disagree without being too disagreeable.

On our panel today we have folks you know very well. Lamar Alexander needs no introduction. He is a former secretary of education under George Bush; in that post, he spearheaded an effort to enact a voucher test at the federal level called the G.I. Bill for Kids. The plan would have spent $500 million in new federal dollars to give the parents of half a million low- and middle-income children each a $1000 voucher to use at the schools of their choice. He is a former governor of Tennessee and a former presidential candidate in the last race and in this race. I asked Lamar the other day if he thought maybe he didn't drop out too soon, considering what's been happening these days.

We have Clint Bolick from the Institute of Justice. He's the vice president and director of litigation there and is perhaps the leading litigator in the country on behalf of school choice programs that are facing constitutional challenges. We have Andrew Rotherham, who is a special assistant to the President for domestic policy. Andy was formerly with the Democratic Leadership

NOTE: Andrew Rotherham's remarks in this article were made in his capacity as a federal employee; therefore, they are in the public domain.

Council and the Progressive Policy Institute, and he's now at the White House, where he coordinates education initiatives and advises the President on education policy.

We have Sandra Feldman, who is the well-known president of the American Federation of Teachers and has been active for many years as a leader in the teaching movement and the union movement, both domestically and internationally.

We had invited Kweisi Mfume to join us, and he declined. He did not turn us down in a huff; I don't want to leave that impression. But he's a very busy man.[1]

I'll ask everyone to speak, I would say again, for the same seven or eight minutes if you can, laying out your thoughts on whether a grand bargain somehow is possible between Left and Right. In a nutshell, a bargain that I proposed in the *Atlantic Monthly* was as follows. Take a handful of towns where everyone agrees that the school system is not producing the results we want; it's dysfunctional for various reasons. Don't pick cities that are outliers in school spending, like Washington, D.C., and Newark, New Jersey, where spending is excessive and seems to be very ineffective. But take one of the many cities where per pupil spending is substantially lower than in the surrounding suburbs, and raise per pupil spending, say, 20 percent, giving the schools what the Left says are the resources needed for kids in districts that come with many more troubles, many more needs, more dilapidated schools, and so forth. Raise per pupil spending, but

implement that higher spending only via something like a universal choice program, or at least a program that would give this higher voucher to poor kids, who, sadly, as you know, in our urban districts may compose a large proportion of the student population: about two-thirds of the kids are on the federal school lunch program. That's an idea which, when shopped around at least through my *Atlantic* piece, seemed to draw some interest from some differing points on the political spectrum. I just mention that as one option. I'm sure we'll hear about others, and then we'll have a debate. Let me start with Lamar Alexander.

THE G.I. BILL FOR KIDS

LAMAR ALEXANDER: Thank you, and thanks for the opportunity to be here. I'd like to pose a question, recall a little history, and make a specific proposal in my seven or eight minutes. Here's my question. Why don't we try an idea that worked spectacularly well to help create the best colleges over the last 50 years and see if it will help create the best schools? I'll add a little history to this.

About eight years ago, almost exactly, it was a beautiful spring day, and I was walking with President Bush on the South Lawn, where he was about to make an important announcement, when his wife, Barbara, sent him back inside because his coat didn't match his pants. So he went back, changed his clothes, came out, and made that important announcement.

Let me be specific about what President Bush said in April of 1992. This was a result of about a year of work, and a broad coalition of support was behind it. He proposed a G.I. bill for children. The G.I. Bill for Kids would give $1000 annual scholarships in new federal dollars to each child of a middle- or low-income family in a participating state or locality. In other words, you had to want to be a part of this to do it. Families could spend the scholarships at any lawfully operated school, public, private, or religious. Up to $500 of each scholarship could be spent on "other academic programs," for example, a Saturday program to learn more math, an afternoon program for children with speech disabilities, or a summer accelerated course in language or the arts.

Let me emphasize here that the President said what most people miss with this proposal. These are $1000 scholarships, new federal dollars that may be spent at any school. That means most of the dollars—"I would expect," he said, "more than 75 percent"—would go to public schools. Now let me underline that one more time. This is a different way, a different proposal. It would mean that if you were a principal of a middle school with 600 kids in it—let's say it was an inner-city school, and 80 percent of the kids qualified for this scholarship—the kids would show up at that public school, if they chose to go there, with $1000 pinned to their blouses or their shirts. That would be approximately a half million new federal dollars for that school, to be spent the way that faculty, under the supervision of that local school board, thought it ought to be spent. These were not dollars to be taken away from that school to go to some private or religious school.

Now those children could have chosen to go to other schools. Actually, the proposal gave them a series of five new choices. They could have taken their $1000 to a different public school, or to the Catholic school down the street, or to the same public school, as I just mentioned. If there was something about it that dissatisfied them, the moms could go in and say that they didn't want to go to the school. Or they could say they did want to go there but ask if the school could stay open until 5 o'clock because they worked. With that new money, perhaps the school could stay open until 5 o'clock.

The money could go to a new school, one that might be at the hospital where a mom worked, for example. Or the money could be spent for other academic programs. That was the proposal.

Now what happened? What happened was the bill never got out of committee. The usual voices arose to object. They said it wasn't enough money, even though it was a half billion dollars. It was the largest new dollar program in the federal budget that year. It was more money than was used to start the Head Start program in 1965. They said it would hurt public schools, even though we've had 50 years of experience that the same idea helps public universities. They said it would help the rich, when it was really for the poor and middle-income; those who would be eligible would be anyone with less than a median income, which then was a little under $50,000 a year.

They said it was unconstitutional, even though tens of thousands of veterans went to Catholic high school after World War II on the G.I. bill for veterans. They said the poor can't make wise decisions, even though we allow them to do that with food, with hospital, and with day-care vouchers. And they said it would discriminate, even though there were anti-discrimination provisions in the law. That's what happened to that specific idea.

I believe our nation missed a terrific opportunity in 1992 by not recognizing the difference between President Bush's G.I. bill for children and a typical state voucher proposal. So this morning, this is my specific proposal. I'd like to up the ante, in the spirit of the day. Instead of a $500 million new federal program, let's make it a $5 billion new federal program, ten times as much. Instead of $1000 for 500,000 American schoolchildren, let's make it $1000 for each of 5 million American schoolchildren. That's 1 out of every 10 American children. That's 1 out of every 6 children who would be eligible if the eligible children are those who come from families with less than the median income, which today is more than $50,000 a year. Instead of enough money to make it available for 24 cities the size of San Jose, which President Bush's proposal was, this would make it available for all the eligible children in 240 cities the size of San Jose; instead of 30

cities the size of Little Rock, it would be 300 the size of Little Rock; or instead of 7 cities the size of Milwaukee, it would be 70 cities the size of Milwaukee.

And a participating school district would have to do what Arizona does in this sense. It would have to allow parents to choose among the schools. If they chose among all the public schools, that would be all right with me. I would not have a federal requirement that state money must be spent at a private or religious school. But the federal money would have to go to any lawfully operated school.

Now what would have happened if the Congress and the nation in its wisdom had adopted President Bush's proposal in 1992? Well, it was a five-year demonstration proposal. We would have known by 2000 that it didn't work, that it actually hurt public schools or hurt poor children, or that the money wasn't enough money, or that there was something unanticipatedly wrong with it. Or, as I suspect, we would have found out another answer, that it did work. That it worked just as well as the G.I. bill for veterans and as the Pell grants.

I was president of a university. I sat there at the University of Tennessee every day knowing that a great many students could go to Vanderbilt or Notre Dame or Yeshiva or even for-profit institutions. It never occurred to me to come to Washington and say, Please don't give any more Pell grants to students who might go to Notre Dame or even to a poor private institution. I knew they were bringing new dollars to our university, and the choice and the change helped us as well as the money did.

So we would have, after five years, a successful program, I would think. Today we would be competing with this G.I. Bill for Kids with all the new money in our economy, to broaden the program, to fund it. We would be getting poor parents more choices; we would be funding the change. We would be finding a more equitable way to help pay for the extra cost of educating children who come often from poor families.

You might say $5 billion is an unreasonable, unrealistic amount of money, but we're spending $5 billion new federal dollars this year just on technology in the schools. If you add up all the federal programs that have to do with computers, that's $5 billion. We could easily fund $5 billion for a demonstration program for the G.I. Bill for Kids.

Then I would end where I started. Why not try the idea that helped create the best colleges in the world to see if over a five-year period it will help to create the best schools in the world for our children?

MILLER: Clint Bolick, vice president of the Institute of Justice.

TRUE SUPPORT FOR PUBLIC EDUCATION

CLINT BOLICK: It is a pleasure to be here today. Thanks, Matt, and to the Annenberg Center for putting together a very provocative forum. I do think that the question of the day does bring people out of the woodwork to determine whether a person really supports the goals of public education or is out to preserve the status quo.

I am very skeptical about greater spending on education. If spending were the answer, the Newark, New Jersey, school system, which is now spending close to $14,000 per student, would be one of the finest school systems in the country. It is not. More money in recent years has tended to buy more bureaucracy. While over the last decade or so the number of schoolteachers has risen slightly, the number of administrators has risen dramatically. That has made the educational mission in many instances harder, not easier.

I'm also skeptical because this is how the grand bargain often works. You say lots more money and also some school choice. Then the other side agrees to go halfway with you. They'll compromise on the more-money part, but they'll get rid of school choice. So we have a compromise that just looks like more of the same.

I think it is far more important who has control over the money than how much money is actually being spent. That's why I favor Lisa Graham Keegan's proposal to put an equal amount of money on the back of every schoolchild, and that is the way every school would be funded, not through a local bureaucracy that shaves off a tremendous amount of money. That money is spent by the consumer, and then it is controlled by the school, whether that school is public or private.

Nonetheless, I do think that the grand bargain is possible. We have never had a school choice plan without substantial liberal and minority support, whether it was Polly Williams and John Norquist, the mayor of Milwaukee; Fannie Lewis, the Democratic council member from Cleveland; or T. Willard Fair and many black Democratic members of the legislature in Florida. The United States Congress has passed school choice programs only to have them vetoed by President Clinton, who, Polly Williams has often quipped, is an example of the only person in public housing who gets to send his child to private school.

Here in the District of Columbia, we've even supported it with people like Joe Lieberman, Pat Moynihan, and others. But Florida is a concrete example of an aspect of the grand compromise in practice. The Florida opportunity scholarship program is a tiny part of a much larger school reform program that delivers as much as $1 billion of new money to public schools. But Jeb Bush insisted that accountability and choice be a part of that system, so we now have the first state in the nation that offers a money-back guarantee on public schools. If the public schools fail, the kids are no longer held hostage there. While we're fixing the school with a bailout program, the kids get to go to either a better public school or to a private school.

One of the things that I love about the Florida program is that the peo-ple who are shrieking so loudly opposing vouchers have it within their power to prevent a single voucher from ever being issued in the state of Florida. The way they could do that is by doing their jobs. If they don't fail, there are no scholarships. If they do fail, there is no argument against scholarships.

Nonetheless, I do think that this grand compromise is possible, and elsewhere than Florida, but I don't think that this panel is reflective of the Left-Right debate. The American Federation of Teachers gives lip service to reform, and it actually has supported some positive reforms in the public schools. But when it comes to school choice, they have built a Berlin Wall around it, and they have blocked the schoolhouse doors in state after state, going to court in Ohio, in Wisconsin, and in Florida. In fact, in Florida, they are not support-ing the grand compromise. They are vigorously litigating that issue.

The NAACP shamefully, shame-fully is opposing school choice every-where in unholy alliance with People for the American Way. In Milwaukee, the NAACP litigated the issue of school choice despite the fact that the *Milwaukee Community Journal*, the largest African American newspaper in Milwaukee, found that 90 percent of the black community supported the program. The numbers support-ing the Milwaukee program continue to grow. And the Clinton administra-tion is emblematic of the Democratic Party at the national level, being totally beholden to its special inter-est constituency. The debate between

Al Gore and Bill Bradley is a perfect example: the fact that Bill Bradley at one time voted for school choice programs is apparently a part of the disqualification, at least in the eyes of Al Gore, for ever being president of the United States.

I agree with Senator John Kerry, not exactly a raving conservative, that the Democrats are in real danger of losing the crown jewel of their policy arsenal by being so militantly opposed to school choice programs and to other systemic education reforms. They are in danger of ceding that issue to the Republicans, if we ever have a Republican presidential candidate who is capable of articulating a rational position on educational policy. It may be high on a wish list.

My bottom line is, yes, it is possible for our nation to have a grand compromise. It happened in Florida. And not only that, but I predict that it will happen. Once we get to the point in our society where we recognize that the goal of public education is not about preserving a particular system at all costs, that the system exists to serve the needs of all children, and that education can take place outside of the public school system, we will make it happen. As Kurt Schmoke, the former mayor of Baltimore, said, over time and through dialogue, "Critics of school choice will come to see this movement for what it is—part of an emerging civil rights battle for the millennium, the battle for educational equity."

MILLER: Thank you, Clint. Up next is Andrew Rotherham, the education adviser to President Clinton at the White House.

CHARTER SCHOOLS: THE REAL GRAND BARGAIN

ANDREW ROTHERHAM: There have been a number of great viewpoints already presented today, and I think we'll hear some more that illustrate that vouchers are obviously a contentious public policy issue that honest people with good intentions can disagree on. Something Dr. Peterson said earlier I think is really worth heeding: since we're debating something that's as important as what's the best thing for our kids, it's unfortunate in many cases that this debate has become so toxic and that it's not productive. The blame for that can be shared by all sides.

There is a division in our schools in this country. There's no doubt about that. But the division is not between public and private, as the lines in the voucher debate are commonly drawn; it's between good schools, the kind that the people in this room would want to send our kids to, and mediocre or low-performing schools, which we would not. However, these schools are not delineated by their governance, public or private, but rather by their performance.

As we think about vouchers, I'd really encourage you all to look at them through this lens. A private school is not by default a good school, nor is a public school by default a bad school. The reality, as in many things in education, is a lot more complicated than that, but that often gets lost in the crossfire of this debate.

Two principles, access and accountability, should define public education. For a school to be considered a public school, part of our system of public education, it should have to be open to all students and publicly accountable for its performance. It's important that we look at public schools in this light. Are they open to all and publicly accountable for their performance? For the past 40 years, we've made great strides on access to public schools. They now serve a more diverse population than ever before. Students with disabilities, minority students, those with exceptional needs, and other groups that were previously excluded now have access to elementary and secondary education. In all the hand-wringing over what's happened to schools in the past 40 years, it's really important we recognize this reality, that we not lose sight of these important accomplishments.

We have not, however, made the strides that we must in terms of accountability. Too many children, especially in our poorest communities, are not receiving the education that they need in order to be competitive in our new economy. I think there's general consensus about that. As Hugh Price, president of the National Urban League, who was discussed earlier, has written eloquently, in the past we had a public school system that did a very good job of educating a sufficient number of children with really strong minds to support the economy, but for most Americans a strong back was a more important attribute than a strong mind. Relying on our strong backs is not a luxury that we have in the new economy. Our economy is changing, and we cannot afford any children to

come out of our schools without the skills they need to succeed.

So our challenge as policymakers and policy leaders is to figure out how to replicate success and foster the conditions that allow excellence to thrive. In terms of vouchers, we must continue to look at this debate, to look at the issues simply in terms of how we finance schools. Make no mistake about that—that's all vouchers are at their core. They are a discussion of how we finance our schools. To look only at that fails to address the core issue of fostering excellence, and in the process it fails our children. The issue of achievement of excellence is not as simple as just taking kids from public schools and putting them into private ones. However, defining excellence is an area in which we've made tremendous progress in the past few years. Forty-eight states now have standards in at least math and reading. Not every state is where it should be in the process, but overall we've made real progress.

Standards enjoy bipartisan support. It's worth noting that in 1989 President Bush and Governor Clinton came together on this. Standards enjoy bipartisan support, and they also enjoy support from all across the education community. Al Shanker, Sandra Feldman's predecessor at the AFT, was a leader in the standards movement. However, vouchers without accountability, without a link to standards, would move us away from the progress we've made on standards rather than closer to it. We have finally reached the point where educational resources are being invested in schools that are held accountable for meeting standards. Why would we want to walk away from that by allowing public funds to be invested in schools that aren't required to meet a state's agreed-upon content standards?

So I think the grand bargain that we should be assessing, and one that's been alluded to this morning in various ways, is not one about public and private or more money in exchange for vouchers, but rather one that recognizes access and accountability, increases choice for parents, makes education more competitive, but includes accountability. We have this bargain already, though. It's not as sexy as vouchers, not as controversial, but it's more widespread, also has bipartisan support, and, rather than affecting just a few thousand kids around this country, it's affecting more than a quarter million. I'm talking about charter schools and the charter movement.

Charter schools are public schools open to all students and held accountable to a public authority for results. They are free from many of the regulations that govern traditional public schools in exchange for meeting defined performance goals and staying open as long as they do. And unlike traditional public schools, public entities including museums, universities, community groups, parents, and teachers can open charter schools, not only the local school district. This increases the range of options for parents, increases competition between schools, but at the same time increases accountability for performance in public education.

When they first appeared on the education landscape, the common assumption was that charter schools were just a compromise on the way to vouchers, something that Democrats were doing to compromise. That view has been shown to be clearly wrong. Charter schools are proving to be a dynamic reform in states across the country and a means to better schools, not a way station. As I said, more than a quarter million students now attend charter schools in 36 states and the District of Columbia. There are more than 1700 charter schools operating right now. In 1992, there was only 1, in Minnesota.

Already, evidence of a positive, competitive dynamic is emerging. Parents in charter schools are satisfied. Seven of 10 charter schools have a waiting list. Overall, charters are working. Charters increase choice in competition, which is something that voucher proponents purport to want, but at the same time charters increase accountability both to parents—schools without students don't stay open—and to the public because charter schools are accountable for meeting performance goals, and those that don't are shut down.

In terms of the public-private debate, it's also worth noting that 1 in 10 charter schools are former private schools that have converted to charter status by agreeing to stay open to all kids and be accountable for performance. So rather than unproven theories and politically catchy ideas, we ought to be replicating what is working in communities across the country by encouraging this grand bargain.

Regarding the bargain that Matt laid out, let me say a few words. Increasing funding in exchange for vouchers, I would argue, is a grand bargain on both ends that is not good for kids. Simply increasing funding without a link to standards and a link to demanding more from our schools is not an answer. That's not going to do anything for kids who are currently in dysfunctional school systems. On the other hand, without a link to standards, vouchers themselves are meaningless.

Now don't take my word for this. E. D. Hirsch, one of the fathers of the standards movement in this country, has written that we have to be careful to link choice with standards, or we're not going to get the results we want. Checker Finn wrote a fascinating paper for the national education summit getting into the same issues. Just spending more is not the answer and won't improve the schools or kids in them, and the kids who don't receive a voucher under the model we're talking about would be a real issue; they would still be in those schools. For the kids who do get vouchers, the parents don't care about a public school versus a private school. That's not their issue. They want a good school for their kids.

I'd also note that in terms of creating new schools, something people are talking about, if you look at where we've had vouchers and where we've had charters, charter laws have been incredibly more effective in increasing the number of high-quality options and opening schools, something that Ms. Keegan talked about. The resources that are available for entrepreneurs who want to get into this field under charter schools are much greater than under any voucher proposal being discussed, including the ones today.

Let me close by saying we should not tolerate failing schools. The President has been very clear on this. We just had a radio address on it the other day where he talked about this issue. And he's enacting the Accountability Fund. For the first time, states and localities are being given resources specifically dedicated to addressing the needs of failing schools, overhauling them, and getting them back on their feet.

We've also invested in charter schools, more than $375 million over the past three years, and our budget this year includes a $30 million increase. So while the American public is much less familiar with charter schools than they are with vouchers, they tend to support charter schools upon learning what they are. I'm reminded of a story from a couple of months ago. I was on a fishing trip and we were at this diner out in central Virginia. There was a guy sitting next to us having apple pie. The waitress asked him whether he would like his pie à la mode. He looked at her and he said, "No, but I would like it with some ice cream."

The American public very often doesn't know what charter schools are under that specific moniker. When you describe what they are, open to all, publicly accountable, the American people support charter schools. Is every charter school perfect? No. As Ms. Keegan alluded to, there are issues in a lot of states, but overall the formula of public money, public accountability, and public access is proving to be a grand bargain for kids.

MILLER: Thank you, Andy. And now we'll hear from Sandra Feldman, the president of the AFT.

AN EXPERIMENT IN
EDUCATIONAL EQUITY
FOR POOR CHILDREN

SANDRA FELDMAN: Thank you very much. I'm coming at this subject really from my own experience, not only as someone who grew up poor in Coney Island, which was a slum then, is a slum now, but also as someone who was saved by the public school system. I have a grandson and a nephew in the public schools in New York City. In fact, my nephew goes to the very same public school that I attended in Brooklyn. I've been fighting all my life for our nation to provide the sources of educational excellence to children, particularly in urban schools, because that's where I spent my life.

I've been a plaintiff in cases involving educational equity for poor children. I'm a plaintiff right now in a case that's trying to get some funding for refurbishing schools in New York. So many of the schools that poor children attend are a physical disaster. I've stood in front of members of my union in failing schools and urged them to support the closing down of their very own school because it had been failing for years. So I come at

this with a fundamental concern, which is how to improve the education and lives of poor children. That's what I care about; that's my major concern.

I have to say that both my mind and my heart shrink from the idea of doing this theoretical bargaining between the so-called Right and so-called Left over real children and over their real educational needs. We shouldn't be bargaining over vouchers or even over money. What I want to discuss is how we get the best possible education for poor children because, while policymakers all say they're very concerned about that, unfortunately, there's really precious little of that kind of discussion because it's not politically correct these days to talk about how to provide more resources to better the education of poor children.

I am not ideological about vouchers. If I thought they would work, I'd be for them. But they haven't worked. They haven't worked in Cleveland. They haven't worked in Milwaukee. They haven't worked in Chile, which tried them in the entire country; the program has left the poorest children of that country bereft educationally. They haven't worked in the Netherlands, which has a voucher-like program that probably would warm Jack Coons's heart, with all the things in place that supposedly create equity and opportunity for poor children. But it hasn't worked, and now that country, coming from the liberal side of things, as compared to Chile, is trying to figure out a way for its voucher system to provide better education and equality for poor children. So when all the smoke is cleared in the voucher research debates, the case for vouchers just isn't there.

The discussion of vouchers, as evidenced even by the fact that we're talking about a bargain between Right and Left here, has instead been ideological. It is divisive, and it's a diversion from what needs to be done to educate poor children. It's also a diversion from the very real progress that's being made in improving student achievement as a result of the standards movement.

I'm not even ideological about money, even though I've spent a lifetime fighting for adequate resources for poor kids. I can't just grab at a 20 percent increase—it's attractive, even if it's only theoretical—without asking what that money would go for. And I have to confess that I find it almost immoral that the theoretical possibility of spending 20 percent more on poor children, whose education is so underfunded by any reasonable measure, would have to come at the cost of embracing a voucher system that is radical, that threatens the progress that we're making in public schools and public schooling itself, and that also just doesn't work to improve achievement.

Does anyone talk about extracting that kind of price when it comes to the education of advantaged kids? In New York City alone, it would take a 50 percent increase—not the 20 percent on the table but a 50 percent increase—to have the same resources that the highest-achieving

school district in New York State has. Not highest-spending, mind you; I'm saying highest-achieving. And if you wanted to factor in all the special needs of the children that New York City public schools are educating, have to educate—kids that no ordinary private school would take in—it would take up to an additional 33 percent, for a grand increase of more than 80 percent.

In the end, vouchers would be even more expensive because ultimately all kids, including those already in private schools, would have to participate, and so on. So rather than bargaining—and I'm a bargainer—over vouchers and abstract sums of money, I want to talk about putting in place the things that we know work, on the basis of solid research evidence, for the education of poor children. I have seen, and I'm sure there are many in this audience who've seen, schools that are successful despite being in the most devastated of environments. I've spent a lot of time in those schools. We have to put policies and programs in place that make these successful schools the norm and not the exception. We have to make a system in which schools that work for poor kids are not just the achievement of extraordinary people doing extraordinary things but are instead an ordinary event.

Some of the things that need to be in place are high-quality preschools, early childhood education. Now, you probably all saw that kindergarten study that came out two weeks ago, done by the National Center for

Education Statistics. There's no question, according to that study and many other studies, that because of the effects of poverty, poor children start kindergarten way behind advantaged children. Any teacher in an inner-city school will also tell you that poor kids start school far behind more advantaged kids. So even at the start, our schools have a huge gap to overcome. And while they do narrow this gap, they have not been able to overcome it altogether. They need help.

So let's provide high-quality early childhood education for 4-year-olds, maybe for 3-year-olds. Poverty cannot be an excuse for poor achievement, but neither can its effects be ignored, especially today, and with the particularly brutal aspects of the poverty that so many kids live with in America.

Our public schools have done a terrific job. They've done an amazing job of narrowing the achievement gap between rich and poor, and they're doing an even better job as we speak. But we know that, with quality preschool, that gap is far narrower when poor children start school, and it's far narrower as they go on. Other countries have instituted high-quality preschool. France, which has a large immigrant population, has universal, high-quality, early childhood education. France has a national system, a core curriculum; it has lots of other things, but early childhood education helped close the gap between poor immigrant kids—mostly kids of color, by the way—and middle-class French kids. I think the United States ought to do that.

How about guaranteed class-size reduction in the early grades, from kindergarten to grade three at a minimum, which the President is trying to get done? The research evidence is crystal clear that smaller class size, especially in the early grades, has achievement benefits that last all the way to high school graduation. The gold standard of class-size research was done in your state, Governor Alexander, and it found that lowering class size in K-3 improved achievement and other educational outcomes for all children, but especially for poor children. Poor children tend to have the largest class sizes. So why are we talking about vouchers instead of lowering class size, which works?

How about ensuring that every poor child has a highly educated and qualified teacher? Let's face it, since it's so fashionable to talk about markets in education these days, that does mean ensuring competitive salaries and professional conditions and other incentives that are necessary to attract and retain such teachers to work in schools in our poorest and most difficult neighborhoods.

How about being able to offer poor children an extended school day and an extended school year, which we know works, so they can get the kinds of things that more advantaged parents pay for their children to get, like tutoring if they're falling behind, or enrichment, or extra support meeting higher standards—which we have strongly supported and which most states are putting into place—or maybe just an educationally sound place to be after school?

Why can't we support that for our poorest children in America in the year 2000?

How about upgrading the deplorable school buildings where so many of our really poor children attend class in the year 2000 in the United States of America, the richest country in the world? This would mean that poor children don't have to constantly get the message—they may be poor, but they're sure not dumb—that they're second-class citizens, and it would mean that they don't have to be continuously left behind in the technology revolution because the wiring in their schools is so ancient that their schools can't even be connected.

I could go on, but the fact is, even if I didn't add to this list that I just gave you—and I think it's a reasonable, commonsense list based on what advantaged kids have and what we know works for poor kids—even if I didn't add to it, the 20 percent increase in spending on education for poor children that's being offered in return for buying into a risky and already failed voucher experiment might or might not cover what needs to be done, depending on the community. We've heard a lot about the inequities of funding here this morning. I agree with all of it. Vouchers would make that inequity worse.

So I would like to make a counterproposal, a proposal for a much safer experiment, but one that has never been tried before on behalf of poor children in this great, wealthy nation of ours. It's a good time for this proposal because we're in a period of unprecedented surpluses at every level of government. Let's do an experiment in educational adequacy for poor children. Let's try doing what is needed, what the evidence has solidly demonstrated as successful, and paying what it costs. Let's do that for at least the same amount of time that the voucher experiment in Milwaukee has been going on, which is 10 years, so it's not a fly-by-night experiment. And let's evaluate the results of that experiment in educational adequacy for poor children for the full 10 years and not do what they did in Milwaukee, which was to stop all evaluation and accountability to the citizens who foot the voucher bill after 5 years, when the results showed that the voucher system was failing to improve voucher children's achievement relative to that of their public school peers in the ways that were promised. Let's keep the educational adequacy study going for the full 10 years. Let's have real accountability.

If we're going to experiment or bargain over the education of poor children, then my starting proposal is this: provide educational adequacy. Not just more money turned over wholesale to a school management such as in Newark or elsewhere that hasn't done the job, but money targeted specifically on what works. Then we'll have a level playing field that puts our poor kids in the game.

Now, will my colleagues be willing to bargain about that, about what poor children really need, rather than abstract rhetoric about choice or competition?

* * *

QUESTIONS AND ANSWERS

MILLER: Thank you, Sandra Feldman. Now if you were listening closely, you're probably wondering whether we have a deal yet. Let me try during the discussion period to suggest, taking from what everyone has said, a possibility that would move this discussion. I'm a hopeless optimist.

Let me ask Sandra Feldman what is wrong with Lamar Alexander's proposal, which is a fresh $5 billion a year. He would do it, he said, with 5 million vouchers of $1000. Lamar, if I could offer just another option, maybe a million vouchers of $5000 each, which—

ALEXANDER: Before you do that, remember that's on top of what they're already getting. So if you're getting $6000 your proposal would be—you'd suddenly jump up to $11,000 a year, and I don't think there's any justification for that.

MILLER: Okay. If it's on top so that they can take the money—

ALEXANDER: That's the point that people missed in 1992 and probably missed this morning. What I proposed was a 20 percent increase on the average in funding for every child who received this scholarship, and the only children who would receive it would be those who were poor and those who were middle income. So that is a 20 percent increase.

MILLER: Let me throw one other thing into it, though, because I wanted to address what Sandra was talking about. This is an era of surplus. At least for purposes of discussion, I'm willing to spend money so I'm willing to say, let's enact Al Gore's education agenda of $110 billion over 10 years, which is about $10 billion a year, which is nothing in terms of the amount of resources that we're looking at now in these surpluses.

What if we, just for purposes of discussion, enacted that Al Gore agenda and do this $5-billion-a-year experiment of new fresh money that involves choice?

FELDMAN: I don't have a problem with choice in the public school system. But I think we should enact Al Gore's program. It's a very good idea. As for Governor Alexander's program: how about putting that fresh $5 billion in a truly needs-based program that already includes poor children in private and parochial schools? We have a federal program that already does this in a much better way; it's called Title I, and it's the result, by the way, of a truly grand compromise. With that fresh money, we'd probably come close, at last, to funding it fully.

You want to talk about grand compromises? We had not had much federal funding for K-12 education until we were able, in the Johnson administration, to get a grand compromise between the people who cared about public schools and the people who cared about Catholic schools and other religious schools. Because both groups cared about getting poor kids desperately needed resources, a grand compromise called the child benefit theory was developed. Today we have over $8 billion going to supplement the education of poor children, mostly in inner cities, and it is going to public schools, it's going to private schools, mostly Catholic schools, and it gets the support of all of the people on the scene because it works to provide help to the poorest children, extra help that they need to meet standards; it's not money for abstract theories about school markets and competition.

Title I has helped to close the gap between rich and poor over the approximately 30-year life of its existence, and in the past several years, as it's become improved to be part of the higher-standards movement, poor kids have actually accelerated their progress in reading and math. So why don't we put 20 percent more into Title I?

ALEXANDER: That would be fine as long as it attaches to each child. The way for the federal government to help pay for local schools is to let the funding follow the children who need help the most. I've listened to this for years, and I'm really trying to think about this in the simplest way. If a single mom has a kid stuck in a school where she wishes he weren't, what would she want to do? I think she would want some options. All I'm trying to say regarding your proposal about Title I is it actually follows the school. As for options, one, the mom could send her child to another public school; two, she could send him to the Catholic school; three, she could team up with the other moms and tell the principal of the current school that if this school doesn't get safe, or if it doesn't stay open until 6 p.m., they can't send their children there anymore. Or they might start a new public charter school at the place where they work, or they might use half the $1000 to send their chil-

dren to an after-school program somewhere.

I think the real difference that I hear on the panel is that some people think they know what's best for the children and other people want the parents to have more choice. Sandy, I think you want what's best for the children, but you want to tell parents what that is. I want to give the mom or dad more of a choice in deciding what that is. So let's increase Title I radically, 20, 30, 40, 50, 60 percent, and let's just say the money will follow the child to any school where the parent wants to enroll the child. I'm glad you came round at the end of your comments to being in favor of bargaining. I was beginning to wonder if the head of the AFT was offended by the idea of a bargain.

MILLER: Would you like to respond?

FELDMAN: Well, I'll sit at the table with you any time you want to, Governor. I am totally in favor of parents' having choice within the public school system. I am in favor of making sure that schools are accountable, which vouchers to private schools don't provide, and that there's a level playing field and that all schools are good schools. I'm for closing down failing schools; I'm a participant in the closing down of failing schools. But what the child benefit theory does is provide the extra resources to schools that are serving poor children, generally large concentrations of poor children. That money gets you more bang for the buck because it goes into programs and services. Dividing that money on a per child basis leaves you with very little money per child to do much at all and also takes money away from schools where poor children are concentrated to the detriment of those kids.

ALEXANDER: If you put the money where the poor people—

FELDMAN: It's very interesting that in the discussion over whether or not Title I should be voucherized, we had an agreement between all of the public education organizations, the National Catholic Educational Association, the National Association of Independent Schools, and a number of other denominational associations of private and religious schools not to voucherize Title I but to leave Title I as the program that it is, which is a program that supplements and supports the schools that are educating poor children. There is absolutely no support for the notion of—

ALEXANDER: What you're saying is that the schools, in their opinion, are educating poor children. But if the mother of a poor child believes the child is stuck, she can't wait five years for a great political revolution. She needs to do what my mom could do, or anybody who has any money can do, and that's take her child to another school.

ROTHERHAM: The other day the President announced again that a parent should have the option of transferring his or her child from a low-performing public school to a high-performing public school. You look at Title I—

ALEXANDER: The mother could send her children to a Catholic school because she didn't believe in the public school that was available.

ROTHERHAM: Title I has been a mixed bag throughout its history. No one denies that. However, in 1994, standards were embedded into Title I. This was something that President Bush tried to do, and he was unsuccessful. It fell prey to the political crossfire in Congress. After President Clinton was elected, we were able to get it enacted. We now have standards as part of Title I, and you're seeing tremendous gains. As Sandy said, poverty is not destiny. One of the real reasons impoverished kids have not done so well in our inner cities is we're teaching them different things from what we're teaching our kids in the suburbs. There is a watered-down curriculum; they aren't getting the same kind of high-quality content and so forth that suburban kids have gotten.

Through Title I we finally eliminated that. All kids have to be held to the same standard. You have to ensure that kids, regardless of where they live, are being held to the same high standards and have the resources they need. Why, when we're finally making progress, are we turning back on a lot of hard-earned progress? It doesn't make sense.

———

COMMENT FROM THE AUDIENCE: My name is Patrick Armiho. I'm with the *Albuquerque Journal*. It seems to me that, when I hear people who are against vouchers, what they have not considered is that to fail is quite natural and human. It happens all the time. That's why there's only going to be one president while a dozen candidates started out seeking the presidency. Vouchers are appealing in part because they clearly identify failure for everyone to see, since parents stop sending their children to the school and it has to close down. The public institutions essentially protect failing schools.

People have talked about accountability, but I don't think the citizens buy it. There are always new ideas about accountability and standards, but when you have a public school that's run without competition, I don't think, given the way America is organized and people's natural way of living every day, they're going to buy it—they're going to believe that a competitive system is just far better at identifying successes and failures.

QUESTION FROM THE AUDIENCE: Are charter schools a step in the right direction?

ALEXANDER: I think real charter schools are step one in the right direction. What Andrew is really saying, with respect, is that he's not for charter schools; he's for more restrictions. I'd be for fewer. I don't think we really have an education problem in this country; we just have a political problem. We know exactly what to do, and a lot of people are doing it. We've just got schools that are smothered with overhead. Charter schools get rid of that. And then every school board really ought to just write every parent in February and say, "Where would you like your child to go to school next September?" and do its best to see that they go there. Just those two things alone would do it.

Charter schools are step one, but the more freedom teachers and

principals have to use their own common sense, the more likely they are to succeed. Of course, there are going to be mistakes, but I mean, look at Berkeley and Brown, two of the best universities in the world. There are plenty of weird things going on there that we wouldn't all exactly approve of, but we don't want to close them down or stop people from going there with their vouchers.

FELDMAN: I think that the whole notion of just having a total free-for-all in education is so totally radical it's hard to respond to. I mean, there is no country in the world among the countries that we're competing with, whether Japan or France or Germany or any advanced industrialized country, that has a free-for-all for its education system. In fact, most of them have core curricula; they have national tests; they really do have much more accountability than we have in the United States. So I just can't respond to this free-for-all idea. I think it is not workable.

I participated in the establishment and development of a number of charter-type schools in my school district in New York, and I think that charter schools that are accountable and that adhere to the same standards that are required of all other public schools can be a way for teachers and parents to work with each other and be creative. In fact, it was my predecessor, Al Shanker, who actually proposed the idea of charter schools. But I have to agree also that, unfortunately, there are a lot of charter schools—and I know that the superintendent of Arizona just actually found this—that are not adhering to the appropriate standards and have not been held accountable. I think that if they're not, then they ought to close down.

I think any failing school—whether it's part of a public school system, whether it's a voucher school like the Hope Academies, which were disastrous in Cleveland, the city where allegedly vouchers worked—a failing school, a school that is not working for children, ought to be closed down. I think that's true with charter schools. It's true with any public school. It certainly ought to be true with voucher schools but would never be because private schools do not have to be accountable to the public, and voucher advocates have no intention of allowing that to happen.

We're in favor of good charter schools that adhere to high standards, that are accountable in the way that public schools have to be accountable. We're not for charter schools that can just go off and do their own thing without being transparent in their curriculum, in the way they spend their money, and in the way in which they teach the children and with what results.

ROTHERHAM: We have Ms. Keegan here, who, of everybody here, is uniquely qualified to comment on this because she's actually going to be charged with the task of figuring out what to do about failing charter schools. I thought the question from Patrick Armiho from the Albuquerque paper really hit the nail on the head. What are you going to do with low-performing schools, regardless of whether they are traditional public or charter schools? That's going to be the crux. I'd be very interested in hearing what Ms. Keegan thinks. Can we shut these schools down? I don't mean to put you on the spot.

KEEGAN: No, you didn't put me on the spot. I appreciate the opportunity. First of all, this generation of charter schools is the first time I think this nation has taken very, very seriously our responsibility to know how every school is doing. There is a group of schools out there, as in the voucher programs, that people want to say are working or not working. The fact of the matter is that there were no evaluative systems in the whole public school sector. Perhaps there are states that have had fabulous systems by which to track every student's academic achievement every year, but, quite frankly, I don't know about them if they're out there. I don't think there has been good information. Hence the standards and accountability movement.

The fact of the matter is that public charter schools in Arizona performed well for grades K-8 in our studies; a class in K-8 moved more quickly there than in the traditional public schools. In the last assessment that we had, those students progressed further. That was not true for grades 9-12. It was just the opposite. More to the point, a school is not a school is not a school. Governance does not dictate quality of education. The school itself will dictate quality of education. I will make a proposal at the end of this year, after three years of evaluation of traditional public schools and public charter schools, for those that have not progressed year to year and that have abysmal scores and that we should recommend for closure.

It is important to know that the vast majority of the public charter schools are extremely successful. They should not be cast as a failure because a few public charter schools fail. In a traditional system, on the other hand, a vast number of schools fail. Those schools should be closed.

MILLER: Because we are running long and we do have panelists who have to be somewhere else, I'm going to have to close this discussion. Let me just invite all the panelists to use 10-15 seconds to offer a last thought you want people to take away.

BOLICK: Two of us, Lamar Alexander and I, are willing to invest more in public education provided that the broadest possible range of options is provided to kids. Not letting a parent give public funds to a good school down the street to serve his or her child even though it may be the best school for the child is, to me, antithetical to public education.

ALEXANDER: I propose that the federal government appropriate $5 billion new dollars per year and give 5 million children $1000 scholarships. The money would go to the poorest and middle-income children. It would follow them to the school that their parents think is best. Under this arrangement, we would see whether the most successful social program we've ever enacted, the G.I. Bill and its successor, the Pell grant, works in schools as well as it did to help create the best colleges in the world.

FELDMAN: I would propose that we experiment in a way in which we absolutely just never have done before in the United States of America; we would have an experiment in educational adequacy for poor children. Provide our poorest children with what they need, with what we know they need, and level the playing field for them in education. Give them the opportunity for high-quality early childhood education. Give them smaller class sizes in the early grades; give them a school that is staffed by the highest-quality, best-prepared teachers; give them a building that is wired for technology and the ability to have access to that technology. Let's provide whatever resources are needed, whether it's more or less than what you propose. We're the richest country in the world; there are surpluses all over the place. Give our poor kids what they need and what we know will work for them because it already works for advantaged children. Let's experiment with doing that because we've never done it before.

MILLER: Andy Rotherham, with the last word from the White House.

ROTHERHAM: Money does matter. Money does matter, and it's important we're talking about investment. At the same time, choice and accountability, accountability and performance are important. We've made great strides in improving the educational opportunity for poor kids through the standards movement. We ought not walk away from that. Schools that are innovative, open to all, and publicly accountable, that's the grand bargain. The President said we should institutionalize charter schools, and that's a bargain, a good bargain for our kids and a good bargain for our society.

MILLER: Thanks to our panel and our audience for a great discussion.

Note

1. The representative of the NAACP who participated in this panel discussion at the forum declined to have his comments published in the present volume.

ANNALS, *AAPSS*, **572**, November 2000

Don't Knock the Folks on the Bus

By E. J. DIONNE, JR.

ABSTRACT: It is important for journalists to write about issues in a political campaign. It is the responsibility of the candidates, however, to make the campaign issue-oriented. This essay examines how journalists report on issues and the value of that reporting. It also inventories the issues addressed by candidates in the presidential campaigns in 2000.

E. J. Dionne, Jr., joined the Washington Post *as a reporter in 1991 and began his op-ed column for the* Post *in 1993. He is author of the best-selling book* Why Americans Hate Politics *(1991) and* They Only *Look* Dead: Why Progressives Will Dominate the Next Political Era *(1996) and editor of* Community Works: The Revival of Civil Society in America *(1998), and with John DiIulio,* What's God Got to Do with the American Experiment? *(2000). Dionne joined the Brookings Institution in May 1996 as a senior fellow and is a regular commentator on politics on both television and radio.*

IT is said so often that journalists do not like to report on or write about issues that I particularly enjoy the story about two journalists who were so intensely interested in issues that they drove to distraction a ward leader in the late Mayor Daley's legendary machine. These two journalists kept pressing this ward leader not on patronage, or on organization, or on loyalty—matters about which he knew a great deal—but on the issues of the day. Finally, in frustration, the ward leader looked at the journalists and declared impatiently, "Look, if you can't be loyal to a friend, how in the world can you be loyal to an idea?" I have always taken that as an important statement about politics.

But today, if we sang a hymn for the present collection of articles, it might be, "What a friend we have in issues." I have always thought that issues could be covered more, and more entertainingly, and that the criticisms made of us journalists almost always have some merit. I would also confess that it is easier for those of us who are newspaper columnists to make this argument, because it is easier for us to write about issues than it is for many with day-to-day responsibility for covering campaigns. Before I conclude, I want to issue a defense of those folks, because I think a lot of times criticism directed at them often ought to be directed elsewhere.

There are some remedies to the sparse coverage of issues. Giving candidates longer sound bites on TV and radio and longer "ink bites," to use my friend Marty Plissner's phrase, is one. Plissner, formerly of CBS, got so sick of reports on the shrinking sound bite on television that he started counting the words in quotations in newspapers. He argued that not only were the television and the radio folks quoting candidates less extensively but so were we in print. Marty has successfully put the shrinking ink bite issue on my radar screen.

I think it is possible to link good, old-fashioned horse race reporting to the coverage of issues. This is the real genius in the work of the late Theodore White. We have some lessons to learn from him. He is so often credited with taking us into the back room of politics, with covering the managers and the scheming of consultants (although they were not called consultants back when he started writing those books in 1960). People forget that he did two other very important things in those books that we do not do nearly enough of in political coverage. First, he paid very, very close attention to what candidates actually said. All of his books include whole pages or even a page and a half that carry excerpts from important speeches that candidates made in the course of the campaign—and then very thoughtful analysis of what they meant, why they were saying it, and what ideas lurked behind the words in the speeches.

When I wrote *Why Americans Hate Politics* (1991), I discovered that when I wanted to read a major campaign speech, I often found it right there in my old Teddy White books on the shelf. That is a credit to him, and it is something we all need to think about.

Teddy White (1961) also used the campaign to paint both a political and human portrait of the country. In *The Making of the President, 1960*, one of the most powerful chapters is on the U.S. census. There are people who think the census is a boring subject, but it certainly isn't in the hands of Teddy White. White, in fact, began to describe way back in 1960 some of the trends that my friend Bruce Katz describes (this volume). White was one of the first and most articulate describers of the trend to move to the suburbs.

I think those are some lessons we can take. But in the end, I am not one of those people who thinks that journalists all by themselves can make a campaign issue-oriented. The main responsibility for that really does lie with the candidates. For that reason, I think the 2000 election has some good news for issue mavens.

First, I do want to point to one piece of potentially bad news here. Although it is bad news, it confirms something I believe, so, of course, I welcome it. Adlai Stevenson used to talk about the man who declared, "These are the conclusions on which I base my facts." The Annenberg Public Policy Center's report on political knowledge (Jamieson et al. 2000) has offered me convenient facts. I am heartened and troubled by the data in this Annenberg study. I am heartened because they confirm a view many of us have long had, namely, that in the New Hampshire primary and in all other states where voters get a lot of time from candidates and a lot of concerted television advertising— yes, television advertising, which can convey a good deal of information—

political knowledge is much, much higher than it is in states where there is much less of that.

We have talked a lot in this campaign period, as we do, it seems, in every campaign, about having national primaries or moving to regional primaries. The Annenberg study is useful because it points to some questions we have not asked about what would happen if we moved to national or regional primaries. In the Super Tuesday states, where candidates did not have either the time or the resources to really engage their electorates, political knowledge was significantly lower. We talk about how to increase participation, but it is not clear that regional primaries would increase participation, and it could well be that they will not increase knowledge. I do not say this as the definitive word on the subject, but I think these questions need to be introduced into the debate.

ISSUES RAISED BY CANDIDATES

The topic of this essay is issues that were not covered in the presidential campaigns, but I would like to address this by way of talking about the issues put on the table by the candidates, because I think they are quite significant. It is clear that John McCain has changed the national discussion of campaign finance reform. He has made this such a national issue that Al Gore, I think, is going to change his name to John McGore. He is trying to embrace that issue.

McCain, in his exchanges with George W. Bush, and Bush, in his arguments with McCain, did something that I think was going to happen inevitably, but they made it happen earlier. They created a national battle on taxes and spending, with an emphasis on tax cuts and whether they can be afforded, what kind we need, and whether tax cuts create growth. I think this is an issue that will be seen throughout the campaign. It is an issue that should be on the agenda of every campaign. The fact is that our politics are quite responsive to public debates about taxes. Contrary to what many think, the tax changes made at the beginning of the Reagan era, then the Bradley tax reform, then the tax increases at the end of the Bush era and the beginning of the Clinton era indicate that we have a capacity to change taxes quite a lot, and we do so in response to the public mood. I think that this debate is going to be very important.

However generally expressed, McCain also put on the table the role of the religious conservatives. One can argue a lot about how he did it and why he did it, but I think that issue is going to be with us. In addition, I think Governor Bush is going to try to redefine that issue as the campaign goes forward.

The Annenberg report showed that Bradley pushed health care to a more dominant position in the debate, and there is evidence that Al Gore is going to do what he can to pick up that issue, especially as a battering ram against George W. Bush. Bush himself is interested in diffusing that issue. As a result, we may actually have a Republican candidate proposing some sort of national health care plan—although watching what Gore did to Bradley might make Bush a little reluctant to put out too many details of such a plan.

Again, Bradley, as the Annenberg report showed, also put campaign finance reform on the agenda, though less effectively, it would appear, than McCain. I also think the issue of child poverty will be discussed in part because Gore, with his emphasis on universal preschool and after-school programs, can link to that Bradley issue quite effectively.

Gore and Bush also have substantial disagreements, and both have an interest in talking about them. I have always been of the view that candidates cannot be made very often to do things that are against their own interests, a fact worth discussing when people talk about the press and the issues. The press has some capacity to affect how candidates interpret those interests, but I do not think the media can ever get a candidate to act against his or her own interests.

In this campaign, it is in the interest of both Gore and Bush to raise some substantial issues. Taxes is one of those issues. Medicare and Social Security will receive a great deal of attention, and Gore clearly has a powerful interest in that. I think education will become a more important issue because of George W. Bush. This may be surprising, because education is seen traditionally as a Democratic issue. That is precisely why Bush is emphasizing it. He is using a strong position on education and a rather detailed proposal on educational issues to neutralize recent

Republican disadvantages among women, especially married women, a group the Republicans very much need now.

It is worth noting that Bush is taking a lesson from Governor Gilmore of Virginia, who, if you might recall, ran a campaign about cutting the car tax. Gilmore was able to run that campaign on cutting the car tax because, very early, he announced a program to put 4000 new teachers in the schools. That move made it very difficult for the Democrat to use the education issue against him—and Gilmore was then free to make the car tax the issue.

China and Russia will also, I believe, be on this agenda. They will be forced there partly by events: the upcoming debate on trade and also the results of the Taiwan election. I think it is striking that the Annenberg study found that, despite what many of us think, McCain and Bush talked a good deal about foreign policy. On these issues, Gore may end up being primarily reactive to Bush, but I think these issues are going to be talked about more than we thought.

Finally, there is an issue that may emerge depending on the price of gas at the local gasoline station. We seem to be talking again about energy. I must say, listening to some of these discussions, this is a case of Yogi Berra's déjà vu all over again. We do not think we need an energy policy when prices are low. We do think we need an energy policy when prices go up. Then we decide we don't need an energy policy when they go back down again.

JOURNALISTS AND CAMPAIGN ISSUES

If candidates give us these openings, what can journalists do with them? Will we run with them? Will we use these issues to open up other issues? One question is, When candidates talk about poverty, do advocates manage to broaden the discussion to include issues such as smart growth? And do journalists try to unpack what the candidates are saying in ways that are useful? Will we try to demonstrate the link between campaign strategy and issues, on the one hand, and voter interests and worries about the issues, on the other?

Our goal as reporters ought to be exploring the issues without being cynical about a campaign or unrealistic about what we can accomplish. We can learn a lot by looking at the way a candidate is talking about issues because it can reveal not only what the candidate might really think but also the candidate's vision of and for the country.

I always felt we missed the boat as journalists on that famous issue from the 1988 campaign, the Pledge of Allegiance, when George Bush attacked Michael Dukakis for vetoing a bill requiring students to recite the pledge. Although we covered that mostly as a civil liberties issue or as a phony issue, there was a reason Bush was using that issue. Underlying what he was saying was an argument about the values schools are teaching children. Should patriotism be one of those values? There is almost always a real issue lurking underneath what we like to call a phony issue. I think we will have that opportunity again in this campaign.

Now, I'd like to close by saying a strong word in defense of my colleagues who cover the campaign day to day on those buses and airplanes. Covering a campaign day to day is hard and exhausting work. There is constant competition between the need to keep moving and the need to keep thinking, and sometimes they collide. Great campaign reporters manage to do both, and I think nothing makes campaign reporters happier than when their candidates raise a real issue. I think one of the myths of journalistic criticism is that reporters do not like covering issues—we like covering only the horse race. In fact, people on the campaign bus in particular get sick and tired of reporting exactly the same thing. They long for a good issue discussion.

In the past, those of us off the bus regularly critiqued the failures of those on it. But I think the task of getting issues discussed falls especially to those who are not on the bus, who are in the offices, who are the producers, the editors, the commentators, the issue specialists, and, yes,

even the think tanks, who I think can help us with reports like the one that tells us: "Please, dear reporters, don't say candidates aren't talking about issues, because in fact they are—in their way." And, yes, especially the candidates. But I think this year there is hope. The differences between Gore and Bush are much more substantial than has generally been advertised. I think the candidates, because they each have an interest in highlighting these differences, may actually help us out, and God bless them if they do it.

References

Dionne, E. J., Jr. 1991. *Why Americans Hate Politics*. New York: Simon & Schuster.

Jamieson, Kathleen Hall, Richard Johnston, Michael Hagen, David Dutwin, Kate Kenski, Kimberly Kirn, Suzanne Morse, Daniel Orr, Erika Prosper, Lesley Sillaman, and Paul Waldman. 2000. *The Primary Campaign: What Did the Candidates Say, What Did the Public Learn, and Did It Matter?* Philadelphia: Annenberg Public Policy Center.

White, Theodore. 1961. *The Making of the President, 1960*. New York: Atheneum.

ANNALS, *AAPSS*, **572**, November 2000

The Black Hole of American Politics: Foreign Policy

By CHARLES KRAUTHAMMER

ABSTRACT: Foreign policy has been neglected in American political campaigns, a remarkable situation given American dominance of the world. Ignoring foreign policy, in presidential campaigns and in politics in general, could make the world a dangerous place for the country. To keep the United States safe in the world, presidential candidates must bring foreign policy to the fore.

Charles Krauthammer was educated at McGill University (B.A. with First Class Honors in political science and economics, 1970), Oxford University (Commonwealth Scholar in Politics at Balliol College, 1970-71), and Harvard University (M.D., Harvard Medical School, 1975). He is a syndicated columnist for the Washington Post *and an essayist for* Time *and the* Weekly Standard. *He won the 1986 Pulitzer Prize for commentary.*

I would like to address one very major issue that I think has been remarkably absent from our discussion both in campaigns and generally in politics. But let me just start with two process points raised by E. J. Dionne (this volume). I must say that one of the reasons I wanted to participate with E. J. in the panel that yielded this article is that I have been admiring E. J. for decades, yet he and I have never actually been on a panel together. I thought that this might be a nice opportunity to have a little rumble, but I find that I agree with almost everything he said.

Regarding the first point of process, E. J. pointed out that the responsibility for raising issues in a campaign belongs to the candidates. It is somewhat grandiose and, I would say, presumptuous of reporters to decide that they ought to be deciding the agenda. The candidates have the wisdom, the experience, and the self-interest to choose the issues that they think are at the heart of what people care about.

Second, we go around and around every four years and decide that our last election was terribly marred by the structure of the primary system and that we have to reform the primaries again. The latest fad in the last 10 or 15 years was to change to regional primaries because people were saying how unusual, idiosyncratic, and uncharacteristic states such as Iowa and New Hampshire are compared to the rest of the country, and what right do a handful of New Hampshirites, all of a certain class and race and segment of American society, have to decide who the next president is going to be?

The lesson that we have learned in this campaign is that there may be some wisdom in the old, haphazard system. The regional primary, which was the great idea proposed to cure the idiosyncrasies of the small states, is a disaster. The regional primary, Super Tuesday, is a disaster because there is no time to be everywhere. There is no way to really have a discussion. Having elections all over the country at the same time actually is a national primary, and it turns out to be seriously impractical in terms of having a real debate.

Perhaps what might work in the future—and I would offer this as a tentative proposal—would be to have particular states serve as representatives of their respective regions. New Hampshire is a wonderful state to represent New England in a general way. South Carolina turned out to be a very good state by which to judge the feelings of people in the South. Michigan spoke for the industrial states of the Midwest. Maybe rather than having a regional primary in 8 or 10 states, with enormous burdens on candidates financially and personally to spread the message everywhere, we should pick one state and have it speak for the region. Perhaps we could rotate representative states in cycles so it isn't always South Carolina or New Hampshire serving as the representative state.

FOREIGN POLICY NEGLECTED

The major topic I would like to address has to do with the one issue that I think has been remarkably neglected not just in this campaign cycle but for the last 12 years. Richard

Nixon recognized it shortly before he died when he commented on how the last two elections he witnessed in the late 1980s and early 1990s were the most devoid of discussion of foreign policy he had ever seen in his lifetime. That was true in 1988 and in 1992, certainly in 1996, and again in 2000. I think it is absolutely remarkable that the one country that so dominates the world in everything it does, even haphazardly and by inadvertence, is amazingly unconscious of its role in the world.

Our insularity is seen as absolutely staggering abroad. It is understandable from American history and geography, however. We are protected by two oceans. We have friendly neighbors to our north and south, and, since the Cold War, we have faced no threats. But, to have a slight difference with E. J. on this point, I think while there was a modicum of discussion of foreign policy in the Republican primaries, it was pro forma. The only candidate who had a passionate position of any kind on foreign policy was Gary Bauer. He made China one of the centerpieces of his campaign, and he did not get very far with it: people are simply not interested.

On the Democratic side, I did not discern a single foreign policy issue at all. There was a discussion of trade, but, of course, that was really about economics and about class.

We are in a position of dominance in the world unseen not only in 500 years of the modern state system but in 1500 years. Since the fall of Rome, there has never been a country as dominant militarily, politically, economically, culturally, linguistically—

in every possible way—as the United States today. The world feels it. We are living in a totally unique time. I think part of the reason that there is so little discussion of foreign policy is that, (1) due to our dominance, there are no current threats, and (2) we are so dominant that we are in a position that is utterly unique in all of modern history.

There has never been a time when the disparity in power between the number-one and number-two powers in the world has ever been remotely what it is today. Even the British empire at its height in the mid-nineteenth century had rivals who mirrored it in military reach, in population, and in economic strength.

The more general and abstract issue, and the one that I'm not surprised does not make it into presidential campaigns, is how we maintain this position of dominance and what we do with it. This notion that what we have now is inevitable, that it is sort of God given, is shortsighted. The reason there has never been a country as dominant as ours is because inevitably when one country achieves hegemony as ours has, coalitions of rivals arise to counter it. This happened with, for example, Napoleonic France, with Hitler, and with Stalin and the Soviet empire. There are many reasons why it is not happening now. Our kind of hegemony is far less intrusive, far more benign than that of any of the previous empires. But I do not think it is inevitable by any means. The Russian election is very telling. The threats that the Chinese have made to Taiwan are telling. Even more important is the quasi-alliance between China and Russia. There were several summit communiqués between Yeltsin (who was quite pro-American) and the Chinese that openly denounced what they call the "unipolar" structure of the world, which means the United States. Whether the Chinese and the Russians can form a coalition that would be stable, no one knows. But it certainly is in the cards. Let me give an example of how what we do has an effect on that.

EFFECTS OF FOREIGN
POLICY NEGLECT

The U.S. involvement in Kosovo, I believe, was largely responsible for the election of Vladimir Putin, ex-KGB, a man who has very little attachment to democracy, a man who could turn out to be a rather nasty surprise for the United States. We, of course, were not calculating the effect on Russia or China of our involvement in Kosovo. The intervention was justified purely on humanitarian grounds—we did not justify it even in terms of American interest in the Balkans. But the furthest thing from our minds was what ricochet effect this would have on the Russians. The Russians have a long history of involvement in the Balkans. They have often seen the Balkans as part of their sphere of influence. This goes back at least 100-200 years. We sort of stumbled into the situation in our benign, truly humanitarian, and totally selfless way, with not an iota of national interest in the control of or occupation of the Balkans. We do not want the Balkans, but we wanted to help suffering Albanians. The effect of this good intention was to give a very rude shock to the Russians.

Up until the Kosovo intervention, there was a lot of anti-Americanism among the Russian elites—part of it had to do with the expansion of the North Atlantic Treaty Organization (NATO). But the Kosovo intervention elicited a visceral nationalism and an anti-Americanism from the general population. There were demonstrations and opinion polls showing resentment of NATO heavy-handiness. This very strong nationalist response in Russia was obviously not a result only of our intervention in Kosovo. But we contributed to creating a possible new center of opposition in Russia.

This points to one of the blind spots in our thinking. Kosovo, as far as I know, was not discussed at all in the campaign by anybody. Basically, there was a general agreement. At the time, there was some argument over tactics, with John McCain saying we ought to use ground troops and other potential candidates being rather silent on the issue. But there was no discussion of the general issue of what America should be doing in the world. Why are we in Haiti? Why are we in Kosovo? Why are we in Bosnia? Why are we not in parts of Africa that have suffered far more than any of the areas in which we have intervened? As the dominant power in the world, are we to be involved in these humanitarian adventures, or are we to reserve our strength, as I would argue, for the kinds of situations where only American power and only American strength can be effective? I am thinking here of the Persian Gulf war and the protection of Taiwan. There is nobody who can substitute for us in containing and controlling a country like Iraq or Iran. There is nobody who can substitute for the United States in defending Taiwan if and when it is threatened by China. That is the role for a great superpower. That is the role for a hegemon like us.

There are two reasons, I would argue—and this debate is not heard at all in the current campaign—why the kinds of policies we have had for eight years are very destructive. First, they bleed our resources. We are spending tens of billions of dollars in the Balkans. We have not lost any soldiers, but ultimately this expenditure is draining our resources. It endangers the readiness of our army and of our military capabilities. Second, these policies cause secondary effects, such as the one I described in Russia, which could help to galvanize opposition coalitions against us. This issue is not discussed at all. There seems to be a general acceptance, and perhaps it is a national consensus rather than an ignorance or avoidance of this issue, that we ought to be the good guy on the planet, helping out wherever we are needed.

This is a debate we have to have. I think the reasons that we have not had it are that we have not lost any soldiers—thank God for that—and the cost to our military is very subtle. The cost does not appear on the front pages or make the evening news. But I suspect that if and when one of these operations turns bad, as hap-

pened in Somalia; if and when we lose a soldier or a platoon; if and when the cost becomes so great that when there is a crisis—as, for example, in Taiwan—our carriers are not in place, then it will become an issue.

The only other place where foreign policy impinges on debate is missile defense. I think this could be an issue between the Democrats and Republicans. I am surprised that the Republicans have not made it more of an issue in the past. If Americans were asked in a survey what would happen if we were right now under attack by a single missile launched accidentally, say from Russia, I think the majority of Americans would say that we should shoot it down. And they would be shocked because, in fact, a majority of Americans do not know that we have no way whatsoever of stopping a missile that is headed for the United States.

I have long thought that this would be a post–Cold War issue for the United States, for a candidate in a general election, given the fact that the great issue of the struggle between us and the Soviet empire is over. The actual question of danger from rogue states or from accidental launches of weapons of mass destruction is the single greatest threat to American safety in the world, and I am surprised that it has not gotten traction as an issue. The reason, again, is the absence of a crisis, the absence of an example of what could happen. I suspect that if there were more instability in South Asia, where they are bristling with nuclear weapons, if there were missile attacks by

Middle Eastern states on each other, as happened in the Iran-Iraq war, our discussion of this issue might be galvanized.

OPPORTUNITY FOR DEBATE

I think the Republicans now have the opportunity to challenge the eight years of foreign policy of the Clinton administration, to question the squandering of our resources on humanitarian interventions. We ought to have a debate—we have not had one at all—about the wisdom, the efficacy, the future of humanitarian interventions. We have had only a muted debate on missile defense, an issue that I think is another opportunity for the Republicans to exploit if they can dramatize it, if they can make Americans aware that even in our current position of dominance, we live in a world where a very small number of people with a very concentrated source of power—meaning weapons of mass destruction—could eliminate an American city overnight.

It would be interesting to see if and how these issues can be discussed. If we in the press are to throw our weight around and insist that some issues are overlooked and ought not to be, I would argue it be foreign policy.

ANNALS, *AAPSS*, **572**, November 2000

Big Issues Missing from the Presidential Campaign

By MATTHEW MILLER

ABSTRACT: When it comes to the nation's pressing social problems, there is a depressing gap between both parties' aspirations and the federal resources now available. The nation has moved from an era of $200 billion deficits to equally outsized surpluses, but bipartisan ambitions have paradoxically shrunk. The author reviews problems where money would indisputably make a difference—such as the 44 million Americans with no health insurance, growing inequality in wages and wealth, and the myriad challenges facing urban education—and suggests promising directions for reform that are not being discussed in the presidential campaign. He also analyzes other issues not being debated, such as the size of the defense budget and the burden of payroll taxes, and urges the press to play a role in raising these issues when candidates will not.

Matthew Miller, a senior fellow at the Annenberg Public Policy Center of the University of Pennsylvania, is a nationally syndicated columnist, a contributing editor at the New Republic, *and cohost of* Left, Right & Center *on KCRW-FM in Los Angeles. Miller served as senior adviser to the director of the White House Office of Management and Budget from 1993 to 1995 and was previously a management consultant with McKinsey & Company.*

I am still mulling over the most interesting finding of the Annenberg report *The Primary Campaign: What Did the Candidates Say, What Did the Public Learn, and Did It Matter?* (Jamieson et al. 2000): the gender difference in the way men and women process political knowledge. I am trying to figure out how I can use that at my own breakfast table. I live in California; my wife and I are both Clinton administration refugees. When we moved out there a few years ago, we were immediately confronted with this long list of ballot measures—California leads the way in long lists of ballot measures. We process this very differently. My response is, "I don't want to vote on things that I know nothing about," and I'd like to be able to delegate that to some elected official. I vote on only 2 or 3 of the 10 or 15 every time they come our way. My wife's response is, "My uninformed vote is as good as anybody else's." We have this fight over these different philosophies of democracy every year.

Let me start this essay by building on something that Felton Earls offers in his article (this volume). To me, the biggest omission on the domestic side in the presidential campaign so far is the incredible disconnect between our aspirations and our resources. We are in a time now when the fiscal, financial, and economic situation of the country is dramatically different from what it was in the early 1990s. We had deficits that were nearly $300 billion and scheduled to go to $500 billion, with the debate over how to reduce them paralyzing all action in Washington. Now we have surpluses as far as the eye can see, and yet the scope of our ambition, across the board in domestic policy, in areas where money does matter and can make a difference, is totally crimped. That paradox is, to me, the overriding, glaring fact—domestically, at least—of this 2000 campaign. It is a mystery that ought to be explored.

Let me offer the most compelling illustration of this. George W. Bush sometime soon will unveil a health plan that will almost certainly be far smaller than the one his daddy unveiled in 1992, back at a time when deficits were much higher. The idea that the "compassionate conservative" son will now offer something that is just a fraction of what his father offered—when the latter's plan in 1992 was by some measures larger than the plan Bill Bradley put out this year—should stun us because the fiscal situation has changed so dramatically. That captures, I think, the great missing debate.

NEGLECTED ISSUES

Let me go through one man's brief hit parade of things along these lines that are not being discussed and toss out some ideas that might stir the pot on ways in which columnists, the press, moderators, and others who are trying to shape the debate might try to inject them. First is the growing wage and wealth inequality that is often a staple of both sides' speeches. Both George Bush and Al Gore talk in variations about prosperity with a purpose, about leaving no one behind, but they do not offer the kind of resources or creative policies, I would argue, that might address this. Even if one puts aside the so-called "undeserving" poor and those on welfare, the fact that millions and millions of families work full-time but remain in poverty is a scandal. We have the resources now, which we did not have a decade ago, to actually try to do something about this.

There are very creative ideas offered by economists like Ned Phelps at Columbia and others for dramatically higher wage subsidies for the working poor than we have now through the Earned Income Tax Credit (EITC). That concept, of something like a super EITC, which would take measures to reward work, to make it pay for people to move from welfare to work, to assist those who have made the transition off welfare but find that their economic situation is no better off and may, in fact, be worse, is something that ought to be on the radar screen. The reason it is not is that it is expensive. And expensive things, as Bill Bradley learned, have a hard time being discussed, especially by Democrats. The paradox is that the Democratic Party is the natural location for concern about those who are poor or those who are left behind. But the imperatives of getting elected are deemed to require that Gore and others position themselves in a way that cannot be branded liberal or big-spending in any way. That is a political fact of life that is shaping the debate.

Then there is the question of how we teach poor children. Education is going to be a huge issue. My concern is that vouchers will end up being the focus of the debate. There are a lot of interesting things to talk about in terms of vouchers and school choice and doing much bigger experiments. But putting aside the question of structural reforms that would lead to competition or innovation in the public schools, a central fact remains. No matter what we do—charter schools, vouchers, you name it—if we cannot attract quality teachers and the best and brightest of the next generation to replace the 2 million teachers who will be retiring in the next decade— that is two-thirds of the current teacher core—none of the systemic changes is going to have much impact. Gore is talking about this more than Bush is. I suspect Bush will talk about it more. But even the things that Gore is talking about, and some of the resources he is talking about putting in to help pay for teacher raises (he offered modest teacher raises for urban teachers), tend to be very small compared to the reality of the situation. When urban school teachers with a master's degree in New York City after five years make $38,000, and in Scarsdale they make $60,000 or $65,000, it is going to be a lot harder to get good people into the urban schools. If we do not stop relying on those folks to be essentially missionaries, we are going to have trouble, no matter what kind of structural reform we offer.

In the same spirit, the whole question of school finance equity remains one of these "elephants in the room" that do not get discussed at the national level. Even after decades of litigation on school equity, there are still major differences between spending in wealthier suburbs and in inner cities. It is true that there are a number of cities that spend more per pupil than most of the rest of the country. Washington, D.C., is one. Most of New Jersey is another. Conservatives are always able to use those examples to render impossible the discussion of financial equity in other poor areas. But the fact remains most poor kids in America go to school in districts that spend less than their state average. One in four of them go to schools that get 10 to 30 percent less per pupil. These are kids who have much higher needs, who come to school with all the problems associated with poverty that suburban kids don't have. The strange thing is that the only person who has raised this issue, who has a hope of getting this on the national agenda, is someone who was John McCain's education guru. Her name is Lisa Graham Keegan. She is the state superintendent of education in Arizona. She talks more like Karl Marx than Barry Goldwater about school finance equity. But it is very difficult to get school finance equity to be considered a national issue.

On defense, let us talk about resources. I echo what Charles Krauthammer (this volume) has argued: there is an absence of debate on nuclear policy. It is more than 10 years after the end of the Cold War, and we still have essentially an unrevisited nuclear strategy of mutually assured destruction. By some estimates, we spend $30 billion a year on our nuclear stockpiles. In its 26 March 2000 edition, the *Washington Post* reported that the Energy Department was looking for another $4 billion or $5 billion a year to refurbish 6000 weapons as part of a strategy to keep them in the inventory.

Why is it that the only people who talk about these things now are retired generals on both sides? They include Lee Butler, who ran the Strategic Air Command, and some of the former Russian generals responsible for the nuclear arsenal there. These and other voices were inventoried in a wonderful book by Jonathan Schell. Schell was very smart. Since he is way on the left, he was smart to use the voices of retired military men to say it is nuts that we are not talking about dramatic reductions, because this does remain the gravest threat to U.S. safety.

The defense budget gets no debate, because both sides agree that we should be spending close to 90 percent of our average Cold War budget a decade after the Cold War, when Russian defense spending has fallen off a cliff. In fact, both parties agree that we should be taking it toward full parity with what we spent at the height of the Cold War. I would argue there are a lot of ways to rethink the kinds of deployments we are doing now, which do have the troops running ragged, and the kinds of structures of the divisions we have, which lots of experts say are crazy and caught in "old think" (for example, where the Pentagon is preparing to be able to go to Europe on a day's notice to stop the Russians from rolling into Germany). Instead, we should be responding more flexibly to this whole panoply of new threats from terrorism, biological weapons, and computer attacks—things that are going to be much more important in the next decade or two.

The only hope I see for getting the new threats on the radar screen is a commission chaired by Warren Rudman and Gary Hart that is due to come out, sometime during the campaign, with recommendations on the new security threats. Maybe that will be a hook for the media to pose these questions to the candidates.

Let me mention a few issues briefly. One is drug policy. Two million folks are in jail now in the United States, many of them for minor drug offenses. Drug treatment is getting short shrift in ways that are probably wrongheaded. The last person who talked about this intelligently was Richard Nixon—as was the case on so many domestic policy issues, as it turns out.

Another issue is the Social Security surplus. Both sides say we should not touch it. I would be in favor of spending some of it. We have spent some of it for 30 years. We are talking about taking $2 trillion of the projected surplus and saying that it cannot be part of the debate now— both sides agree—and that we talk only about how to use the non–Social Security surplus. Using some small portion of the Social Security surplus, however, could do a lot for a number of causes where money would make a difference, yet this notion is off the table and will not get on the table unless it gets raised from outside.

Finally, a third issue is payroll taxes. We talk a lot about tax cuts. George Bush has proposed a big tax cut. If the cuts are applied to income taxes, they will not resonate too much since, according to a front-page story in the *Washington Post* (26 Mar. 2000), income taxes are actually lower for average Americans than they have been in decades. The payroll tax, however, is higher and, for most workers—between what they pay and what their employer pays, which comes out of their wages— ends up being a much bigger tax for them than the income tax.

All these issues could easily be on the radar screen. Why aren't they? They are perceived as too risky, I think, by both sides. I think that, in the press, we have some obligation to try to inject these things into the debate. The 1988 debate proceeded without the savings and loan crisis being given a peep. It was *the* first order of business for George Bush when he came into office. Both sides did not want to discuss it for obvious reasons. They were both knee-deep in it. But it became *the* defining use of resources—over $100 billion—during the next four years for George Bush. It deserved attention. So do these issues.

Reference

Jamieson, Kathleen Hall, Richard Johnston, Michael Hagen, David Dutwin, Kate Kenski, Kimberly Kirn, Suzanne Morse, Daniel Orr, Erika Prosper, Lesley Sillaman, and Paul Waldman. 2000. *The Primary Campaign: What Did the Candidates Say, What Did the Public Learn, and Did It Matter?* Philadelphia: Annenberg Public Policy Center.

Youth Development

I would suggest that a candidate's policies and issues have a holistic framework into which they fit. Many candidates espouse more than one issue, but when the thinking behind each of those issues is examined, the candidate's approach to an issue is revealed to be not comprehensive but fragmented, perhaps even based on just one solution to solve a complex problem.

I would recommend that, first, a candidate create not an agenda comprising unrelated issues that he or she claims to be able to address in a one-shot manner, but holistic plans for tackling several large issues. For instance, contributors to this volume have discussed early childhood education and drug policy, but we have not discussed how one has an effect on the other—how they are connected—nor did we talk about the larger issue of which these problems are components, and that is youth development.

It is really a shame that when something happens in this society, we frame our response in terms of one answer that is expected to address that specific issue. Yet there may not be a single, specific program or approach that will deal with why an issue is playing itself out in a particular way. There may be a multiplicity of reasons for a particular action, and the only successful way to intervene may be with a plan that deals with each of those myriad reasons.

If a candidate could come forward with a holistic plan of actions for tackling a problem or issue—a plan that is systemic in nature—that plan could provide the framework from which he or she could govern. I recommend this strategy for tackling youth development. There is no reason why we cannot implement a strong, comprehensive youth development policy or agenda in this country, one that takes into account early childhood through postsecondary education needs. This kind of approach would serve us well by helping to build a strong common culture and strong individuals in this society.

I would ask the candidates what they expect a child born in 2000 to be like in 15 years. What would they want that new adult's ideals, ethics, and values to be, particularly in light of our fast-moving technology? Technology is moving our society along so fast that most of us adults cannot keep pace. But our young people must keep pace. So I would ask each candidate to profile that child. Having done that, they would know better how to craft a policy for youth development in this country.

BOBBY AUSTIN

Bobby Austin is president of the Village Foundation.

ANNALS, *AAPSS*, **572**, November 2000

Old Habits and Old Myths

One of the problems with this general discussion of issues omitted from political campaigns is the problem of multiple issues. We all talk as if somehow we can introduce different issues. But people can't vote on them. Candidates need some central issues between themselves and the parties. Bush is for this; Gore is for that.

In terms of issues that I think candidates should discuss, one is the question of the military budget, including the legitimacy of continuing all sorts of Cold War patterns.

Second is the question of educational standards. Governor Bush has talked about the fact that it's a disgrace that children receive different levels of education depending on which part of the country they're from or which state or class they're in. Texas, it should be noted, has had more emphasis on internal standards than other states, which is often not recognized.

But, as a society, we're committed to localism. The French, on the other hand, have a system in which every French school, whether it's in France or, in the old days, in the colonies—in Dakar or Saigon—teaches the same subjects at the same time. At 10:00 a.m. on Monday everywhere in the French-speaking world, including *lycées* in Washington or Los Angeles, classes go over the same textbooks and teach the same subjects, and the students have to pass the same exams.

We're at the opposite extreme, where we think there's advantage in localism. New York went to local school boards, and about 5 percent of the population votes in these local school board elections, and a lot of them make a mess of it.

A third issue, which I think is an interesting one—and which isn't discussed at all—is what I call the myth of Social Security. Do we have a Social Security surplus or a Social Security deficit? Every country in the world, every developed country, has an old-age pension system, supports old people, by different methods. Many of them do it simply out of their general tax revenues.

We have a myth that we have a Social Security fund that has to have enough money in it to pay. There's no question, however, that the United

States will support people who have retired or are of retirement age, whether the Social Security fund is in deficit or not. The Social Security myth was created by Franklin Roosevelt in 1935 or 1936 because he wanted to attract middle-class people in a climate in which there was a tremendous revulsion against being on relief or taking government welfare. As a result, old-age pensions were not cast as relief or welfare. Instead they were called insurance.

To sell the idea, all sorts of wealthy people, including Hollywood stars, applied for their Social Security check to show this wasn't welfare but was something everyone was entitled to. Although the myth of an insurance system is unnecessary today, it sets the framework of a debate that is fundamentally irrelevant. In addition, we have a special tax, the so-called payroll tax, which is today the biggest income tax on lower-income people and which is essentially a regressive tax, because people pay the same rates no matter how much money they earn.

If I were limited to one question, I'd ask how we can get education standards established in the country.

SEYMOUR MARTIN LIPSET

Seymour Martin Lipset is the Hazel Professor of Public Policy at the School of Public Policy at George Mason University.

ANNALS, *AAPSS*, **572**, November 2000

Religion and Politics

Whether our military actions should be for humanitarian purposes or not cannot be debated without addressing the religious question, because all the religious groups say that the humanitarian side must be considered. Agreements on international human rights or trade with China cannot be discussed without finding that Jews, Catholics, evangelicals, everybody across the board is asking how highly issues involving human rights will be ranked in those agreements.

Religion is not an issue in itself. Rather, it hitchhikes on issues. It barnacles to issues. It subverts issues. It is a penumbra around issues. It is part of a constituency on all sides of all issues. If you reduce religion to where one stands on abortion or gay marriage and so on, you're going to get on the killing side right away and not on the healing side. I think most of the religious groups are looking for ways in which candidates can pose issues that will bring out their constructive and healing side.

If I were near the people who are making the campaign speeches, I would ask them, "When you get near these questions, can you help frame them so that what Abraham Lincoln called 'the better angels of our natures' might show, and that we would bring forth those qualities of mercy, justice, fairness, and equality in dealing with poverty and life-and-death issues, instead of distracting us by misusing religion, which is still the most volatile subject in American political life when brought up badly?"

MARTIN E. MARTY

Martin E. Marty is the Fairfax M. Cone Distinguished Service Professor Emeritus at the University of Chicago.

Religion and a World Rule of Law

Faith-based efforts to support policies that are needed in the inner city are extremely important. They can work very effectively, especially if the religious groups are able to get together across lines of race and religion. This can happen. It is happening in a number of cities.

There are about 14 cities in which such coalitions have been built. It is unfortunate that many of us ignore or derogate this kind of civic action out of exaggerated respect for the separation of church and state. The success of ameliorative projects in the inner city requires the element of personal concern, demonstrated in face-to-face relationships. Volunteer citizens often can contribute this element more readily than overburdened professionals working in bureaucratic structures. Religious commitment is one source, though obviously not the only source, of personal concern.

But inner-city policy isn't the question I would raise to the presidential candidates. My colleagues have done so, very effectively. The question I would raise has to do with foreign policy. How do we address a world that is so divided, as Samuel Huntington (1996) has pointed out, in terms of religious orientations? He foresees a "clash of civilizations" between the West (with its Judeo-Christian tradition) and the rest, especially the Islamic and Sinic civilizations. Huntington says that, since these civilizations are so different from ours, there is a danger that we will have a clash of civilizations that will replace and be more horrendous than the Cold War.

I believe that the reconciliation of these differences is both important and achievable. There are common themes among the great religions of the world, and these themes can be used as a foundation for constructing a moral consensus that would provide support for the emergence of a world rule of law. So far, that has not been done effectively. I would ask whether, in the foreign policy area, there is not the potential for bringing together these various religions in a way that helps to support the emergence of a worldview that all nations and religions can share. All of the religions have in common the principles of peace, justice, and compassion. If exclusivist doctrines can be relaxed, the religions should be able to find common ground in the context of guiding and supporting a world legal order.

In my view, we ignore Huntington's question at our peril. If we do not find a way of addressing that question, an enormous danger awaits us. I'm afraid we might encounter it sooner rather than later. The thought that bothers me is one that I take from Edward Gibbon in his description of the decline and fall of the Roman Empire. I think that the United States, the one remaining super-power, has reached a position that may be analogous. If we are lulled by our own success and ignore future imperatives, our world might also collapse.

Gibbon (1963) described the Roman situation as follows:

The decline of Rome was the natural and inevitable consequence of immoderate great-ness. Prosperity ripened the principle of decay. The causes of destruction multiplied with the extent of conquest. And as soon as time or accident had removed the artificial supports, the stupendous fabric yielded to the pressure of its own weight. (642)

I think there is a remedy for the analogous danger, but it's a difficult rem-edy. It requires that the nations of the world, in concert, examine the possibil-ity of moving in the direction of a world rule of law. If we want specific issues to be discussed in the presidential campaign, we can talk about the Comprehen-sive Test Ban Treaty, signed by the President but not yet ratified by the Con-gress. Beyond such specific issues, however, we must find a way of thinking about the fundamental interests of all the world's people: peace and justice for all. That vision cannot be adequately realized unless we move toward a world rule of law. I would ask our would-be next presidents, "If not now, when?"

RICHARD D. SCHWARTZ

Richard D. Schwartz is Ernest I. White Professor at the College of Law of Syracuse University and professor in the Departments of Sociology and Social Science in the uni-versity's Maxwell School.

References

Gibbon, Edward. 1963. *The Decline and Fall of the Roman Empire*. Abridged, with an introduction by Frank C. Bourne. New York: Dell.
Huntington, Samuel P. 1996. *The Clash of Civilizations and the Remaking of World Order*. New York: Simon & Schuster.

ANNALS, *AAPSS*, **572**, November 2000

Racism

I worry about racial integration not only because of the past but also because of the future. We all know what the U.S. census projections tell us; in 50 years, half the population will be white and half the population will not be. The U.N. projection is that instead of having 6 billion people in the world, we will have at least 9 billion, and 80 percent of those 9 billion people will be poor.

In 50 years, the American population will be very different from its current composition, and the world will have in it more poor people than there are right now on the planet. What do poor people do? They go to places where there are jobs, where there is money. People right now are leaving China hidden in cargo containers. Some of them arrive dead. It is only going to get worse over time, and therefore the pressures on the United States, on the psyche of the people of the United States, are going to be more intense.

After all, this country started with the idea that it was going to be a white country. The first Congress passed an immigration law that indicated that only white people would be eligible to become citizens. The people who came to Jamestown in 1607 thought of this as a uniracial country when, in fact, the minute they set foot on it, it became a biracial country. Even before the first blacks were imported in 1619 into Jamestown, the habit of racial hatred, in the form of the hatred of Indians, had already become established in that colony.

Racial animosity beset this land and our politics for a century and a half before we became a country. It is like an awful beast that constantly haunts our culture. But some politicians are like kids who can't stop playing with fire. We had it in George Wallace's presidential campaigns. We had it in the Nixon campaigns. The Democrats have figured out a southern strategy, which is called the Democratic Leadership Council, and triangulation. The elder George Bush certainly could not avoid it when he dealt with the Willie Horton image.

Divisiveness and division keep us from addressing the kinds of problems that the contributors to this *Annals* issue have dealt with. When I was in the government, I used to say the things about cities that Dr. Madden (this volume) has said. If you destroy the cities, if you permit the cities to disintegrate, it is as though a society is sticking a pencil in its own eye.

But our inability to see other human beings fully and richly, and our need in our politics to divide people, makes that human rights issue that Dr. Earls (this volume) has discussed the most difficult third rail in American politics, far more difficult than Social Security ever was.

I will steal a question from one of my favorite American philosophers, Rodney King. My question for the presidential candidates would be, "Can't we all get along?" I would ask the candidates what the impediments to that are and what their solutions are. What are their suggestions for overcoming those impediments?

ROGER WILKINS

Roger Wilkins is Clarence J. Robinson Professor of History and American Culture at George Mason University.

ANNALS, *AAPSS*, **572**, November 2000

Utopia and Campaign Spending

We are often sanguine about the prospects for recommendations that we feel have a lot of merit. Yet we need to be candid and think through the problems of implementation that they face. I was struck by the remarks of Mayor Edward Rendell about the importance of sensible limits on campaign spending and the obstacles to it that he perceived. He concluded that we may have to have a constitutional amendment to get such limits through.

That seems to me to be tantamount to confessing that there is no way to implement campaign spending limits in the next decade or more. Accordingly, we will have to think in terms of second- and third-best alternatives. That applies, moreover, to many other overarching proposals. We will have to back away from utopian formulations and address these in terms of the political and economic realities. That will mean less posturing and maybe less fun. But I think that that would be a good thing for the political dialogue as it plays out over the next several years.

OLIVER WILLIAMSON

Oliver Williamson is Edgar F. Kaiser Professor of Business Administration at the University of California, Berkeley, where he is also professor of economics and professor of law.

Book Department

INTERNATIONAL RELATIONS AND POLITICS

CIMBALA, STEPHEN J. 1998. *Coercive Military Strategy.* Pp. ix, 229. College Station: Texas A&M University Press. $39.95.

As a strategy, military coercion has at best enjoyed mixed success since the end of the Cold War. Policymakers in Washington and elsewhere have nevertheless attempted it frequently during the 1990s, the most recent example being the North Atlantic Treaty Organization air campaign in Kosovo. Earlier in the decade, many commentators had predicted that the end of the East-West confrontation and the demonstration of American military prowess in the Persian Gulf had created a security climate well suited to coercive strategies, at least when employed by the remaining superpower. Yet coercion has proved disappointingly difficult. Threats and/or limited applications of force failed to stop the warlords in Somalia, to oust Haiti's military government, to stop the fighting in Bosnia during 1992-95, or to prevent Saddam Hussein from brutalizing the Kurds or defying U.N. resolutions.

Given this track record, the time is ripe for a fundamental reassessment of coercion as a strategy and of the conditions under which it is likely to succeed or fail. That is the subject of Stephen J. Cimbala's latest book. In it, Cimbala traces the evolution of military coercion as a strategy since 1945 and attempts to distill this understanding into a set of attributes that inform successful coercive strategies.

His examination is essentially divided into three parts. The first part follows the evolution of coercion from the related but distinct concepts of nuclear deterrence and compellence, and the interaction of conventional and nuclear deterrence and coercion in the Cuban Missile Crisis. (He attributes the American success there to a nuclear and conventional superiority understood by both sides coupled with judiciously limited objectives.) The second part analyzes the failure of coercive strategy in Vietnam (attributed to the failure of U.S. decision makers to appreciate the steadfast commitment of the North Vietnamese leadership and to gradualism in the coercive approaches adopted) and its employment in the Persian Gulf war. The last part discusses how shifts in the post–Cold War security environment will constrain and complicate coercive strategy. Here Cimbala focuses on the reemergence of collective security and the need for international legitimization of uses of force and on the decline of interstate warfare and the resulting complexities of coercing nonstate participants in "operations not war." He notes that a preference for military action only by coalitions will make goal setting and agreement on credible action at early stages of crises difficult. He also argues that the mismatch between the (limited) interests of the United States and other intervenors and the (strong) interests of participants in internal conflicts will make the intervenors themselves susceptible to coercion due to their intolerance for casualties.

While useful in focusing attention on problems of coercive strategy, the book is, however, ultimately disappointing on two scores. The first is its largely inductive approach to understanding coercion. Coercion as a concept and phenomenon is only briefly introduced at the beginning of the book. A comprehensive theory of cause and effect is never articulated. Consequently, the reader lacks a context for the substantive material that follows. One is forced to wait until the final twenty pages of the book for any attempt at synthesis, and there the second disappointment is encountered, for conclusions and suggestions for improvement are scarce. Greater focus on theory development and testing might have produced a more robust set of ideas for successful coercive strategies. Robert A. Pape's earlier study of coercion (*Bombing to Win* [1996]) did a better job of framing issues and suggesting conclusions precisely because it began with an extended treatment of coercive theory. Readers looking to improve their fundamental understanding of coercion may wish to start there.

WADE P. HINKLE

Institute for Defense Analyses
Alexandria
Virginia

GRAYSON, GEORGE W. 1999. *Strange Bedfellows: NATO Marches East*. Pp. xxxiv, 268. Lanham, MD: University Press of America. Paperbound, no price.

Strange Bedfellows celebrates the successful efforts of a band of disparate brothers (and an occasional sister) to win the Clinton administration and then the Senate over to the cause of North Atlantic Treaty Organization (NATO) enlargement. George W. Grayson, of the College of William and Mary, follows its tortuous course with the enthusiasm of an insider. Since his sources were mostly interviews and telephone conversations with the policymakers, it is not surprising that he appears as a cheerleader for the enlargement process.

While the cast of characters is large, the single most influential figure in lobbying for the admission of Poland, Hungary, and the Czech Republic into the alliance was the young official Jeremy Rosner, head of NATO's Enlargement Ratification Office (NERO). Grayson attributes the inspiration for enlargement to an influential 1993 article in *Foreign Affairs* by RAND senior analysts Ronald D. Asmus, Richard L. Kugler, and F. Stephen Larrabee. He likens it to George Kennan's famous X article in 1947, also published in *Foreign Affairs*. Again like Kennan's containment thesis, the ideas of Asmus and his colleagues had a ripple effect that lapped over to Senator Richard Lugar's office, then to the State Department's Policy Planning Staff, and ultimately to NERO as the nerve center of the operation. Two key figures—Deputy Secretary of State Strobe Talbott and Senator Jesse Helms—were vital to securing American support for the formal admission of the three new members to NATO at the 50th anniversary meeting of the North Atlantic Council in 1999.

Pressures abroad for enlargement emanated from the eloquent pleas of Czech president Vaclav Havel and Polish president Lech Walesa, buttressed by the political backing of Polish American and Hungarian American groups. Among West Europeans, German defense minister Volker Ruhe was the most aggressive statesman lobbying for NATO's new direction. The allies in general presumably accepted with few reservations the arguments of the proponents, namely, that NATO's enlargement would erase the strain of Yalta and stabilize Europe at a modest cost. The danger of alienating Russia would be minimized by the Founding Act of 1997 that would ensure cooperation between NATO and the Russian Federation.

Grayson's breezy style effectively transmits the excitement generated by the principals who claimed responsibility for NATO's enlargement. His account will be of considerable value to historians examining the process after relevant documents become available. But there are some troubling problems with his approach beyond the too hasty account of the history leading up to the invitation tendered at Madrid in 1997. What roles did the allies, besides Germany, play in NATO's march to the east? Were the views of Britain and France, both in support and in opposition, mirror images of those of their American counterparts? And if there were influential opponents, would they have been demonized, as American opponents were? Professor Michael Mandelbaum in particular was ridiculed for switching from supporting to opposing expansion, while Talbott was praised for moving in the opposite direction. The one opponent spared criticism was Kennan, whose views are patronized even as the book was dedicated to him.

There are issues that are either finessed or trivialized in this book that historians will want answered. The cost element is given short shrift, although Grayson recognizes the uncertainties surrounding them in 1999. But he does not ask what impact they may have on the economies of the new members as well as on the budgets of the older members. Nor does he look closely into future enlargements and their potential impact on the alliance. How does an organization run by consensus function as it grows beyond 19 members? And what may be expected of Russian relations if the Founding Act is denounced? For the most part, these questions cannot be answered at this time, but they should be given more attention than they receive in this readable book.

LAWRENCE S. KAPLAN

Georgetown University
Washington, D.C.

VERDERY, KATHERINE. 1999. *The Political Lives of Dead Bodies: Reburial and Postsocialist Change.* Pp. xvi, 185. New York: Columbia University Press. $21.50.

This book presents the Harriman lectures delivered by Katherine Verdery at Columbia University in December 1997. The topic Verdery chose—the curious phenomenon of the reburial of bodies, both famous and anonymous, in the postsocialist era in Eastern Europe—was motivated in part to interest a broad audience of social scientists and humanists. Yet Verdery's choice serves another, more important purpose: to move the discussion of the Eastern European transition beyond the dry calculations and dull observations of much economic and political analysis. She would rather we embrace a "richer and more meaningful conception of what politics itself consists of . . . a more enchanted view of politics, one that gives special importance to political symbolism, life experiences, and feelings."

The book is divided into four sections. The first is a short introduction describing the variety of bodies being transported, removed, and reburied. Her analysis covers the reburial of local figures (such as rehabilitated figures and anonymous war dead) and the "repatriation" of famous personages from abroad. She also considers the removal of statues from many public sites as constituting another instance of "body politics." Chapter 1 offers a clear explanation of why a study of the political lives of the dead (or, alternatively, the politics of reburial) may illuminate significant features of the postsocialist period. Three issues make this story of mobile bodies in the Eastern European transition different from comparable instances of reburial elsewhere: (1) several crucial issues, such as "property restitution, political pluralization, religious renewal, and national conflicts," are being negotiated simultaneously; (2) when attempts are being made to revise the past, dead bodies are particularly effective tools; and (3) dead bodies are sufficiently profound symbols to convey the enormity of the changes taking place. Chapters 2 and 3 are case studies, one case being the reburial of an eighteenth-century Transylvanian bishop, the other chronicling the dilemma of mass graves and war dead in the former Yugoslavia.

By studying the politics of corpses, Verdery wishes to focus our attention on the cultural dimensions of the transition, to aid us in appreciating the complex emotions and moral dilemmas that have characterized this momentous transformation. She is also careful to situate the transition in Eastern Europe within the larger processes of globalization, a point not sufficiently emphasized in much scholarship. Verdery is quick to explain that her approach to the study of culture and politics does not derive from the concept of political culture but is informed by anthropology. As such, it insists upon the analysis of practices, for culture is far more than ideas alone. Politics, Verdery argues, comprises the struggles over meaning and public claims to significance, actions taken not only by political elites but also by the nameless in crowds and demonstrations. Verdery's insistence on analyzing practices is welcome, since much of the work done on the transition suffers not only from a narrow reading of political culture but also from an impoverished understanding of social process and history. Hence in the study of transitions, history is often understood as an ineluctable barrier to change, when in fact history is a complex, often contradictory repertoire of ideas and actions that people refashion continually in the strategic maneuverings and ingenuous moments of everyday life. It is for this reason—that history is a local and heartfelt product—that the transition engages issues of morality, indeed cosmology. Verdery's analysis constitutes, therefore, an important theoretical intervention in the study of transitions, as well as being a good read.

MARTHA LAMPLAND

University of California
San Diego
La Jolla

AFRICA, ASIA, AND LATIN AMERICA

BAY, EDNA G. 1998. *Wives of the Leopard: Gender, Politics, and Culture in the Kingdom of Dahomey*. Pp. xv, 376. Charlottesville: University of Virginia Press. No price.

In *Wives of the Leopard*, Edna Bay has given us a meticulously researched study of precolonial Dahomey that focuses primarily on the monarchy, with special attention to women's roles in shaping the monarchy and the importance of the palace within the polity. She appropriately sets Dahomey in the context of other similar polities, rather than assuming its uniqueness. Her model is consciously diachronic, outlining the large changes that transpired over the eighteenth and nineteenth centuries. She is very careful about her use of sources and relies partly on her own and others' collections of oral histories.

The strongest point of this work is the analysis of changing religious hierarchies instigated by monarchs and those who influenced them. Precolonial African political history has too often been written as if religion were not a key aspect of politics, but in Dahomey and elsewhere, including Europe until the nineteenth century, state religion was essential. Dahomey's preeminent military reputation and achievements were based largely on religion-as-tactic or, as Bay puts it, the neutralizing of the enemy's sources of power. Thus, at various times, Dahomeans used religious sabotage to undermine future victims' confidence, pretend cannibalism to terrorize their enemies, and other tactics. When Behanzin, famous as the last independent Dahomean king, was being defeated by the French, he had his best warriors beheaded to send a message to his ancestors for help, a tragedy that ended with his executing his own mother, all to no avail.

Bay's analysis of the reigns of Tegbesu and Gezo is particularly good, pointing out in the latter case that the outward trappings of success concealed substantial weaknesses. Other strengths are the span of Bay's synthesis of Dahomean history and her use of clear style, making the work eligible for use as a classroom text.

At the same time, there are some weaknesses. Most annoying are the tendencies to write by indirection and to raise but not answer questions. A section heading is likely to be followed by a disquisition seemingly on an unrelated subject that is tied into the heading only after some pages. The speculative nature of precolonial African history is evident in the unanswered questions, but Dahomey is spectacularly documented compared to most polities and a bit more courage at certain points might have been warranted. Also, perhaps because of the past tendency to sensationalize Dahomean history, Bay downplays some aspects that might have been better more fully discussed. The superior documentation might have allowed more interesting detail, but a lot of time is spent on general analysis of changing bureaucratic structure, which, though important, is at times tedious. A few diagrams might have been a more elegant solution.

In the end, Bay's effort is meritorious for pulling together many sources in her synthesis; for adding significant oral sources to the literature; for an important contribution to precolonial religiopolitical history that includes women; for paying attention to both sides in discussing the imposition of European colonialism, including Euro-American representations of Dahomey in venues like the 1893 Columbian Exposition; and for analyzing the political ramifications of changing economic structures and other aspects. Such work is necessary, especially for those of us who are not specialists in precolonial African history, and useful for exploding commonplace stereotypes.

CLAIRE ROBERTSON

Ohio State University
Columbus

NUGENT, DAVID. 1997. *Modernity at the Edge of Empire: State, Individual, and the Nation in the Northern Peruvian Andes, 1885-1935*. Pp. xvi, 404. Stanford, CA: Stanford University Press. $55.00. Paperbound, $19.95.

The central idea in anthropologist David Nugent's study of a truly marginal area of the Peruvian geography (and historiography) is that, contrary to standard notions of nation-state building, in Chachapoyas modernity was willingly imposed by the people, not by the homogenizing forces of capitalism and bourgeois hegemony. This case, moreover, can be considered an illuminating example in a more general Latin American model of nation-state formation, a model that differs significantly from processes in Western Europe (and its colonial dominions).

Dealing with the period 1885-1935, Nugent focuses "on a social context in which commerce, modernity, and the nation-state were regarded as liberating rather than threatening forces—forces to be embraced rather than resisted." A future book, on the years 1935-95, will deal with "the forces that led to modernity being perceived in negative, hostile terms." However, the periodization is at times confusing, since some relevant examples are taken from the 1870s, and some generalizations seem to be applied to the entire nineteenth century of Peruvian national history. If some characteristics were so pervasive, why choose the specific 50 years of 1885-1935? By the same token, why not connect more explicitly the local focus with national Peruvian political processes?

The first three chapters present local power structures and build a fascinating and dynamic model of patron-client power relations. Local elite families, through marriage alliances, constitute rival clans looking for total control of local politics and provincial administration. This dynamic model of successive cyclical periods of stability and instability, breakdown and reconstitution of clans' domination, gives sense to an otherwise constant violence in the area. However, the terminology used by Nugent is somewhat confusing. He calls the clans from the beginning *castas*, a term only later defined; moreover, he uses it confusingly, excluding socioracial (*casta española*) and sociopolitical (*casta política*) meanings. It seems to be a very local usage that typifies a privileged traditional group, as expressed by an informant quoted in the middle of the book. Nugent does not take the Spanish colonial meaning, of racial miscegenation with some degree of African descent, into account.

Building on the opposing concepts of "aristocratic" and "popular" sovereignty (Foucault), Nugent proposes how the *castas* exerted their power based on the former's conceptions of privilege and hierarchy but expressed their rivalries in the latter's rhetoric of individual and equal rights guaranteed by the state (chapter 5). Only when local intellectuals started in the 1920s to question the "schizophrenic" nature of the elite formal discourse did the liberal notions of equality of rights expand into marginalized middle sectors, both through progressive newspapers (Ricardo Feijóo Reina's *Amazonas*, brilliantly analyzed in chapter 6) and political indoctrination (a process ably reconstructed in chapter 7 from interviews with old *apristas*, the political activists of the radical-reformist party led by Haya de la Torre). The construction of a conscious middle sector of urban artisans gave birth to *el pueblo*, the people, as if they represented non-elite sectors in their totality. Through a process of embodiment of popular sovereignty, these provincial middle sectors imposed a democratization, an opening of political and social participation for them, which otherwise excluded the rural peasantry and women.

By the middle of 1930, after the collapse of the 11-year regime of President Leguía, a new alliance between *el pueblo* and a refashioned family from one of the traditional clans had taken control of Chachapoyas. For some few years, the aims of the middle sectors were fulfilled, as these sectors took control of municipal councils and created new "horizontal associations" (chapter 8). For them, modernity had lots of promises to fulfill after being recovered for *el pueblo* from traditional aristocratic clans (or *castas*). As a quote from an old muleteer reveals, the modern-liberal "popular sovereignty" discourse had great appeal to provincial middle sectors in an isolated corner of the Andes: "No señor! I am your equal! We are all equal!"

NICANOR DOMÍNGUEZ

University of Illinois
Urbana-Champaign

OWENSBY, BRIAN P. 1999. *Intimate Ironies: Modernity and the Making of Middle-Class Lives in Brazil*. Pp. xiii, 332. Stanford, CA: Stanford University Press. $45.00.

In an important recent essay, historian Michael Jiménez called attention to "the elision of the middle classes" from Latin American historiography and social science. Even while pointing to the middle class as the best long-term hope for stability and democracy in the region, scholars have "neglected or at best marginalized inquiry into the nature and role of the middle classes outside of the North Atlantic basin" (in *Colonial Legacies*, ed. Jeremy Adelman [New York: Routledge], p. 211).

In this gracefully written, quietly intelligent book, Brian Owensby—probably not coincidentally, a former student of Jiménez's—offers an exemplary model of how to reverse that neglect and "bring the middle classes back in" to Latin American historical narratives. He begins by noting the importance of Brazil's slave past in determining the particularly challenging conditions faced by that nation's middle class. Under slavery, wealth and power were overwhelmingly concentrated in the hands of a landowning elite; at the same time, all forms of manual labor were deeply degraded, socially and culturally, by their association with slavery and nonwhite racial status. Thus, as the country's urban middle class began to form during the period 1870-1920, it did so under conditions of extreme domination by, and dependence on, the planter elite and equally extreme aversion to any connection with the degraded world of manual labor, whether slave or free.

As the 1945 novel *Middle Class* put it, the middle class is "an unhappy class, because it cannot be rich and must not be poor" (quoted in Owensby, 127). Yet the recurrent economic crises and persistent inflation of the period 1900-1960 confronted professionals and white-collar workers with eroding salaries and the specter of falling downward into working-class poverty. During the 1920s and 1930s, members of the middle class formed opposition political movements to defend their class position, most notably Fascist-inspired Integralism. Under the corporatist policies of President Getúlio Vargas (1930-45, 1950-54) and his successors, however, those movements were pushed aside in national politics by the rising power of organized labor.

Trampled and marginalized in the intensifying struggle between labor-based populism and conservative elites, much of the middle class withdrew into what Owensby describes, in perhaps the most interesting chapter of the book, as "apolitical politics." Unable to compete effectively in electoral politics, but unwilling to withdraw completely from the public realm, many professionals and white-collar workers sought to play a political role through working in state bureaucracies, through teaching, or through the new and rapidly growing profession of social work. Other middle-class Brazilians, alienated and disgusted by what they saw as the corrupt, opportunistic world of politics, opted out of political life completely. Instead, they sought refuge in the private world of the home, where they tried to cultivate the tranquility and morality so visibly lacking in national politics. Both these responses—faith in technical competence, or private morality—argues Owensby, help explain middle-class support for, or acquiescence in, the military coup of 1964 that brought electoral democracy to an end.

This short summary cannot do justice to the richness and subtlety of Owensby's arguments. I should also note that, though the story he tells is quite specifically Brazilian, it also forms part of a much larger historical narrative. As the book notes, in an aptly chosen quotation from Norman Mailer's *The Naked and the Dead*, "The natural role of twentieth-century man is anxiety" (Owensby, 236). The Brazilian middle classes suffered (and suffer) from particularly concentrated forms of anxiety, but forms that American readers, I believe, will recognize as unpleasantly familiar. By tracing the Brazilian variant of middle-class experience, Owensby vividly illuminates not just Brazilian and Latin American history but, as his title suggests, the history of modernity more generally.

GEORGE REID ANDREWS

University of Pittsburgh
Pennsylvania

RUF, GREGORY A. 1999. *Cadres and Kin: Making a Socialist Village in West China, 1921-1991*. Pp. xvii, 249. Stanford, CA: Stanford University Press. $49.50.

Based on a total of about a year's fieldwork in rural Sichuan in 1990-91 and 1994-95, *Cadres and Kin* reconstructs the history of a "village" (the term "village" is problematic in Sichuan, as Ruf himself points out in a useful concluding chapter) in the 70 years between 1921 and 1991 that subjected its people (together with all other rural Chinese) to warlordism, anti-Japanese resistance, civil war, land reform and collectivization, the Cultural Revolution, and the reform period. Naturally, all of this is well-trodden ground in Chinese studies, but Ruf's contribution is to relate the historical narrative to the life and times of real people by focusing on issues that are at the core of Chinese anthropology: kinship, family, gender, religion, networks and power, group formation, development, inequality, and identity. Steeped in the anthropological tradition, the book is completely devoid of jargon or intellectual posturing, making it ideal for students not yet well acquainted with contemporary rural China and for China anthropologists searching for a clear account of another place in China for comparison with their own research area.

Cadres and Kin tells us little that we do not already know and carries no great or novel analytical argument apart from questioning the naturalness of the natural village. Yet this does not devalue the book. Over the last 10 years, the ethnographic record of the rural areas in the People's Republic of China has been enriched by a relatively large number (compared to the decades before) of monographs that are, like Ruf's, based on long-term firsthand anthropological fieldwork. While often sophisticated in their analysis and theoretical argument, these monographs rarely present the terse, chronological account that make Gregory Ruf's *Cadres and Kin* so eminently suited as a set reading for introductory courses on contemporary China.

FRANK N. PIEKE

University of Oxford
United Kingdom

TEIWES, FREDERICK C. with WARREN SUN. 1999. *China's Road to Disaster: Mao, Central Politicians and Provincial Leaders in the Unfolding of the Great Leap Forward, 1955-1959*.

Pp. xxvii, 319. Armonk, NY: M. E. Sharpe. Paperbound, $27.50.

The Great Leap Forward (GLF) of the late 1950s is a fascinating period to many China scholars. As a purely Maoist approach to accelerating economic development through mass mobilization, the Great Leap created backyard furnaces, established communal kitchens, and caused the death of at least 30 million people. A leading analyst of the People's Republic of China's first decade, Frederick Teiwes provides a richly detailed explanation of the GLF's elite politics that combines meticulous analysis of newly published Chinese materials with insightful interviews.

Analysts of elite politics during this period adopt either a zero-sum or non-zero-sum game approach. While acknowledging Mao Zedong as the preeminent leader, the non-zero-sum game interpretation emphasizes the relative influence of the other political elites. Analysts such as Roderick MacFarquhar and Kenneth Lieberthal thus argue that Mao and the top elites compromised, co-opted the opposition, or sought stronger coalition allies to achieve their policy objectives. David Bachman proffers a more recent variation that utilizes a neo-institutionalist approach to understanding bureaucratic bargaining within the Political Bureau.

In contrast, the zero-sum game approach advocates that one player's gain is another's loss; interrated games result in one dominant player. The Cultural Revolution's "two-line struggle" model interpreted the political scene as dominated by either capitalist roaders or Maoist revolutionaries. Reacting to this winners and losers paradigm, Teiwes developed the parsimonious "Mao-in-command" school in which political games were concluded by 1949. The sole winner—Mao Zedong—was responsible for all subsequent dramatic policy changes.

According to Teiwes's new study, Mao conceived of China's first "leap forward" in late 1955. Acknowledging a certain degree of inconsistency and complexity, Teiwes argues that Mao immediately reversed course to promote a moderate policy of "Opposing Rash Advance." Perhaps spurred by provincial leaders, Mao again revised his thinking by the Third Plenum of 1957 to support accelerated economic growth, namely, the GLF. Mao subsequently denounced the Party's economic leadership in January 1958, resulting in Premier Zhou Enlai's offer to resign. Mao then led the country forward under the Great Leap banner, as well as initiating intermediate policy readjustment by late 1958 to ensure policy success.

While primarily reacting to Bachman's neo-institutionalist interpretation, which is criticized as another American political science "fashion," Teiwes neglects the other non-zero-sum game views. For instance, Mao could have unwillingly retracted his Rash Advance strategy under pressure from his elite coalition colleagues. Mao actually described this exact situation during the 1958 Nanning Conference, stating that he had resorted to a strategy of "passive resistance" during the previous two years. While omitting this famous passage, Teiwes does relate several pre-1958 incidents in which Mao criticized the moderate approach. Teiwes also describes how such "benign" behavior was quintessential Mao: "Mao would sometimes say nothing and wait for an occasion to state his views."

Are Mao's actions the result of a leader's suffering from "intellectual incoherence" or a masterful tactician's waiting for the right time to wrestle control from the leadership's economic specialists? Was Zhou Enlai's forceful opposition to Mao's Rash Advance strategy the result of "naïveté" or "careless politics"? In view of Mao's "extraordinary outburst" at Nanning and Zhou's previous disagreements with Mao, Teiwes needs to counter more forcefully the view that Mao was formally breaking with his former coalition partners in 1958 to restore his vision of Rash Advance.

Teiwes again has set a high standard for the Mao-in-command approach. It is hoped that other scholars will be inspired to reevaluate their paradigms in light of the new Chinese sources and reengage Teiwes in an enlightening academic debate.

LAWRENCE C. REARDON

University of New Hampshire
Durham

EUROPE

MORAVCSIK, ANDREW. 1998. *The Choice for Europe: Social Purpose and State Power from Messina to Maastricht*. Pp. xii, 514. Ithaca, NY: Cornell University Press. $59.95. Paperbound, $22.50.

It is sometimes obvious when a classic is born. The general sense of anticipation preceding the publication of Andrew Moravcsik's new book shows that it is a classic. In fact, I found myself repeatedly looking up amazon.com to see if the book had already appeared. Having now read *The Choice for Europe*, I am no less convinced that it is indeed going to be considered a landmark publication. Because of its ambitious scope, historical detail, and clear argumentation, it is a must read for anyone seriously interested in European integration. But, as happens to be the case with most classical social science texts, I suspect that we will find its core argument to be flawed.

Before going through the book's pros and cons, a summary of its main argument is in order. Moravcsik sets out to explain five major decisions along the path of European integration, starting with the Treaty of Rome and ending with the Maastricht Treaty. To account for these milestones, Moravcsik employs a hybrid framework based on three stages. For each decision, he derives the preferences of the three major actors, France, Germany, and Britain, from their respective economic interests as opposed to geopolitical determinants. Factoring in these governments' relative bargaining power, the second step postulates that integration advances will reflect the preferences of the most powerful actors. Finally, the process also depends on the availability of credible bargaining positions, typically supported by veto threats against laggard countries. In essence, this elaborate "liberal-intergovernmentalist" position, which has become so closely associated with Moravcsik's name, postulates that national preference convergence drives the integration process.

The book's strength derives primarily from its massive empirical coverage. If many contributions to the integration literature have cut corners and resorted to sweeping theoretical claims, Moravcsik sets new standards in painstaking empirical analysis. He has probably read more secondary literature in English, German, and French, held more interviews with key actors, and fine-combed more archives than any other political scientist. Not surprisingly, then, there is a wealth of interesting material in the volume's half thousand pages. And as we have become accustomed to anticipate from this author, *The Choice for Europe* is exceedingly well written, clearly articulated, and forcefully argued.

The crux is that the book does not hang together theoretically. Preferring to see his study as a part of a general theory of liberalism, Moravcsik has an ambitious agenda, but the internal coherence of the theoretical propositions disappoints, and their link to observable hypotheses leaves much to be desired. We learn that loose paradigmatic clusters of ideas, such as "modern political economy" and "bargaining theory," "predict" unambiguous outcomes in specific cases. I found the references to "geopolitical theory" particularly puzzling. Instead of evaluating alternative theories in their entirety, the book lumps together and "tests" a grab bag of wildly disparate propositions and policies, such as balance of power, Gaullist anti-Americanism, European federalism, and "liberal constructivism," all under the geopolitical label.

As regards research design, Moravcsik's exclusive focus on successful integration decisions has been criticized for its alleged selection bias. While it would have been interesting to see how the main argument holds up in unsuccessful cases, such as the European Defense Community, the book's emphasis on integration advances can be defended if the theory is based on necessary conditions (although Moravcsik does not do that explicitly).

Nevertheless, even if we accept his umbrella terms and research design, the argument still does not stand. Given that European integration is a macrohistorical process, there is no reason to believe any single theory, including Moravcsik's economistic interpretation, to hold throughout the entire period. The author makes much out of the observation that only in 8 of his 15 country cases does geopolitics have causal clout. But because there is no clear theoretical rationale for why the five particular decisions should be treated as "salient," such comparisons become meaningless. Indeed, if we add the path-breaking and successful European Coal and Steel Community (ECSC) as a sixth case—given its historical salience and subsequent impact on the process, to do anything else seems seriously misleading—and if we exclude Britain from this decision and the Rome

Treaty since that state did not participate in the decision making in either case, geopolitics—or, more precisely, the attempt to transcend historical conflict between France and Germany—looms large. In fact, Moravcsik admits that the ECSC was geopolitically motivated (104), and he only partly succeeds in discounting its importance for France in the negotiations leading up to Rome. Even more revealing, he suggests that European integration minus geopolitics would have equaled a large free-trade area rather than a suprastatist organization (90). In sum, it seems hard to avoid the conclusion that at least the first decade of European integration was fundamentally a peace project in the name of Franco-German reconciliation.

Moravcsik's insistence on framing his arguments as relatively context-free and implicitly universal hypotheses while treating the five decisions as isolated "data points" obscures the historical logic that lies at the very suprastatist core of the European integration process. Having reduced integration to mere interstate cooperation by definition, he throws away what makes the European experience so unique, incidentally together with the liberal theme of progress. All the same, Moravcsik's crisp style and provocative argumentation make him as worthwhile reading as ever.

LARS-ERIK CEDERMAN

University of California
Los Angeles

UNITED STATES

ANDREWS, RICHARD N. L. 1999. *Managing the Environment, Managing Ourselves: A History of American Environmental Policy.* Pp. xiii, 463. New Haven, CT: Yale University Press. $65.00. Paperbound, $30.00.

Environmental policy is not just the result of the explicit regulatory legislation of the past few decades but is deeply rooted in fundamental values and policies that have been pursued on the American continent over the past four centuries. That is the message of Richard Andrews's superb new history of U.S. environmental policy. He defines this policy broadly, to include all public policies that have shaped our exploitation of resources. Indeed, he shows that policies regarding private property, land use, agriculture, transportation, trade, and economic development generally have had far more impact on our environment than have specific environmental protections.

What is most laudable about this work is not only its comprehensiveness and elegance—despite the awkward title— but also the fact that Andrews explains the need for "environmental governance" in an introductory chapter and then maintains a coherent focus on continuities and shifts in governance throughout our many phases of national development. This allows him to explain the often dramatic policy changes from one era to the next in terms of shifting ideas about the role of government and public administration as well as in relation to such contextual factors as new scientific discoveries, new political movements, and ongoing socioeconomic and technological change.

The result is a fascinating story of how different forces interacted to push the goals of public policy in multiple directions, ultimately producing a fragmented patchwork of programs and agencies with conflicting missions and clienteles rather than any coherent national framework for managing environmental resources. Andrews makes it clear that economic interests and "subgovernments" have dominated every major policy sector throughout history, making environmental protection an uphill

battle at best. Yet, since colonial times, there have always been some public restraints on the use of resources, and in some periods such as the Progressive Era, the New Deal, and the 1970s, there have been remarkable policy breakthroughs that achieved immense environmental gains.

The book is organized chronologically, though some chapters focus on more general topics such as the "public health and urban sanitation" movement of the late nineteenth century. Nine chapters cover periods from the colonial era to the post–World War II years of "superpower and supermarket." Three chapters analyze the rise of modern environmentalism in the 1960s and the subsequent revolution in environmental legislation in greater detail, providing an excellent overview of all current policies. The final three chapters take a fresh look at what Andrews calls the "unfinished business" of environmentalism, the potential impacts of unregulated economic globalization, and possible ways of breaking the current political deadlock over environmental policy reform.

Andrews is not sanguine about the "doldrums" that environmentalism seems to be in at the close of the century. He sees environmental policy as having become mired in "pendulum politics," with pro- and anti-environmental ideological forces blocking the emergence of any new majority reform coalition (despite widespread agreement of policy scholars and professionals on many innovative proposals). The conclusion of the book suggests several avenues for reform that might provide at least a partial vision for renegotiating the environmental contract in the future. My only criticism is that Andrews is perhaps too harsh in writing off the efforts of the Clinton-Gore administration to move in these directions.

The book is beautifully written and edited, richly annotated, and modestly illustrated with photos and figures; it contains a useful chronology, bibliography, and index. It will make an ideal textbook for nearly any college or university course in environmental studies.

NORMAN J. VIG

Carleton College
Northfield
Minnesota

DeSIPIO, LOUIS. 1996. *Counting on the Latino Vote: Latinos as a New Electorate*. Pp. xii, 221. Charlottesville: University of Virginia Press. Paperbound, no price.

Louis DeSipio provides the reader with a theoretical and practical tour of U.S. Latinos as a "new electorate." To accomplish this goal, he examines Latino political participation as it relates to incorporation and the potential impact of the Latino vote on the national electorate. DeSipio also evaluates the likelihood that Latinos will form a new electorate as other major groups (particularly women, youths, African Americans, and southern and eastern Europeans) did during the twentieth century. Furthermore, he questions the permanence of ethnicity in the Latino community since ethnicity is a very fluid force in politics. A final evaluative characteristic of this well-written book is the role of naturalization not as a mere tool of citizenship but as a vehicle to fuel political incorporation among what he calls "Reticents" (registered nonvoters), "Reluctants" (U.S. citizens not registered to vote), and "Recruits" (noncitizen adults).

To support these arguments, DeSipio uses data from two surveys on the Latino population. The National Latino Immigrant Survey reveals the potential for naturalization. The second survey, the Latino National Political Survey, examines the political values, attitudes, and behaviors among Latino citizens and noncitizens.

Although the two surveys were limited in scope and already several years old, DeSipio's ambitious research agenda takes us to a different level of understanding of Latino citizens and noncitizens by enlarging the picture of complex and highly diversified Latino communities. In chapter 2, DeSipio argues, for example, that "many of the 'commonsense' understandings of Latino partisanship, ideology, and policy concerns neglect the diversity of these populations and of their continuing adaptation to the political environments and opportunity structures available in different historical periods." To enlarge on this complex picture, DeSipio defines three significant and interrelated factors that affect Latino political development: immigration, acculturation, and the experience of political exclusion (particularly among Mexican Americans and Puerto Ricans).

The author presents a viable and rigorous case for expansion of the Latino research agenda since, with minor exceptions, all Latinos are immigrants, migrants, or descendants of immigrants and migrants. They have a long legacy of political acculturation that has been difficult to appreciate. This legacy is fueled by a continuous high rate of new immigration, with the new immigrants being distant from participatory politics in this nation. In spite of this reality, when the immigrants are asked about policy issues facing this nation, their response is well within the "mainstream political debate." Nevertheless, immigration, acculturation, and exclusion from the political process are significant factors that have contributed to low levels of electoral participation, making Latinos unable to influence electoral outcomes and national policy issues.

Latinos have significantly different experiences than women, youths, African

Americans, and southern and eastern Europeans. These latter groups nevertheless offer multiple lessons for Latino political mobilization. Taking advantage of these experiences, DeSipio outlines several trajectories to increase the Latino vote. The recommended trajectories include following some of the pattern of the southern and eastern Europeans; following the examples of women and youths by organizing to gain mass voter registration; using as models African American experiences, which tie voter registration and participation to sets of policy objectives; and continuing on the current course of action.

Counting on the Latino Vote is an integrative, comprehensive, and significant contribution to the ethnic literature. It addresses some of the problems facing the Latino leadership and community as Latino leaders and followers continue to mature politically into the twenty-first century.

ROBERTO E. VILLARREAL

University of Texas
El Paso

FISHER, GLENN W. 1996. *The Worst Tax? A History of the Property Tax in America*. Pp. x, 245. Lawrence: University Press of Kansas. $35.00.

This book provides a detailed portrayal of one of the most revenue-productive and controversial taxes in American history, the property tax. The tax, which dates back to ancient times, was brought to the colonies from Britain. It was used on a limited basis by the federal government during part of the nineteenth century, and it became the mainstay of state and local government finance during that century. It was the focal point of an intensive debate between those who advocated a strong central government, represented by leaders such as Andrew Hamilton and James Madison, and those who favored decentralized government, led by the likes of Thomas Jefferson and Andrew Jackson.

The book identifies the crucial interaction that exists between constitutions and political philosophy, on the one hand, and the begrudging acceptance of taxes to finance the public goods desired by a laissez-faire populace, on the other. The American public sector, which is the most decentralized in the world, with its 50 sovereign states and thousands of nonsovereign local governments, could not have achieved this status without the presence of a strong revenue source for its subnational governments. The property tax has performed this role in an impressive fashion, especially during the nineteenth century, when it served as the principal revenue source for both state and local governments, but even in the present time, when it supplies 75 percent of local government revenues. Meanwhile, the states have now substituted general retail sales and personal income taxes for their reliance upon property taxation.

In keeping with the strong egalitarian preferences of American society, the concept of a general property tax prevailed in the nineteenth century. This consisted of a flat or proportional tax rate imposed upon the value of all property, both real and personal as well as tangible and intangible. However, as implemented, the tax was unevenly applied across different types (classes) of property as well as across the many jurisdictions that employed the tax. It is seemingly impossible to tax all forms of wealth at a uniform percentage of their respective values. Subsequently, it has become largely a tax upon real property, and even then one with differential tax rates.

While the primary orientation of the book is a history of the property tax in the nation as a whole, a seemingly disproportionate number of chapters are devoted to a case study of the tax in the state of Kansas—even though the Kansas experiences are linked to the national scene. Moreover, the discussion might have been strengthened by use of the conventional tax performance criteria of fairness, in ability-to-pay terms, and tax efficiency, in the economic resource allocation sense. The concluding discussion considers the future of the American property tax, ranging from policies that would (1) improve its administration; (2) abandon its use; (3) abandon its use for public school finance; or (4) continue the historical muddle-through approach that allows it to evolve in an ad hoc fashion depending upon localized conditions and political interests.

Overall, the book provides a great deal of information regarding the history of the property tax, and, appropriately, the reader is left to answer the enticing question encompassed in the title of the book: Is the property tax America's "worst tax"? The tax appears to deserve this label if one is guided by the conventional tax performance benchmarks of ability to pay and economic efficiency. However, if the question is answered in terms of the capacity of a large, highly decentralized, local government sector to survive in the long run, the property tax may well escape the label of "America's worst tax."

BERNARD P. HERBER

La Jolla
California

GARRISON, JEAN A. 1999. *Games Advisors Play: Foreign Policy in the Nixon and Carter Administrations*. Pp. xiv, 192. College Station: Texas A&M University Press. $34.95.

Scholarly research on presidential decision making often focuses on conflict and cooperation between presidents and their advisers. This book concentrates on the latter half of that equation—presidential advisers—which has received relatively less systematic attention to date. Garrison's purpose is to examine "how and why advisors manipulate the group process, under what conditions foreign policy advisors engage in power games, and in what situations they are most effective."

The study analyzes three types of "games" that advisers play to exercise influence: structural maneuvers to determine who participates in the decision-making process; procedural strategies to set the agenda, frame the issues, and build support for a position; and interpersonal tactics to influence other decision makers. The significance of the topic and Garrison's extensive primary research on the development of arms control policy under Presidents Richard Nixon and Jimmy Carter make this book a valuable addition to the scholarly literature on U.S. foreign policymaking.

National security adviser Henry A. Kissinger capitalized on strong presidential support to exercise the most influence on arms control policy in the Nixon administration. Nixon employed a hierarchical advisory system that delegated primary responsibility to Kissinger for shaping the 1972 Anti-Ballistic Missile and Strategic Arms Limitation Talks (SALT) Treaties. Kissinger furthermore took the initiative in developing other resources, such as a "back channel" of communication between himself and Soviet Ambassador to the United States Anatoly Dobrynin, that solidified his central position in the administration. Yet other advisers such as Secretary of State William Rogers and Secretary of Defense Melvin Laird, also participated more than is commonly recognized. As Garrison puts it, "Despite [Kissinger's] organizational advantages, he could not unilaterally determine the content of policy." Garrison concludes that Nixon's hierarchical system "created the best-case scenario for the national security advisor to be influential but did not leave him invulnerable to the maneuvers of others."

Carter created a more open advisory system in which several officials, particularly Secretary of State Cyrus Vance and National Security Advisor Zbigniew Brzezinski, shaped the administration's position on the SALT II Treaty. While Carter's open system permitted advisers to present their views freely, it did not produce a careful vetting of all policy options. Because of Carter's commitment to arms control, advisers focused more on building support for the president's views than on evaluating criticisms of his position. Carter also was reluctant to resolve advisory disputes, thereby permitting conflicts to fester and ultimately undermine the administration's image. Garrison finds that "the collegial and open setting that the president set up at the beginning of his administration evolved into an openly competitive system." Consequently, the Carter case study reveals "the central role that the president must play in the open advisory system, in order to bring some order to a potentially chaotic process."

Garrison identifies a number of important strategies that advisers employ in policymaking and uses both archival research and interviews to illustrate the application of those strategies in the Nixon and Carter administrations. The "strategic impact" of advisers on policymaking clearly merits attention; yet one might conclude that this study serves to illustrate the primary role of presidents themselves in the decision-making process. Both case studies show that an adviser's role depends foremost on presidential management of advisers and awareness of advisory "games." Studies of decision making therefore need to examine both presidential leadership style and advisory games. This well-researched study lays the

foundation for such scholarship and will be of interest to students of the American presidency, American foreign policy, and international relations alike.

MEENEKSHI BOSE

United States Military Academy
West Point
New York

GILENS, MARTIN. 1999. *Why Americans Hate Welfare: Race, Media, and the Politics of Antipoverty Policy.* Pp. ix, 296. Chicago: University of Chicago Press. $25.00.

Even though African Americans represent 36 percent of all welfare recipients and only 27 percent of poor Americans, Martin Gilens convincingly demonstrates that whites' attitudes toward welfare and antipoverty policy are dominated by their beliefs about blacks. Gilens marshals an impressive array of primary and secondary sources to support a twofold proposition as to why white Americans hate welfare: they hate it because they erroneously believe that most welfare recipients are black and because they continue to cling to old stereotypes of blacks as lazy, unmotivated, and lacking a work ethic. Such perceptions, rooted in our nation's history but fueled by distorted portrayals in news magazines and television news, have rendered poor urban blacks most representative of the "undeserving" (able-bodied) poor in the minds of the whites—despite the fact that only 6 percent of all poor Americans are blacks living in urban ghettos. While students of racial attitudes and antipoverty policy will find these basic findings quite familiar, the illustrative examples provided by Gilens of how, when, and why race shapes and directs Americans' views of welfare, coupled with the prominence that welfare continues to hold in the foreground of policy debates, make this book an important contribution to what has already been written on the subject.

Gilens, however, claims that his contribution lies in the rarely understood finding that, when questioned about the poor in general, white Americans express a willingness to "devote their time and money to charitable causes, they want their government to do more to help the poor, and they consistently express a willingness to pay higher taxes to help poor people and welfare recipients obtain better wages, better housing, medical care, child care, education, and job training." This theme attempts to course its way through the narrative of *Why Americans Hate Welfare*, giving us, ever so slightly, something to feel good about. But if Americans are so benevolent, why, Gilens queries, does the United States consistently rank second to last among affluent industrialized nations in social welfare spending and dead last among 16 nations in overall efforts to reduce poverty through taxation and transfer programs? To answer these questions, Gilens returns to his main thesis: race, as refracted through the prism of the "deserving" and "undeserving" poor is *the* central factor that informs and subsequently sustains white perceptions of welfare recipients and opposition to welfare spending. From beginning to end, it is this theme, and not the discussion of American benevolence, that truly dominates Gilens's story.

Gilens does a yeomanlike job doing what is typical of books in this genre of social science: reviewing prior survey findings and testing competing explanations for Americans' opposition to welfare. We learn that white Americans' cynicism toward welfare recipients, and their specific attitudes toward blacks, are stronger determinants of their opposition to welfare than their feelings of personal self-interest or their commitment to the American ethos of hard work and individual responsibility. These findings are quite consistent with most recent research, but the discussion of the advanced statistics upon which they are based makes large segments of the book less accessible to a general readership.

However, more accessible and atypical is Gilens's analysis of how media images of the poor are produced. Here a content analysis of poverty-related stories on the nightly news of the three major television networks, and three news magazines (*Time*; *Newsweek*; and *U.S. News and World Report*) is buttressed by in-depth interviews with photo editors at these magazines. The findings bring the significance of race to center stage: news professionals have a "tendency to portray the black poor more negatively than the nonblack poor; pictures of poor blacks are abundant when poverty coverage is most negative, while pictures of nonblacks dominate the more sympathetic coverage."

Important parts of Gilens's argument seem tautological and somewhat contradictory at times. We are told that white opposition to welfare does not signal antiblackness per se because human-capital-enhancing programs such as Head Start, job training, welfare-to-work, the minimum wage, and so on all enjoy widespread popular support since they allegedly help the "deserving poor" lift themselves out of poverty. At the same time, it is poor blacks, and not poor whites, who are associated with the "undeserving" poor in the minds of whites. Also, the most infamous human-capital-enhancing program of them all, affirmative action, has generated so much opposition among whites that even black intellectuals have predicted its impending demise. In not readily acknowledging this vicious circle, Gilens fails to offer a way out.

If the American distaste for welfare is based on the faulty equation that welfare equals black equals lazy and undeserving, how then can such perceptions be changed? Equally important, how can welfare and antipoverty policy be deracialized in a way that will make them palatable to the American public? A short section entitled "Policy Implications" derides proponents of race-neutral antipoverty policies (which enjoy some measure of public support), but it falls short in completely answering these questions.

In the end, Gilens shows, perhaps without meaning to do so, that lying dormant between the chasm of "deservingness" and "undeservingness" in the American psyche is the sleeping giant of racism. The racialization of welfare, just like the racialization of affirmative action, suggests that the race card remains an effective tool for generating opposition to social programs designed to assist not only blacks but poor whites, women, and other minorities as well. Beyond the acknowledgment that there are those who abuse the welfare state (both on the individual and corporate level), we are still left with the tired question often observed by students of racial attitudes but woefully abandoned by political leadership: How do we go about changing the grossly exaggerated, deeply held stereotyped impressions of blacks in America? Gilens does not provide an answer to this query, but it is a question that practically leaps off the pages of *Why Americans Hate Welfare*.

RYAN ALAN SMITH

Rutgers University
New Brunswick
New Jersey

HANSON, CHARLES F. 1998. *Necessary Virtue: The Pragmatic Origins of Religious Liberty in New England.* Pp. x,
277. Charlottesville: University Press of Virginia. $35.00.

By standard historical accounts, an unlikely coalition of humanists and evangelicals laid the theoretical groundwork for religious liberty in America. In a fascinating portrait of American pragmatic proclivities, Charles Hanson revises this conventional perspective and supplies a "missing chapter in the history of American religious liberty" by viewing the American Revolution through the lens of Franco-American alliances. Focusing on the New England response to these alliances, Hanson examines the invasion of Quebec in 1775; the formal treaty of 1778, which pledged French monetary and military support; and the legacy of the French presence on American soil. Although traditional religious-political hostilities naturally placed Catholic French and Protestant Americans at odds, Hanson argues that New Englanders willingly jettisoned religious convictions—that is, an intolerant anti-Catholic animus—for pragmatic political considerations. Taking his cue from the philosopher Richard Rorty, he views the French Alliance as an example of American pragmatism driven by the contingency of events.

Throughout his study, Hanson skillfully dissects New England's ambiguous, paradoxical, adaptive, and accommodating responses to the French alliances. How to make despised enemies into tolerable friends? Physical contact is one way, and, indeed, during the Quebec military fiasco, Americans discovered that ordinary Catholics, though duped by papists, were not so repugnant after all. Of course, Tories delighted in exposing the hypocrisy of these Protestants cavorting with "the Whore of Babylon" for political ends. On the Patriot side, attitudes toward French alliances ranged from reluctant, temporary support to gushing Francophilia. Whereas some Patriots feared moral and religious pollution, propagandists defended the French as worthy allies by emphasizing (among other things) the loosening grip of Catholicism in France. For their part, the Congregational clergy expressed similar conflicted responses. Some retained the traditional anti-Catholic posture and viewed the alliance as a precarious gambit, but never to the point of sabotaging the alliance. More overt pro-French clergy resorted to biblical symbolism and portrayed King Louis XVI as the providentially sent King Cyrus, the pagan Persian who protected the Jews.

Hanson suggests that the French Alliance softened hard-line, intolerant attitudes toward Roman Catholicism, split opinions within the Standing Order, weakened the influence of the Congregational establishment, and thus indirectly contributed to religious toleration and eventual religious liberty. However, if the seeds of religious toleration were sown in the rich soil of the French Alliance, they dried up in the suffocating heat of the radical stage of the French Revolution. And so it was that in the early stage of the French Revolution, Ezra Stiles anticipated a coming age of enlightenment and religious freedom, whereas in its bloody, godless aftermath, Timothy Dwight held the French responsible for America's descent into moral and religious turpitude. Dwight's revisionist account won the day, but at the price of obscuring the pragmatic origins of religious liberty in New England.

Although Hanson has uncovered fresh sources and subjects to illumine the contact between two very different cultures, his thesis is not entirely novel. Curiously, he neglects scholars who support his claims. Perry Miller, Sidney Mead, and, more recently, Nathan Hatch have argued that the theoretical contribution of the humanist-evangelical coalition was chronologically prior and hence secondary to pragmatic considerations in advancing Americans toward religious

liberty. To be sure, these scholars ignored the French Alliance as illustrative of this pragmatic bent, and here one must recognize Hanson's original contribution. But the religious accommodation of New Englanders to the French, however exceptional to them, was not unique in a country that had come to accept extraordinary religious diversity by the middle of the eighteenth century. Surely, any discussion of the origins of religious liberty in New England must take note of these broad developments.

In addition, Hanson claims that the Standing Order's divided response to the French Alliance contributed indirectly to religious disestablishment in New England. Perhaps so, but he fails to mention more direct influences. Indeed, theological and ideological fissures within the Congregational establishment, namely, a culture war between evangelicals and liberals—no doubt exacerbated by divided reactions to the French Alliance—contributed decisively to the breakdown of the Standing Order and the eventual separation of church and state.

These reservations aside, *Necessary Virtue* is a valuable contribution to a rich body of literature on religion and politics during the American Revolution. Thanks to this work, "Yankee pragmatism" has wider application.

DAVID W. KLING

University of Miami
Coral Gables
Florida

HERO, RODNEY E. 1998. *Faces of Inequality: Social Diversity in American Politics.* Pp. vii, 192. New York: Oxford University Press.

Rodney Hero continues to perform a valuable service by calling the profession's attention to the role that minorities play in state politics. His 1998 book builds upon his earlier work, *Latinos and the U.S. Political System: Two-Tiered Pluralism* (1992) and recent journal articles, but it also expands the focus to consider several types of diversity. Hero's measure of minority diversity includes the proportion of blacks, Latinos, and Asians in a state; his white ethnic diversity measure encompasses Southern and Eastern European populations. States that have relatively high proportions of both populations are referred to as "heterogeneous"; states with large minority populations and few white ethnics are termed "bifurcated." States with neither— those populated mainly by whites from Northern and Western Europe—are labeled "homogeneous." These differences in social complexity are important explanations for state differences in political institutions, processes, and policies, Hero argues.

In this book's early pages, Hero compares his social diversity framework with extant political culture frameworks such as that by Daniel Elazar, noting that whereas Elazar's categories are fixed according to earlier migration streams, his own demarcations change as current migration patterns change. Indeed, one of the book's most valuable contributions is Table 1.1, which lists each state's score on the two diversity indices for the year 1990. Other scholars can now incorporate Hero's measures into their own research, just as many state politics scholars have done with Elazar's demarcations.

Having developed and justified his measures, Hero's own use of them is less successful. Subsequent chapters of the book examine various explanatory factors commonly used in state politics research, beginning with political process variables such as voter turnout, party competition, ideology, and interest group strength. Next Hero tries to explain differences in state governmental institutions on the basis of current diversity differences. He does not have much success, presumably because states set up their institutions long before 1990 population patterns came about. The bulk of the chapters focus on public policy; social diversity reasons better explain majority-minority gaps in social policy outcomes than levels of average policy outcomes. Such gaps have been too long ignored by other scholars in state public policy.

However, in the empirical chapters, too often a relationship is asserted on the basis of a scattergram of minority diversity by some factor plus noting the bivariate correlation in the text. When multivariate results are included, the coefficients are cited in the text without a table giving the complete information that other scholars need to interpret the results. Alternatively, when tables are used, they report only a plus or minus for the relationship instead of stating the values of the coefficients and the size of the standard errors. These omissions were quite deliberate in that Hero explained his purpose was to emphasize the "forest" rather than the "trees." However, I think most scholars will not want to accept this summary as scientific evidence. They will want to subject the social diversity measures to empirical scrutiny themselves before accepting his arguments. Fortunately, Hero has provided the state-by-state data so that others can build upon his intriguing work. Many state politics scholars will want to read this book.

VIRGINIA GRAY

University of Minnesota
Minneapolis

PENNOCK, ROBERT T. 1999. *Tower of Babel: The Evidence Against the New Creationism.* Pp. ix, 429. Cambridge: MIT Press. $35.00.

The Scopes Monkey Trial was held back in 1925. On that celebrated occasion, a young schoolteacher, John T. Scopes, put himself up to be prosecuted for having supposedly taught his students in high school that humans are descended from apes. Prosecuted by three-time presidential candidate William Jennings Bryan and defended by noted attorney and free thinker Clarence Darrow, Scopes was indeed found guilty as charged. He was fined $100, although on appeal, thanks to a technicality, the conviction was squashed.

Since then, creationism—the claim that the true story of origins is to be found in the early chapters of Genesis—has had a somewhat varied fortune. It peaked in 1981, when the state of Arkansas passed a law mandating the teaching of creationism alongside evolution in the state schools. The law was thrown out as unconstitutional, but in the last decade of the twentieth century we have seen a real resurgence of the doctrine. Interestingly, the new creationists (as one might call them) are an altogether different breed from the people who supported Bryan: many are drawn from the best universities and often come with impressive credentials. Particularly noteworthy are the Berkeley lawyer Phillip Johnson and America's leading philosopher of religion, Notre Dame–based Alvin Plantinga.

I am not sure that one would want to say that the new creationists have better scientific arguments. In fact, it would be hard to claim that they do since creationism is so obviously false. However, they do have much more sophisticated wrappings and now make much appeal to supposedly philosophical and like arguments. It is therefore very welcome news that the bright young philosopher of science Robert Pennock (who is, incidentally, a practicing Christian) has taken up the whole evolution-creationism debate. In *Tower of Babel*, he examines in great detail all of the arguments pro and con showing unambiguously how truly inadequate and, in many respects, unsavory is the case being made for the new creationism.

The work starts with a brief history of the creationism controversy. We then go on to a good and useful discussion of evolutionary theory. This is a very helpful overview and can in many respects stand on its own. We move on next to questions of language and the way in which evolution throws light on the development of language (and, incidentally, gives this book its title). From there we go to sections that I find particularly interesting as Pennock takes on the whole Johnson-Plantinga argument about the so-called philosophical underpinnings of evolutionary thought and its apparent atheistic naturalism. Pennock has little trouble showing how Johnson particularly conflates various senses of naturalism and comes up with the kind of conclusions that he wants.

We then move on to some of the alternative views being pushed by the creationists. In particular, there is very good criticism by Pennock of the so-called design arguments of people like Michael Behe (which Behe put forward in his best-selling *Darwin's Black Box*). Next comes consideration of the important issues underlying the creationist attack, showing how people like Johnson are not so much interested in some of the details of the scientific argument but feel that there are broader moral and social factors at work here. In other words, the creationist critique is an attack on modernism generally and not just on one particular area of science. This revelation leads naturally to Pennock's final topic, where we look at some issues to do with science education, showing that good science education does not mean offering every possible view that anybody has ever held at any time and purveying it indifferently. Good science education requires selection, offering students the best of what the scientific community has to offer.

This is a long book and detailed. It will take some considerable time to read, particularly for those who are not philosophically or scientifically trained. However, all who are concerned about this topic—and, indeed, we should all be concerned about this topic—should study this book with some care. There is much to be learned, and there is a very real threat out there, as Pennock convincingly demonstrates. What he also does is give us a very effective tool for rebuttal.

MICHAEL RUSE

University of Guelph
Ontario
Canada

VIGIL, ERNESTO B. 1999. *The Crusade for Justice: Chicano Militancy and the Government's War on Dissent.* Pp. xii, 487. Madison: University of Wisconsin Press. $60.00. Paperbound, $24.95.

This work is three books in one. The volume is more about Chicano militancy and the government's war on dissent than on the Crusade for Justice, an important community-based organization in Denver, Colorado, during the Chicano struggle for civil rights between 1962 and 1987 in that state. In 1987, the Crusade for Justice building was sold, and its founder suffered an automobile accident that left him with permanent disabilities. The Crusade for Justice ceased to exist in its physical location, and it was leaderless.

This work is also a book about the travails of the author beginning in 1968 as a member of the Crusade. In the opening chapters, Vigil provides an insider's view of the workings of the Crusade and a short biographical sketch of its founder, Rodolfo "Corky" Gonzales. In the preface,

Vigil writes, "When I decided in 1980 someday to write the history of the Crusade for Justice, it was already evident that its decline was inevitable." Unfortunately, Vigil did not fully describe or analyze the demise of the organization or its leader in these pages. The biographies of the Crusade and Corky Gonzales will have to wait for other researchers. Most assuredly, these future students will profit immensely from what Vigil has produced by obtaining government documents through the Freedom of Information Act and from similar research done by others.

The area of government surveillance of Chicano groups and leaders, particularly by counterintelligence programs, has been grossly neglected by social scientists, among others. Often, social scientists have found it more convenient and facile to find fault with the organizations and leaders of the Chicano group than to probe into the government's complicity in disruption, harassment, cover-up, character assassination, and violence directed at these organizations and leaders. Vigil, in this pioneering work, methodically builds his case that the government, particularly the Federal Bureau of Investigation and local police, waged a war against the Crusade and its members. Chapter by chapter, he amply documents that war through successive battles, such as the Poor People's Campaign; the school protests and youth conferences held in Denver; the antiwar moratorium in East Los Angeles; community control of local parks in Denver; collaboration with Reies Lopez Tijerina's land recovery movement in New Mexico; and La Raza Unida Party. He also documents the government's interest in the relations between the Crusade and its members and black nationalists, the American Indian Movement, and the Puerto Rican nationalists.

As a participant in much of the Crusade activity that he depicts and as an emerging scholar in the decade of the 1990s, Vigil has been able to decipher the alphabet soup of government spy agency acronyms. He goes so far as to link government surveillance programs with the document file numbers of the specific Chicano groups or persons being investigated. The documentation in the notes is extensive, and many of the notes are as rich in detail as the actual text, if not richer (see, for example, p. 444, n. 30).

This book is must reading for those interested in government surveillance of domestic groups and, more broadly, public policy and ethnic groups, the nation-state and minority groups, Chicano studies, and intergroup relations during the civil rights era.

JOSE ANGEL GUTIERREZ

University of Texas
Arlington

SOCIOLOGY

ARNEIL, BARBARA. 1999. *Politics and Feminism*. Pp. vi, 284. Oxford, UK: Blackwell. Paperbound, $29.95.

In *Politics and Feminism*, Barbara Arneil successfully describes the intersections of feminism and politics, including the political bases of feminism, and summarizes the history of American feminism in the late nineteenth and early twentieth centuries. Her goal is to show that politics—here understood as Western political theory—reflect gender imbalance and that feminism—through different eras—has resisted this imbalance in various ways. In the end, Arneil stresses that diversity, a diverse range of viewpoints, must characterize both politics and feminism if we social animals are to thrive.

Indicative of the clear style Arneil uses to present her ideas and conclusions, she begins in chapter 1 with definitions of "politics" and "feminism." Acknowledging that one current difficulty in the feminist movement is the broad or changing definition of "feminism," Arneil defines it as "the recognition that, virtually across time and place, men and women are unequal in the power they have, either in society or over their own lives, and the corollary belief that men and women should be equal; the belief that knowledge has been written about, by and for men, and the corollary belief that all schools of knowledge must be re-examined and understood to reveal the extent to which they ignore or distort gender." This "pinning down" of feminism, in contrast to trends in the last twenty years to break feminism into numerous schools of thought, is the first indication that Arneil will move away from relying on multiple feminisms to solve the many problems of the world, and instead proffer one ideology that can incorporate the extant diversity of women, issues, cultures, contexts, and politics.

A second indication of Arneil's dissatisfaction with the feminism of the 1960s, 1970s, and 1980s (which may be referred to as second-wave feminism) is her attack on the culture-nature and private-public dualisms. She contends that for feminism to focus on and try to rehabilitate these dualisms is misguided, for the dualisms themselves are the products of patriarchal Western political thought. Arneil suggests that instead of working with these categories, feminists should begin anew by recognizing the diversity inherent in our world and that people and ideas cannot be compartmentalized so easily. Therefore, Arneil moves to a thoughtful discussion of what is now termed third-wave feminism, which has at its core "the deconstruction of dualistic theoretical frameworks." Third-wave feminism rejects dualities that imply that "there must be an 'other' against which the reference point, concept or perspective is defined. Third wave feminism(s) take (a) new perspective(s): beginning with 'women's' points of view, this new wave embraces the diversity and differences in perspectives among 'women.' "

This discussion of third-wave feminism is the most enlightening aspect of Arneil's text. She identifies the problems in using terms such as "liberal feminism" or "Marxist feminism" that not only make feminism dependent upon political theories but also fracture feminism so that nonfeminists may not even understand the basic goal of feminism. Arneil urges us feminists to join together in third-wave feminism, worrying less about the differences in opinion between us and focusing more on the original task of feminism: eradicating the oppression of women.

This book, due to its clear style and organization and comprehensive bibliography, will be an excellent resource for undergraduate students and scholars focusing on feminism at the end of the twentieth century. Arneil succeeds in summarizing the feminist movement of the nineteenth and twentieth centuries, while also pointing us in the direction of the future, toward a unified feminism celebrating its diversity.

ROSEMARIE TONG

University of North Carolina
Charlotte

GAMSON, JOSHUA. 1998. *Freaks Talk Back: Tabloid Talk Shows and Sexual Nonconformity*. Pp. xi, 288. Chicago: University of Chicago Press. $22.00.

In the debate over the moral and social consequences of tabloid talk shows, *Freaks Talk Back* offers an engaging analysis of the changing presence of gender and sexuality as part of these productions. Sudden media visibility for gay men, lesbians, bisexuals, and transsexuals occurs within a flamboyantly scripted entertainment product pursuing moments of spectacle while persevering and protecting traditional gender norms. Gamson follows the work of authors such as Vicki Abt, whose assessment of the cultural significance of talk shows demonstrates the network of political and social interests that influence the production. The book also supplements the literature on gender and sexuality in popular culture and the current social and historical analysis of these groups.

A departure from the usual inadequate representation, the dramatic materialization of gays, transsexuals, and bisexuals on talk shows was initially regarded with excitement. Investigation of the talk show industry and interviews and focus groups with viewers, guests, and gay and lesbian activists reveal conflicting agendas, most significantly an incompatibility between the talk show genre and the interests of the gay community. Colorful stories about recruiting guests, backstage coaching to create outrageous dramas, and an industry shift targeting urban, nonwhite, and poorer populations are dissected to present the use of transsexuals and bisexuals as an object of curiosity and a means of entertainment. While Gamson's portrait of a carnival atmosphere indicates the limitations of accurate representation of any group, it also demonstrates how the show and audience employ heterosexual norms to restrict and control non-heterosexual behavior and its form. Most disturbing is the coupling of gays, transsexuals, and bisexuals with violent and vulgar topics, which Gamson proves attaches a stigma to the group—standing in center ring in a poor person's circus is unflattering and damaging. Central to the study is an analysis of the audience members, a role the author periodically took on. At their most benign moments, the spectators are depicted as clashing with anti-gay guests. However, when faced with confusion over nontraditional gender and sexuality roles and forms, the crowd reasserts the gay-straight dichotomy, ultimately for the protection of heterosexuality. "Can you guess" exhibitions of transgendered individuals nourish the audience's convictions. The union of audience and production interests, framed by the foundation of spectacle, encourages further disturbing structures. This seemingly liberal soundstage, with its young and diverse staff and audience, erects ridged boundaries; through talk show choreography, bisexuals and transsexuals are judged promiscuous, deceitful, and morally suspect. Aroused by the new opportunities for visibility, gay and transsexual leaders plot and secretly conspire to use the shows for activist work, sometimes successfully tricking staff. Fettered by the lack of true voices available on the shows, gay, bisexual, and transsexual representatives become either unwilling "freaks" in the performance or silenced. This is a complex process, which Gamson untangles; media visibility for gays and other non-heterosexual individuals is exploited, with disfiguring results. Alarmed by stereotypes, "freak" treatment, and class boundaries, gays, transsexuals, and bisexuals are impeded from forming advantageous alliances and from having healthy representation.

Drawing in virtually every important player in the talk show industry, Gamson creates a rich and exhaustive study. Interviews and focus groups provide in-depth perspectives but omit any significant discussion of how the author positioned himself within these dialogues. Jerry Springer's circus of midgets, Klansmen, and transsexuals is often easily dismissed by critics as television waste. *Freaks Talk Back* is a provocative uncloaking of resistance to gayness and the dilemma of media visibility. As Gamson illustrates, ignoring "trash TV" is dangerous in that it risks surrendering power in the political battle over ownership of public space.

AIMEE DELMAN

Syracuse University
New York

SCHNEIDER, BARBARA and DAVID STEVENSON. 1999. *The Ambitious Generation: America's Teenagers, Motivated but Directionless.* Pp. xiii, 321. New Haven, CT: Yale University Press. $26.00.

Barbara Schneider and David Stevenson have written an important book about adolescent development. They show that, contrary to popular perception, America's teenagers are highly ambitious (for example, over 90 percent expect to attend college). Why do so many fail to reach their lofty goals?

Using a seamless integration of qualitative and quantitative data from the Alfred P. Sloan Study of Youth and Social Development—one of the most comprehensive studies of adolescents in the 1990s—Schneider and Stevenson suggest that many adolescents have ambitions that are not realistically connected to specific educational and career paths. In other words, teenagers may be motivated, but many do not possess the kind of information that would provide them with direction and meaningful feedback.

The key distinction explored in the book is "aligned" versus "misaligned" ambitions. Adolescents with aligned ambitions have educational expectations that are consistent with their occupational aspirations. In traditional sociological models, these two variables are often used separately to predict social mobility. Because both have become skewed in a positive direction (that is, this generation of teenagers has such high educational and occupation goals), Schneider and Stevenson introduce the concept of alignment and look at the relationship between the dimensions of educational expectation and occupational aspiration. Students who under- or overestimate the amount of education needed for their desired occupation are classified as misaligned. Students with aligned ambitions, on the other hand, know what type of job they want, and they know the steps they need to take in order to get it. They have a richer and more detailed understanding of the world of work and the educational pathways to achieve their goals.

Unfortunately, more than half of teenagers (56 percent) have misaligned ambitions—they can be called "drifting dreamers." A number of findings from the study demonstrate that these teenagers are at a disadvantage when competing for desired educational and work opportunities. For instance, they are less likely to construct a life plan that can chart their course for success. Life plans provide an orientation to the future and a sense of order. They help teenagers to see the historical context more realistically, use their time and effort wisely, weigh alternatives and evaluate feedback from their actions, and take advantage of familial, school, and community resources.

Schneider and Stevenson are not content to document the problem, however. They present detailed case studies of familial and school contexts that facilitate or hinder the formation of aligned ambitions. They contrast the challenges that contemporary adolescents face by presenting case studies of teenagers who came of age in the 1950s. They were able to accomplish this fascinating juxtaposition by tracking down, in the University of Chicago's Regenstein Library, the original source materials from Robert V.

Havighurst's landmark study of adolescents in "River City." This extra effort pays off in a highly readable account that brings to life historical changes in school curriculum and organization, the family, adolescent friendship patterns, and the organization of the economy. Summaries at the ends of the chapters are full of good advice about how school and family contexts must take seriously the task of helping to guide adolescents toward their goals. Schools, for instance, might focus on creating internships with community organizations. Internships provide an insider's look at particular occupations. Parents, especially, have a vital role to play. By communicating often, providing resources, and creating a personally supportive and intellectually challenging environment, parents help teenagers recognize their strengths and weaknesses and create the life plans they need for eventual success.

An important dimension of this book, one that should get the attention of social scientists, educators, and others interested in social and educational policy, is that the distinction between aligned versus misaligned ambitions cuts across boys and girls and all racial and ethnic groups. That is, connecting dreams or ambitions with realistic information is a strength that can facilitate the efforts of all teenagers, not just a select and advantaged few. In fact, adolescents whose parents had high levels of education (more than a college degree) tended to have misaligned ambitions; that is, they expected to obtain more education than was typically required for their occupational choice.

Finally, it is worth noting that Schneider and Stevenson do not suggest that teenagers with aligned ambitions have all the answers they will ever need. On the contrary, life plans inevitably change. The authors argue, instead, that operating with a realistic plan exercises skills of choice and evaluation that are essential for cultivating one's path in life. Insights such as these make this a timely book that should be read by anyone who is interested in adolescent development.

KEVIN R. RATHUNDE

University of Utah
Salt Lake City

SICK, DEBORAH. 1999. *Farmers of the Golden Bean: Costa Rican Households and the Global Coffee Economy.* Pp. xx, 169. DeKalb: Northern Illinois University Press. No price.

In this succinct and intriguing monograph on a contemporary coffee-farming area of relatively recent settlement in southern Costa Rica, Deborah Sick brings to bear both anthropological theory and detailed oral testimony to explore the past, present, and future of farming households. The strengths and contributions of this brief work are many and include the following. By using theoretical works most often focused on Asian or African cases of householder agriculture, Sick, curiously and counterintuitively perhaps, actually gets closer to her subject than she would have if she had relied for theory or comparison primarily on the coffee in Latin America literature so long committed to Costa Rican exceptionalism as a framing device. She avoids any linear assumptions about agrarian class structure so typical of much of the earlier debates in the Latin Americanist literature on (semi-)proletarianization. Her analysis of gender and household as they intersect with labor, land ownership, inheritance, and labor migration patterns is very revealing. Finally, she reports not only on the dominance of petty property holders' values and aspirations among the local population but also on the strikingly Costa Rican phenomenon of leadership and civic standing among the poor and those not yet, if ever, benefiting directly from the values of the "Yeoman's Republic" and self-help so deeply imbedded in the collective imagination.

Weaknesses of the analysis are far fewer than its strengths, but at least two areas deserve mention here. For a study so heavily based on oral testimony in a region of post-1940s colonization, there is surprisingly little on the early history of the cooperative movement, which is so critical to the region's coffee-producing households and their history. Moreover, the much more abundant material offered on the contemporary role of the co-op and its processing and marketing facilities can be faulted both for seeming to assume that earlier patterns of conflict and challenges from private processing firms were similar to today's and for not going far enough in analyzing today's competition. Conflict in the 1950s and 1960s was over the very existence and financing via state banks of co-op processing plants and production credit, quite different from client and price competition in the 1980s and 1990s, when their existence was no longer politically contestable. Indeed, the crisis of the late 1980s did not threaten the existence of the coffee production co-ops precisely because they had been the beneficiaries of nearly three decades of substantial public investment and preferential finance.

Today the radical redefinition of processor and price competition (what Jeffery Paige calls the emergence of the "mega-processors," the Peters company locally) in peripheral and formerly inaccessible regions is, as Sick so clearly shows, the single most visible consequence of the price collapse of the late 1980s. If these processes are so clearly crucial for Costa Rica's coffee-farming households and their future, then one could only wish that this study of the pivotal case of its southern coffee frontier might have given us even greater detail to work with on this score. Sick's finding that producers of all sizes and political backgrounds seek to diversify their potential processing outlets/buyers is an important one. But an even more important question is what will be needed to ensure that oligopoly and price fixing, the very pattern that led to the formation of the co-ops in the 1950s and 1960s, not reemerge in the hands of either a private cartel or a confiscatory state–co-op alliance. The early co-ops worked their magic not by monopolizing the activity but by ensuring a competitive alternative under producer control. Any statist monopoly, however unlikely in current circumstances or justified in response to some hypothetical future cartel formation, would almost inevitably repeat the very same mistake of noncompetitive practices, with potentially devastating consequences for coffee and for the households that produce it.

Farmers of the Golden Bean will not disappoint readers interested in theorizing the household in market agriculture and the global economy. Nor, happily, will it disappoint those looking for the flavor of San Isidro del General and its coffee-farming village pioneers.

LOWELL GUDMUNDSON

Mount Holyoke College
South Hadley
Massachusetts

TOLBERT, LISA C. 1999. *Constructing Townscapes: Space and Society in Antebellum Tennessee.* Pp. xvii, 294. Chapel Hill: University of North Carolina Press. $49.95. Paperbound, $19.95.

Constructing Townscapes represents something of a tour de force, arguing aggressively for the crucial significance of the small town in the social history of the American South, the special value of spatial study in community history, and the benefits of including building chronology within the purview of urban history. It reflects current scholarly interest in stressing geographical space, gender, and race in community study, delivered under a voguish title obeying today's gerundial imperatives.

The study examines four county seat towns in central Tennessee (Columbia, Franklin, Murfreesboro, and Shelbyville, all south of Nashville) from the 1790s to the outbreak of the Civil War. Towns like these were indeed the quintessential and ubiquitous commercial and public anchors of an agrarian antebellum South. The book contains six chapters grouped in two parts, the first dealing with the collective physical growth of the towns, and the second with selected daily life experiences within them.

The towns passed through three general growth phases: implantation (1790-1825), filling out (1819-49), and rebuilding (1850-61). Using primitive maps, photographs of individual buildings, and imaginatively interwoven descriptive archival materials, Tolbert presents an engaging if unsystematic impression of the spatial history of the towns, emphasizing their central courthouse squares, their Main Streets, and the appearance of small colleges on their fringes. The visual focus on individual buildings rather than streetscapes limits the reader's grasp of the townscapes as wholes, but the presentation of particularistic information about one town or another does nevertheless highlight general processes in these towns' evolving built environments. Creative use of a house builder's memoir provides fascinating detail of town housing viewed from a producer's perspective.

For Tolbert, reconstructing this evolution is largely prelude to an exploration of daily life within town space, which she explores in three very selective dimensions: that of adolescent women of good class (whose diaries and letters chronicled their daily movements); that of adolescent men, seen principally through the eyes of a well-born store clerk; and that of domestic slaves, focused dramatically through the legal prism of a slave convicted of murder. These chapters provide clear evidence of the separate ways in which young men, young women, and slaves made use of town space and were influenced by it, especially their varying degrees of social autonomy.

The slave chapter is by far the most comprehensive and persuasive. Missing, of course, in a research design such as this, is a broader sense of inclusive family life, the action spaces of the community decision makers, and interclass dynamics in general. Tolbert chooses rather to stress the fragmented layering in town space of her chosen subjects. This is a history of some socially isolated elements in these towns, rather than of the community as a holistically functioning unit.

For readers who have not previously considered the built environment's role in social history, this study makes an attractive case for doing so. For readers interested in the historical complexities of actual townscapes, it offers incomplete description rather than new concepts. For example, both men's and women's colleges in these towns were peripheral, and their locations can be more fully explained (given their space needs) as contributing to incipient urban fringe belt formation, rather than resulting from gender sensibilities. Furthermore, an intriguing map showing the plan morphology of Columbia in 1852 suggests numerous townscape features never investigated in the work. Research into real estate activity and deeper cartographic analysis would greatly improve the understanding of these townscapes. In the main, however, Tolbert has written a provocative and valuable study of small-town space and society, with

special significance for the settlement history of the South.

MICHAEL P. CONZEN

University of Chicago
Illinois

VALIAN, VIRGINIA. 1998. *Why So Slow? The Advancement of Women.* Pp. xvii, 401. Cambridge: MIT Press. Paperbound, $17.50.

Despite historical gains, a glass ceiling still appears to hold women back from full economic, social, and political equality. Virginia Valian's book *Why So Slow?* tackles the problem of making the transparent glass visible and then sets out to show us how to remove it pane by pane.

The invisible obstacle to women's progress, according to Valian—and backed up by the scores of studies on which her book is based—is the effects of nonconscious gender schemas. These often unacknowledged assumptions about gender create differential treatment of boys and girls, men and women, beginning with the first day of their lives. The argument that people treat males and females differently due to gender stereotypes is a reasonable and familiar assertion. But Valian's analysis is not the same basic story found in every women's studies text. Valian shows that the gaps between men's and women's achievement can be explained by the accumulated effects of seemingly infinitesimal differences in the way males and females are perceived and treated (for example, perceptions of leaders, nonverbal reactions, tolerance of inequity in housework). Valian persuasively argues that these many small gender biases add up to large disadvantages for women relative to men in the realm of professional and economic achievement. Thus, even when obvious impediments (such as exclusion from networking at all-male clubs, hostile coworkers) are absent, women's achievement does not equal that of men.

Valian's book offers a rigor that is missing in much of women's studies literature regarding women's achievement. Perhaps because of her background in cognitive psychology, Valian has taken the unusual steps of relying only upon solid empirical evidence (using especially reliable meta-analysis results when possible) and using anecdote to illustrate rather than make points, staying aware of the strength of nonconscious assumptions and avoiding the logical fallacy that large effects must have large causes.

This book makes a unique contribution to understanding women's and men's achievement because it explains that, however devastating and debilitating exposure to sexual harassment or blatant gender discrimination may be for the individual, seemingly minor biases are more important in explaining why the progress of women as a group has been slower than many expected. Unlike overt sexism, absolutely no one has escaped the experiences reviewed by Valian (if you think there are exceptions, you need to read this book). Furthermore, the biases produced by nonconscious gender schemas are insidiously difficult to detect and often perpetuated unknowingly, even by men and women with egalitarian attitudes.

Valian concludes, "Fairness requires a more sophisticated understanding of social perception [knowledge of social and cognitive psychology] than most of us acquire in the ordinary course of life." At the end of her book, she offers concrete remedies that, like the arguments in her book, are not the "same old same old." Her remedies are grounded in the empirical studies cited throughout the book and, if implemented, could end the apparent stall in the progress of women. Part of the battle may be convincing people that these remedies are important; they are not as flashy as focusing on blatant discrimination or sexual harassment.

Why So Slow? is comparable to *The Mismeasure of Woman* by psychologist Carol Tavris in that it sums up a huge body of research in a no-nonsense, engaging style that is objective but passionate and personal. Yet there is only a small overlap in content between the two books. Both books are also accessible to a wide audience, including students in social science and women's studies courses.

LORI J. NELSON

Shippensburg University
Pennsylvania

WAIN, MARTIN. 1998. *Freud's Answer: The Social Origins of Our Psychoanalytic Century.* Pp. xv, 366. Chicago: Ivan R. Dee. $28.95.

The reader of *Freud's Answer* is confronted by 13 epigraphs before reaching the first chapter. This profusion exemplifies both the undeniable virtues and even more conspicuous limitations of Martin Wain's book. One, 2, even 3 epigraphs might whet the appetite for a feast to come. Thirteen are indigestible and cloying.

Freud's Answer is erudite, intellectually ambitious, and clearly written. It contains much that is thought provoking, particularly a discussion of the religious dimensions of Freud's thought. Nonetheless, Wain cannot be said to have achieved his aim. The problem is by no means that he is too critical of Freud but, rather, that the analytical instruments he wields are too blunt to perform the task of dissection successfully.

As his subtitle indicates, Wain seeks to elucidate the "social origins" of psychoanalysis. This leads him to open his book with two brief chapters that sketch the impact of the French and the Industrial Revolutions on the modern world. The modern world is contrasted with a vision of "the world we have lost" extrapolated from Peter Laslett. Although Wain does not make factual errors, he relies on potted summaries that perforce oversimplify the complex phenomena they purport to describe. Thus a citation from the 1644 *Shorter Catechism* is held to prove that "all knew their place" and to exemplify the "formula" "Take degree away,/ Untune that string,/And hark what discord follows." One would scarcely guess from this that mid-seventeenth-century England was a period of upheaval that, like the French Revolution, culminated in a regicide. Wain appeals to the same passage in *Troilus and Cressida* adduced by E.M.W. Tillyard as the epitome of the "Elizabethan World Picture," but scholars have long recognized that Ulysses' speech on order is a rhetorical performance that does not reflect the range of beliefs actually held in Shakespeare's time, let alone Cromwell's.

Beyond the hackneyed nature of Wain's historical schema, there is the problem that, in his view, "middle-class culture" suffices to explain Freud's thought. He writes in the last chapter, "Freud was a capsule of the culture, not a shaper of it in his time; it shaped him to be its messenger." But to say this of Freud is as reductive as it would be to say of Shakespeare that his art is the product of social determinants. There is no room in Wain's theoretical framework, which is built on a Foucauldian scaffolding, for the genius of the individual artist or thinker or, indeed, for individual experience of any kind. Against the backdrop of Wain's "twin revolutions," psychoanalysis becomes no more than "a vast transference of the social onto the personal," and "Freud's relationship with his father (or anyone's relationship with one's father)

is a mere detail within this theme, which was world-historical in its significance."

Ironically, despite his antipathy to Freudianism, Wain's social determinism leads him to mimic its most dubious tendencies. Every psychoanalytic concept is provided with a "decoded meaning," as the lesson of the Oedipus myth is said to be that "the twin revolutions placed a burden upon all." Although Wain dismisses Freud's theory of neurosis, he believes that it has a "historical parallel" in the advent of psychoanalysis: "After the fall of the old world there was a 'latency' period during which all the ills of the twin revolutions accumulated, until the fin de siècle when Freud developed his theory." Intending to write a critique of Freud for "composing cultural fantasies," Wain lapses into inadvertent parody.

PETER L. RUDNYTSKY

University of Florida
Gainesville

ECONOMICS

WONG, KENMAN L. 1999. *Medicine and the Marketplace: The Moral Dimensions of Managed Care.* Pp. viii, 219. Notre Dame, IN: University of Notre Dame Press. $32.00.

Americans are anxious about their health care. We find ourselves offered managed care organizations (MCOs) as our only choice for health care by employers desperate to reduce fringe benefit costs. Managed care history and theory may promise cost-effective services to large populations (Robert H. Miller and Harold S. Luft, "Does Managed Care Lead to Better or Worse Quality of Care?" *Health Affairs* 16:18 [1997]), but as consumers we worry that we can no longer trust our physicians to be our exclusive agents and advocates. We worry that our physicians are constrained by outside rules and reviewers, and we fear substandard care and limits on our access to needed specialists and the best hospitals (George Anders, *Health Against Wealth* [New York: Houghton Mifflin, 1996]; for a critique of Anders's book, see the review by Robert J. Samuelson in the *New York Times Book Review*, 24 Nov. 1996). Some of our anxiety is justifiable, given excessive cost-cutting by market-driven plans.

Politicians find easy prey in the environment created by these anxieties. In every state legislature and in the U.S. Congress, we see the spectacle of rapid-fire legislation to counter the perceived abuses of managed care: limits on hospitalization for childbirth or mastectomy treatment time; denial of experimental treatment for desperate cancer patients; limits on choice of specialists not in an MCO's panel. Yet managed care has in reality been one rational response to the high level of health care spending in this country. America for decades spent considerably more per capita on health care than other industrialized countries. Spending on health care was growing at almost 12 percent per year between 1966 and 1993. By 1996, the growth rate had slowed to 5 percent (Katherine R. Levit, Helen Lazenby, Bradley R. Braden, and the National Health Accounts Team, "National Health Spending Trends in 1996," *Health Affairs* 17:36 [1998]). MCOs became the major institutions for American health care delivery because they succeeded in slowing health care cost inflation (Timothy N. Troy, "Does Managed Care Work?" *Managed Healthcare* 6:25 [July 1996]). They achieved this by inflicting pain: extracting a discount from physicians, who often reduced their fees by 40 percent to 70 percent to be part of managed care networks; reducing hospitalization rates and lengths of stay; and restricting patients' choices.

Kenman Wong's book, *Medicine and the Marketplace*, offers a refreshing ethical analysis of health care delivery and managed care in particular. Wong makes a good case for the morality of managed care. He offers a moral topology of perspectives on medicine and managed care by dividing the world of health reformers into patient-centered purists, market reform purists, and explicit rationers. Wong begins by disabusing the reader of the view of the patient-centered purist that the world of health care can be divided into the pre-managed-care era of patient-centered physician altruism and the new corrupt world of corporate profit seeking that sacrifices patients to profit. He writes, "Medicine has always been about someone's financial gain. . . . To some degree, medicine has always been a commodity. Unlike priests, physicians certainly do not take a vow of poverty and are usually very well compensated for their work." Under the fee-for-service model, severe financial conflicts of interest existed for medical professionals: kickbacks from hospitals, fee splitting, and patterns of self-referral. Current federal anti-kickback laws and fraud and abuse rules are designed to police such conflicts of interest, on the assumption that such behavior costs us money without giving us any benefits. Wong is clearly correct that factors other than medical need can influence medical decision making. He also reminds us that fee-for-service medicine may serve a given patient well, but its inherent inflationary pressures cause rising costs, limiting access to uninsured citizens.

Managed care is usually unfairly blamed when care is withheld. Wong's market reform purists are critical of both fee-for-service medicine and managed care. They want patients to be informed consumers. Medical savings accounts (MSAs) are their devices of choice to give patients direct financial incentives to be cost conscious. Wong's critique of MSAs is thorough. Only the sickest will be harmed, as only those who are less likely to be sick will use MSAs.

The explicit rationers want more democratic participation in the rationing of scarce medical resources. They do not want physicians to make implicit bedside rationing decisions. Wong notes, however, that

from the sheer volume of medical decisions alone, it would be impossible for community members to establish standards to provide clear guidance for each situation. Even if all situations could be ranked, medicine changes at such a rapid rate due to technology that these priorities for treatment would probably be obsolete before they were issued. (90)

He contends that implicit rationing through managed care arrangements is better than explicit rationing and that the physician is simply the best rationer in many cases.

Wong then analyzes the ethical significance of the dichotomy of nonprofit versus profit in health care, arguing that the differences between for-profits and nonprofits are not substantial. For-profit MCOs may need regulation, but both forms "are in need of a moral framework that binds them to serve patient and societal interests." In chapter 8, Wong draws on business ethics to propose that "an enlightened business model has significant advantages over a traditional medical model, especially when the fiscal constraints of the new health care environment are taken into account." He then argues that we should recognize and develop the concept of stakeholder, demanding that the community, patients, and employers each have distinct obligations.

This book is provocative reading, particularly for those who have been seduced by the rhetorical arguments and the horror stories offered by critics of managed care. Wong's application of principles of business ethics enriches our understanding of the new world of corporate health care. His development of these ethical obligations in his final chapter offers a convincing argument that health care work is more ethically complicated than attacks from the media and others suggest. He reminds us that regardless of the form of the institution delivering health care, we must develop a framework of ethical obligations for the stakeholders in its delivery.

BARRY R. FURROW

Widener University
Wilmington
Delaware

OTHER BOOKS

ABU-ODEH, ADNAN. 1999. *Jordanians, Palestinians and the Hashemite Kingdom in the Middle East Peace Process.* Pp. xviii, 322. Washington, DC: United States Institute of Peace Press. Paperbound, no price.

AKIRA, NISHIGAKI and SHIMOMURA YASUTAMI. 1998. *The Economics of Development Assistance: Japan's ODA in a Symbiotic World.* Pp. xi, 317. Tokyo: LTCB International Library Foundation. No price.

ALFRED, TAIAIAKE. 1999. *Peace Power Righteousness: An Indigenous Manifesto.* Pp. xxvi, 174. New York: Oxford University Press. Paperbound, $19.95.

BAHGAT, GAWDAT. 1999. *The Persian Gulf at the Dawn of the New Millennium.* Pp. vii, 167. Commack, NY: Nova Science. No price.

BARUAH, SANJIB. 1999. *India Against Itself: Assam and the Politics of Nationality.* Pp. xxiv, 257. Philadelphia: University of Pennsylvania Press. $36.50.

BUTTENWIESER, ANN L. 1987. *Manhattan Water-Bound: Manhattan's Waterfront from the Seventeenth Century to the Present.* 2d ed. Pp. xxvii, 308. Syracuse, NY: Syracuse University Press. Paperbound, $19.95.

CABAN, PEDRO A. 1999. *Constructing a Colonial People: Puerto Rico and the United States, 1898-1932.* Pp. xiv, 282. Boulder, CO: Westview Press. $60.00.

CARLSON, LAURIE WINN. 1999. *A Fever in Salem: A New Interpretation of the New England Witch Trials.* Pp. xvi, 197. Chicago: Ivan R. Dee. $24.95.

COX, W. MICHAEL and RICHARD ALM. 1999. *Myths of Rich and Poor: Why We're Better off than We Think.* Pp. xvi, 256. New York: Basic Books. $25.00.

DePAUL, KIM, ed. 1999. *Children of Cambodia's Killing Fields: Memoirs by Survivors.* Pp. xvii, 199. New Haven, CT: Yale University Press. $27.50. Paperbound, $14.95.

DOBSON, ANDREW, ed. 1999. *Fairness and Futurity: Essays on Environmental Sustainability and Social Justice.* Pp. xi, 328. New York: Oxford University Press. $72.00. Paperbound, $19.95.

FELDMAN, OFER, ed. 1999. *Political Psychology in Japan: Behind the Nails That Sometimes Stick Out (and Get Hammered Down).* Pp. xix, 340. Commack, NY: Nova Science. No price.

FIDLER, DAVID P. and JENNIFER M. WELSH, eds. 1999. *Empire and Community: Edmund Burke's Writings and Speeches on International Relations.* Pp. xv, 353. Boulder, CO: Westview Press. $75.00. Paperbound, $30.00.

GINKEL, A. VAN. 1999. *General Principles of Human Power.* Pp. xii, 221. Westport, CT: Greenwood Press. $59.95.

GOIDEL, ROBERT, DONALD A. GROSS, and TODD G. SHIELDS. 1999. *Money Matters: Consequences of Campaign Finance Reform in United States House Elections.* Pp. ix, 215. Lanham, MD: Rowman & Littlefield. $55.00. Paperbound, $18.95.

HERRNSON, PAUL S. and DILYS M. HILL, eds. 1999. *The Clinton Presidency: The First Term, 1992-96.* Pp. ix, 182. New York: St. Martin's Press. $45.00.

KANN, MARK E. 1999. *The Gendering of American Politics: Founding Mothers, Founding Fathers, and Political Patriarchy.* Pp. xvi, 194. Westport, CT: Praeger, $55.00. Paperbound, $19.95.

KHAN, MAZHAR ALI. 1999. *Pakistan: The Barren Years.* Pp. xi, 757. New York: Oxford University Press. $26.00.

LAMIS, ALEXANDER P., ed. 1999. *Southern Politics in the 1990s.* Pp. xv, 490. Baton Rouge: Louisiana State University Press. $39.95.

LATOUR, ARSENE LACARRIERE. 1999. *Historical Memoir of the War in West Florida and Louisiana in 1814-15.* Expanded ed. Pp. xlii, 358. Gainesville: University Press of Florida. $49.95.

LEONARD, THOMAS M., ed. 1999. *United States–Latin American Relations, 1850-1903.* P. 303. Tuscaloosa: University of Alabama Press. $44.95.

LONGLEY, LAWRENCE D. and NEAL R. PEIRCE. 1999. *The Electoral College Primer 2000.* Pp. viii, 253. New Haven, CT: Yale University Press. $35.00. Paperbound, $16.00.

MILKIS, SIDNEY M. and JEROME M. MILEUR, eds. 1999. *Progressivism and the New Democracy.* Pp. vi, 302. Amherst: University of Massachusetts Press. $50.00. Paperbound, $16.95.

OHAEGBULAM, F. UGBOAJA. 1999. *A Concise Introduction to American Foreign Policy.* Pp. xix, 394. New York: Peter Lang. Paperbound, no price.

PURI, JYOTI. 1999. *Woman, Body, Desire in Post-Colonial India: Narratives of Gender and Sexuality.* Pp. xiv, 234. New York: Routledge. $65.00. Paperbound, $17.99.

RAE, NICOL and COLTON C. CAMPBELL, eds. 1999. *New Majority or Old Minority? The Impact of Republicans on Congress.* Pp. xi, 220. Lanham, MD: Rowman & Littlefield. $65.00. Paperbound, $19.95.

ROCHON, THOMAS R. 1999. *The Netherlands: Negotiating Sovereignty in an Interdependent World.* Pp. xvii, 318. Boulder, CO: Westview Press. $65.00.

ROSELL, STEVEN A. 1999. *Renewing Governance: Governing by Learning in the Information Age.* Pp. xii, 316. New York: Oxford University Press. Paperbound, $27.95.

SHIACH, MORAG. 1999. *Feminism and Cultural Studies.* Pp. xi, 597. New York: Oxford University Press. $80.00. Paperbound, $19.95.

SIMON, ANTHONY O., ed. 1999. *Philosopher at Work.* Pp. xiii, 217. Lanham, MD: Rowman & Littlefield. $58.00. Paperbound, $22.95.

SODEN, DENNIS L., ed. 1999. *The Environmental Presidency.* Pp. xi, 366. Albany: State University of New York Press. Paperbound, $24.95.

STEGMAN, MICHAEL A. 1999. *Savings for the Poor: The Hidden Benefits of Electronic Banking.* Pp. xv, 215. Washington, DC: Brookings Institution Press. Paperbound, $18.95.

VILE, M.J.C. 1999. *Politics in the USA.* 5th ed. Pp. ix, 237. New York: Routledge. Paperbound, no price.

YEE, HERBERT S. 1998. *The Political Culture of China's University Students.* Pp. x, 189. Commack, NY: Nova Science. $49.00.

ZIPPERSTEIN, STEVEN J. 1999. *Imagining Russian Jewry: Memory, History, Identity.* Pp. xii, 39. Seattle: University of Washington Press. $30.00. Paperbound, $14.95.

INDEX